INSIGHT **CITY GUIDE**

SYDNEY

D1399588

Discovery
CHANNEL

APA PUBLICATIONS
Part of the Langenscheidt Publishing Group

✗ INSIGHT GUIDE
SYDNEY

Editor
Jeffery Pike
Editorial Director
Brian Bell

Distribution

UK & Ireland
GeoCenter International Ltd
The Viables Centre, Harrow Way
Basingstoke, Hants RG22 4BJ
Fax: (44) 1256-817988

United States
Langenscheidt Publishers, Inc.
46–35 54th Road, Maspeth, NY 11378
Fax: (1) 718 784-0640

Canada
Thomas Allen & Son Ltd
390 Steelcase Road East
Markham, Ontario L3R 1G2
Fax: (1) 905 475 6747

Australia
Universal Publishers
1 Waterloo Road
Macquarie Park, NSW 2113
Fax: (61) 2 9888 9074

New Zealand
Hema Maps New Zealand Ltd (HNZ)
Unit D, 24 Ra ORA Drive
East Tamaki, Auckland
Fax: (64) 9 273 6479

Worldwide
Apa Publications GmbH & Co.
Verlag KG (Singapore branch)
38 Joo Koon Road, Singapore 628990
Tel: (65) 6865-1600. Fax: (65) 6861-6438

Printing

Insight Print Services (Pte) Ltd
38 Joo Koon Road, Singapore 628990
Tel: (65) 6865-1600. Fax: (65) 6861-6438

©2005 Apa Publications GmbH & Co.
Verlag KG (Singapore branch)
All Rights Reserved

First Edition 1993
Fifth Edition 2004
Reprinted 2005

ABOUT THIS BOOK

This guidebook combines the interests and enthusiasms of two of the world's best-known information providers: Insight Guides, whose titles have set the standard for visual travel guides since 1970, and Discovery Channel, the world's premier source of nonfiction television programming.

The editors of Insight Guides provide both practical advice and general understanding about a destination. Discovery Channel and its website, www.discovery.com, help millions of viewers explore their world from the comfort of their own home.

An international city

In historical terms, Sydney is a young city, but during its 225-year story it has constantly reinvented itself to meet the changing moods of the times. Hosting the 2000 Summer Olympics brought the city to the centre of the world stage, and stimulated yet another round of innovative building, improvements in transport and accommodation, and many other cultural and civic advances. In the first decade of the 21st century, Sydney has come to full flower as one of the world's most exciting and cosmopolitan cities.

How to use this book

The book is carefully structured both to convey an understanding of the city and its culture, and to guide readers through its sights and activities:
◆ To understand modern Sydney, you need to know something of its background. The first section covers the city's history and culture in lively, authoritative essays by specialists.

◆ The main Places section provides a full run-down of all the attractions worth seeing. The main places of interest are coordinated by number with full-colour maps. At the end of each chapter, there is a selective listing of the area's most notable restaurants, cafés and bars.

◆ The Travel Tips section provides a point of reference for information on travel, hotels, shops, festivals and activities for the visitor, with a new A–Z listing of practical information. Details may be located quickly by using the index printed on the back cover flap – and the flaps are designed to serve as bookmarks.

◆ Photographs – most of them new for this edition – are chosen not only to illustrate geography and buildings but also to convey the moods of the city and the life of its people.

The contributors

This thoroughly revised edition was edited by **Jeffery Pike**, an Insight stalwart who also edited *Insight Guide: Australia*, and has built on the earlier editions produced by **John Borthwick**, **David McGonigal** and **Zoë Ross**. It retains much of the work of the original contributors, who included **Neil Jameson**, **Anne Matthew**, **Clair Gerson**, **Elisabeth King**, **Kim O'Connor** and **Meryl Constance**, with additional research by **Ingrid Ohlsson**, **A. J. Ohlsson**, **Faruk Avdi**, **Janelle Johnstone** and **Dianne Campbell**.

This edition has been meticulously updated by **Robert James Wallace**, a Sydney-born photographer and writer who now lives in the city's fashionable district of Darlinghurst. Branching out from a career in photography, he has become a successful author on travel topics and has contributed to several Insight Guides. His wide knowledge of the daily details of his home town – from bus fares to bars, from the best beaches to the hippest restaurants – has been invaluable.

Many of the photographs in this edition are the work of **Glyn Genin**, another Insight regular, who was commissioned to shoot all aspects of the city for us in 2004. Other photographic contributions come from **Catherine Karnow**, **Robbi Newman** and **Tony Perrottet**.

The book was proofread by **Neil Titman** and was indexed by **Penny Phenix**.

CONTACTING THE EDITORS

We would appreciate it if readers would alert us to errors or outdated information by writing to:

Insight Guides, PO Box 7910, London SE1 1WE, England. Fax: (44) 20 7403 0290. insight@apaguide.co.uk

NO part of this book may be reproduced, stored in a retrieval system or transmitted in any form or means electronic, mechanical, photocopying, recording or otherwise, without prior written permission of *Apa Publications*. Brief text quotations with use of photographs are exempted for book review purposes only. Information has been obtained from sources believed to be reliable, but its accuracy and completeness, and the opinions based thereon, are not guaranteed.

www.insightguides.com

Maps

Travel Tips

THE BEST OF SYDNEY

Setting priorities, saving money, unique attractions...
here, at a glance, are our recommendations, plus some
tips and tricks even Sydneysiders won't always know

BEST VISTAS

In a city as dramatic and photogenic as Sydney, there
are plenty of stunning views, many of the harbour.
Here are a few of the finest.

● **Mrs Macquarie's Point** Sydney's prime panorama spot: most of the city and the harbour's tourism icons are in view – and within walking distance – from here. *See page 96.*

● **Sydney Tower** The observation deck 320 metres (1,050 ft) above the streets offers the best elevated 360-degree views. On a clear, haze-free day you can see the Blue Mountains to the west and the Royal National Park to the south. *See page 70.*

● **Blues Point Reserve** One of Sydney's nicest harbourside spots for a picnic, with a superb view of the Harbour Bridge and a short stroll from North Sydney's outdoor cafés and slick restaurants. Gets crowded at nights when a fireworks show is planned.

● **Joy Flights** Views from a helicopter or light aircraft can be had courtesy of pilots at Sydney Airport and Bankstown Heliport. (Check the *Yellow Pages* under Aircraft.)

● **Pylon Lookout/ Bridge Climb** Sydney Harbour Bridge has an observation deck with superb views of the harbour. For even loftier views, those with a head for heights can don overalls and climb to the very top of the bridge's arch. *See page 86.*

● **North Head** Although it's a hike from the city centre, this is a good vantage point by day or night, with fine views back towards the Bridge and city centre. The city has a neon glow when viewed from here after dark. *See page 145.*

ABOVE: Bondi Beach is justifiably world-famous for
surfing, swimming, windsurfing – or just hanging out.

BEST BEACHES

Few major cities have so many beautiful beaches so
close to their metropolitan centre. Here are some of
Sydney's favourite stretches of sand.

● **Bondi Beach** (*above*) An icon of Australia, home of surfing, life-saving and, these days, also of sun-worshipping and body-building. *See page 154.*

● **Manly** Sydney's favourite resort suburb has more surfing beaches, fringed by Norfolk Island pines. *See page 145.*

● **Coogee Beach** Swim in the sea (scuba diving is also an option) or in one of Coogee's wonderful sea baths. *See page 156.*

● **Balmoral Beach** One of the best inner harbour beaches. No surf, so no surfing (but safe for children): windsurfing and dinghy sailing prevail. *See page 145.*

● **Tamarama Beach** Sydney's beautiful people display themselves on Tamarama's beautiful white sands, though the surf is notoriously dangerous. *See page 155.*

● **Palm Beach** An upmarket suburb with chic restaurants and a lovely beach favoured by surfers and windsurfers. *See page 147.*

ABOVE: the Australian Museum will keep kids entranced.
BELOW: swim in Bondi's saltwater ocean pool.

SYDNEY FOR CHILDREN

- **Australian Museum** contains Kids' Island for younger children (toys, animal models and props), and the Search and Discover hands-on section for all ages (animal specimens, both living and dead, microscopes and CD-ROMs). Tel: 9320 6202.

- **Fox Studios** State-of-the-art playgrounds with ball pits, giant mazes, tunnels, cargo nets, climbing, jumping, sliding and exploring, plus bungy trampolining, adventure golf and entertainers. (Lang Road, Moore Park, tel: 9383 4333).

- **Tumbalong Park** Open space near Darling Harbour with a free children's playground and a stage area that hosts free theatrical and musical events on weekends and during school holidays. *See page 105.*

- **Rocks Puppet Cottage** Free puppet shows at this unusual venue (in Kendall Lane, off Argyle Street) at 11am, 12.30 and 2pm every Sat and Sun.

- **Powerhouse Museum** Australia's most dynamic museum: children especially enjoy the Kids Interactive Discovery Spaces (KIDS), with loads of hands-on activities.

- **Centennial Park** Let them burn off that juvenile energy with bikes and rollerblades for hire, pony rides, wildlife walks, and acres of open space.

BEST WALKS

- **Mrs Macquarie's Point to Dawes Point** (1 hr) Sydney's shoreline: from Mrs Macquarie's Point follow the foreshore within the Botanic Gardens to the Opera House, past the Opera Quays outdoor restaurant strip to Circular Quay, then to Dawes Point Reserve, the palm-tree-lined park in the shadow of the Harbour Bridge.

- **Bondi to Bronte Beach** (1½ hrs) Find the path behind the baths at the south end of Bondi Beach. Fine views from the sandstone cliffs of Mackenzies Point, down to trendy Tamarama Beach, climb again on to North Bronte cliffs, then follow the path down to Bronte.

- **Historic Rocks** Buy *The Rocks Self-Guided Walking Tour* from the Visitor Centre on George Street (*see page 84*) for 31 places of historical interest on a local heritage walk. Explore a maze of narrow streets and lanes, sandstone cottages and terraces filled with shops, stalls, cafés and restaurants.

- **Manly Scenic Walkway** (2 hrs) An 8-km (5-mile) walking track from the north end of the Spit Bridge to Manly, winding through native bushland and across the top of sandstone cliffs with breathtaking views. *See page 145.*

- **Architecture Walks** (2 hrs) At 10.30 am every Wed and Sat, walks led by an architect start at the Museum of Sydney (*see page 72*) to explore the ideas behind Sydney's urban landscapes and its architecture old and new. Bookings recommended, tel: 9518 6866.

BEST BARS

- **Baron's** This long-established after-hours place in a side-street of Kings Cross oozes atmosphere. Dark wood-paneling, redolent of a seafaring galleon. *5 Roslyn Street, Kings Cross*
- **Palisade Hotel** Situated in the quiet backstreets of the Rocks, an imposing tall, thin building towers over its historic surroundings. A retro feel and relaxed atmosphere. *35 Bettington Street, Millers Point*
- **The Dugout Bar** A secret Sydney gem, cosy and petite. Dimly lit and intimate on weekday nights, gets crowded at weekends. *2 Oxford Street, Darlinghurst*
- **Hero of Waterloo** Possibly Sydney's oldest pub, with a colonial ambience and a reputation as the true blue Aussie watering-hole. *81 Lower Fort Street, Millers Point*
- **Royal Hotel** Located in the chic Five Ways area, the Royal has Victorian decor and large upstairs balconies. *237 Glenmore Road, Paddington*
- **The Cat and Fiddle** A cosy, live music venue in village-like Balmain. A pleasant atmosphere and charm that many newer Sydney hotels seriously lack. *456 Darling Street, Balmain*
- **Horizons** Not for the budget traveller, on the top floor of the Shangri-La Hotel near Circular Quay. Stunning high-rise views and equally stunning cocktail list. *Level 36, 176 Cumberland Street, The Rocks*
- **Kinselas** This old funeral parlour packs in a mixed straight and gay crowd every night of the week. Amazing interior: massive ceilings soaring overhead, art deco decor and a popular balcony overlooking Taylor Square. *383 Bourke Street, Darlinghurst*

ABOVE: vist the historic Observatory and peer through the telescopes for free – see below

FREE SYDNEY

- **Outdoor concerts** Free performances by Opera Australia and the Sydney Symphony Orchestra as part of the Sydney Festival every January. Tel: 9265 0444 for details.
- **Martin Place Amphitheatre** Every weekday from 12.30, the amphitheatre hosts free lunchtime concerts presenting music from all corners of the world, from police bands to string quartets to rock 'n' roll. Tel: 9265 9367.
- **Free art** Two of Australia's finest collections are free to enter: the Art Gallery of New South Wales (*see page 92*) and the Museum of Contemporary Art (*see page 83*) not only do not charge admission, but even offer free guided tours two or three times a day, every day.
- **State buildings** Admission is free to some of Sydney's historic administrative centres, including Government House (*see page 95*), Parliament House and the Mint (*see page 92*). When the NSW parliament is not sitting, there are free tours of Parliament House.
- **Sydney Opera House** It costs nothing to wander round the outside of Australia's most famous building (*see page 94*) and marvel at its extraordinary architecture. And it's free to enter some of the public spaces inside, although to visit some areas you need to join a guided tour (admission fee).
- **Sydney Observatory** Free admission during the day to this historic observatory (*see page 88*), with guided tours and daylight celestial viewing through the telescopes. To view the stars at night, you must book and pay an entrance fee (tel: 9217 0485).

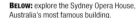

BELOW: explore the Sydney Opera House, Australia's most famous building.

BEST MARKETS

- **Paddy's Markets**, *Hay Street, Thu–Sun*. Sydney's oldest and biggest market (800 stalls). Sells clothes, food, electronics, toys, fresh produce, even pets.
- **Rocks Markets**, *George Street North, Sat–Sun*. A colourful, lively market in the shadow of the Harbour Bridge. Lots of tourist-oriented and arty goods on sale. Vast umbrellas for wet weather.
- **Paddington Bazaar**, *Oxford Street, Sat*. A hip, arty market: lots of new and second-hand clothing, jewellery, ceramics and other arts and crafts. Attracts a big crowd.
- **Glebe Markets**, *Glebe Point Road, Sat*. A laid-back market with arts and crafts, foodstuffs and clothes.

Popular with alternative types and the fashionable inner city set.
- **Opera House Market**, *Sydney Opera House forecourt, Sun*. Lots of tourist-oriented wares, local artists' works, sepia-toned historic Sydney photographs and Sydney-themed souvenirs.
- **Balmain Market**, *Darling Road, Sat*. For homeware, clothing, jewellery and tasteful bric-a-brac. Food stalls indoors and lots of restaurants and pubs nearby.
- **North Sydney Markets**, *Miller Street, 2nd Sat of the month*. A little more upmarket than most. Nearly 200 stalls selling artworks, foodstuffs, jewellery, antiques, also fortune-telling, massage and reflexology.

BEST FESTIVALS AND EVENTS

- **Sydney Festival** A three-week festival of music, theatre, film and visual arts, with Australian and international offerings. January.
- **Chinese New Year** Dancing dragons, firecrackers and exotic food in Chinatown. Late January/early February.
- **Gay and Lesbian Mardi Gras** An outrageous parade watched by thousands and a massive Mardi Gras party. Late February/ early March.
- **Royal Easter Show** The country comes to town: wood chopping, livestock, sideshows.
- **Sydney Film Festival** About 250 screenings in two weeks, many at the grand old State Theatre. Mid-June.
- **Biennale of Sydney** International arts festival. Mid-July, even-numbered years
- **City to Surf Race** Thousands of runners race from the City to Bondi. Early August.

MONEY-SAVING TIPS

Cheap travel There are a range of day tickets and passes to cut the cost of transport. TravelPass allows unlimited seven-day travel on buses, trams and ferries. TravelTen gives you 10 bus or ferry rides for nearly half the cost of individual tickets. Best value of all, a SydneyPass offers unlimited hop-on, hop-off travel on all Sydney buses and ferries, plus the Sydney Explorer and Bondi Explorer, Harboursights Cruises and return transfers on AirportLink trains. *See page 214.*

HalfTix For theatre, concerts, sport and other events, HalfTix offers unsold tickets cheaply – often half price – on the day of performance. You have a better chance of bargains on quieter nights (usually earlier in the week). Some theatre companies also sell unsold tickets cheap a half-hour before the performance starts, direct from the venue. *See page 222.*

BYO Many Sydney restaurants are not licensed to sell alcohol, but are happy for you to bring your own (advertised as BYO), for which they add a small corkage charge. This not only allows wine buffs to drink exactly what they want with their meal, but also seriously reduces the cost of dining out.

Duty-free shopping As well as the usual duty-free outlets at the airport, visitors to Sydney can buy goods tax and duty free at certain shops in the city centre. The DFS Galleria store in The Rocks (55 George Street) claims to be the largest duty and tax free store in the southern hemisphere, stocking international fashion, cosmetics, electronics, watches, jewellery, Australian wines and international liquor.

Direct Factory Outlets Buy upmarket goods at warehouse prices at the DFO shopping complex in Homebush, the clearance centre for over 100 designer shops, selling their wares at up to 70 percent off normal retail prices. *See page 168.*

A MILLENNIAL EDEN

In just over two centuries, Sydney has grown
from a prison colony into an international
metropolis. What can it do for an encore?

Sydney entered the 21st century with a population of 4 million, responsibility for the first major international event of the new millennium,
and the knowledge that it is at the centre of the Asia-Pacific region, the
focus of so many optimistic economic predictions. After the 2000 Olympic
Games drew the world's attention to the city, the hot topic of conversation
has been Sydney's standing as an international city. Does it rank with Paris,
Tokyo, New York and London in the eyes of the world? Some say yes; others
say no. Perhaps the question should be not whether Sydney matches up to
other cities, but whether, with all its energy, light, sensuality, modernity
and beauty, it might come to define what a city really is – a prototype of
the best that an urban environment can offer its residents.

Sydney's greatness lies in its schizophrenic ability to contain the best
of big-city living within a superb natural environment. On the one hand,
Sydney has all the features of a major metropolis – a flourishing arts and
leisure scene, cultural diversity, exceptional tourist facilities, wonderful
cuisine, the capacity for huge events and some noteworthy buildings. On
the other hand, it has a natural beauty so complete that it seems almost
unfair. The rest of Australia sometimes seems to think so – say something
complimentary about Sydney elsewhere and you might get back "Yes, it
does have the harbour, and all those beaches..." almost as if there is something indecent about such a surfeit of scenery.

Undeniably, Sydney has the best harbour in the world as its shining cen-
trepiece, complete with soaring sandstone cliffs, intricately carved bays
and coves, and stretches of green bushland. Then there is the stretch of
coastline forming the city's eastern front, with its stunning surf beaches
fronting the waters of the Pacific. Around these features, the city curves
and twists, opening up to the great natural wonder of its water setting.
From this beauty has also come the open, friendly nature of the citizens,
and a willingness to share the advantages. Development in Sydney has
always succeeded when it has opened up its spectacular environment for
the benefit of the many, and failed when it tried to appropriate it for the
advantage of a few. If Sydney can balance its development against the
beauty that sets it apart, it will continue to be one of the world's greatest
cities well into the new millennium.   ❑

PRECEDING PAGES: the Shangri-La Hotel overlooks the harbour; Doyles seafood
restaurant overlooks Watsons Bay. **LEFT:** Sydney's most distinctive icon, the Opera House.

THE MAKING OF A CITY

It was once a dry valley inhabited by hunter-gatherers. They were displaced by Europeans, whose influence would in turn diminish as waves of immigrants arrived

A successful city exudes a solid feeling of permanence which is reassuring to inhabitants and suggests immutability to its visitors. Even with a top cap of cranes and construction scaffolding, Sydney feels as if it has always been here, despite the fact it has existed as city and town for little over two centuries. Today's children of Sydney will find it hard to recall a time when the Darling Harbour complex didn't exist, just as their parents barely remember when there was no Opera House and grandparents are vague about Sydney before the building of the Harbour Bridge.

When the first people arrived in what is now Sydney, the harbour itself didn't exist: it was a dry valley about 10 km (6 miles) inland. This was over 40,000 years ago, when Aborigines from the north arrived to begin a lifestyle of hunting and gathering that would serve them well for thousands of years. In 1987, stone tools dating back more than 45,000 years were found near the town of Richmond, 40 km (25 miles) from Sydney.

Over the millennia the seas rose and fell as ice ages advanced and retreated. About 10,000 years ago the ice caps melted and the seas continued to rise until reaching the present levels about 6,000 years before the Europeans arrived. At the time of the First Fleet's voyage to Australia in 1788, there were some 3,000 native Aborigines residing in the Sydney area.

Three language groups existed which were

just similar enough to allow communication between the tribes, but there were several dialects and groups within each language. Ku-ring-gai was the language of the north shore, Dharawal was spoken along the coast south of Botany Bay, and Dharug and its dialects everywhere else, from the Cumberland Plains and into the lower Blue Mountains region.

However, everything changed irrevocably on 29 April 1770, when Captain James Cook sailed his vessel the *Endeavour* into a sheltered bay where he noted a "fine meadow". The vessel was on its way back to England after observing the transit of Venus at Tahiti and exploring the New Zealand coast.

LEFT: a European's impression of one of Sydney's native inhabitants. **RIGHT:** Captain James Cook raised the British flag in "New South Wales" in 1770.

A heroic endeavour

When the 41-year-old Cook set foot on Australian soil he was far from the first European to do so. The north and west coasts, and half the Great Australian Bight, had been mapped by Dutch explorers before the end of the 17th century. But none had ventured as far as the east coast, which Cook followed from near the Murray River to Botany Bay and upwards to the tip of Cape York. At Possession Island, north of Cape York, he flew a flag and annexed the east coast under the name of "New South Wales".

The *Endeavour* spent a week in the bay and, although threatened by a couple of Abo-

southern US plantations as a bottomless pit for consigning convicts – until 1776 when the Americans revolted. With that door closed, English jails soon filled and rotting hulks of ships on the River Thames took the overflow.

So suggestions by Joseph Banks and James Matra, a member of Cook's crew, led to proposals that Botany Bay receive a fleet of con-

riginal men, the crew had little contact with the local people. Cook's comment that "all they seemed to want was for us to be gone" made later events all the more poignant. Cook and his crew soon left Botany Bay, but the seeds of destruction of Sydney's Aborigines had already been sown.

In July 1771, when Cook brought the *Endeavour* back to England, the government had little use for the land he had explored, and his return was a major blow to those who cherished the dream of a Great South Land. But a consequence of the American War of Independence brought NSW back into prominence. For 60 years the British had used the

victs. In August 1786, Lord Sydney, the Home Secretary, instructed Admiralty to arrange it. Many English dubbed the new enterprise a "colony of thieves".

The First Fleet sets sail

On 13 May 1787, a fleet of 11 ships sailed from Portsmouth in England bound for Botany Bay. Although many of the 1,030 men, women and children on board were of dubious character, there is no doubting the heroic nature of the endeavour. The journey took them to the other side of the world, some 22,500 km (14,000 miles) from home. They arrived in Botany Bay eight months and one week later, on 20 January 1788. It was soon decided that the bay would never be the fields of plenty Cook had foreseen (there was no water supply), so Captain Arthur Phillip set out along the coast to find a better site.

Phillip sailed into Port Jackson, which James Cook had noted in passing (and named after the Judge-Advocate of the Fleet). Cook had stated that "there appeared to be safe anchorage, which I called Port Jackson", thinking that the harbour finished around Middle Head. Phillip had no misapprehension: he declared it to be "the finest harbour in the world". The whole colony moved to a place by a small creek on "Sydney Cove", so named after Lord Sydney, the British Home Secretary.

On the evening of their arrival, Saturday, 26 January 1788, the Union Flag was hoisted and the history of the new colony began.

Sydney's early days

The first days of the colony were tough for the new arrivals. Ships' carpenters built the marines' quarters and the convicts built their own to replace the tents in which they first lived. Governor Phillip made a well-laid-out plan for the settlement but everyone ignored it, taking the most convenient route from place to place and bringing about the haphazard street grid of present-day Sydney.

Worst of all for the settlers was the unwillingness of the Aborigines to accept the new arrivals – they kept their distance, forcing the settlers to find out for themselves how to survive in this strange land. The male convicts were cast in the role of labourers – the very work most of them had turned to crime to avoid. Delays in sending the next fleet and the shipwreck of supply vessels exacerbated the situation. By mid-1790 the colony was close to starvation, and only the arrival of supplies on the *Lady Juliana* saved it from foundering. The settlement's survival was threatened again when the Second Fleet arrived in poor condition: 267 convicts had died on the voyage and of the 486 who arrived sick, 124 died soon after.

The first bricks were made in the colony within two months of arrival, and the first brick house, built on what is now the corner of Bridge

and Phillip streets, was occupied by the Governor, starting a tradition which continues in the predominantly brick houses of today. The Tank Stream (near today's Circular Quay) was the only water source for several years, and the settlers clung to the foreshore of Sydney Cove.

Simply keeping the colony functioning was a monumental task, so there was an air of "make do" for the first few decades. Phillip was followed by governors Hunter, King and Bligh (who arrived some years after his crew had staged a mutiny against him on the *Bounty*). Often, survival was a fine balance: in 1804, Irish prisoners at Castle Hill Reserve rose against the government, and some 200

THE FIRST GOVERNOR

The son of a German schoolmaster, Arthur Phillip was born in 1738, rose through the ranks of the navy and became Sydney's first practical leader. Small, often ill and somewhat retiring, he took his bleak task of creating a home out of nothing for a bunch of England's most dispossessed and pursued it with vigour. "Upon my soul," exclaimed one of his contemporaries, "I do think God Almighty made Phillip on purpose for that place, for never did man know better what to do, or with more determination see it done." Even so, after four years of intense and often thankless toil, Phillip left Sydney exhausted in 1792.

LEFT: Captain Arthur Phillip lands in Botany Bay.
RIGHT: a 1799 depiction of the founding of the colony.

convicts set out to capture Parramatta, then tried to seize the ships in Sydney Harbour. Troops quickly quelled the rebellion at what became known as the Battle of Vinegar Hill. Nine off the ringleaders were hanged and another nine received from 200 to 500 lashes.

From colony to community

During an inspired 12-year term from 1810 to 1821, Governor Lachlan Macquarie took the strides necessary to convert NSW from colony to fledgling community. If Phillip was the no-nonsense man of Sydney, Lachlan Macquarie was the grand dreamer and schemer. Even now, Sydney bears the indelible stamp of Macquarie

and his principal architect, the forger, convict and architectural genius Francis Greenway.

Soon after he arrived as governor, Macquarie began a series of expensive public projects, not wanting to reside in less than elegant surrounds. He was criticised roundly for creating buildings and streets that were far too grand for a convict settlement, and was eventually sent home to England for spending too much money. As is always the case with visionaries both in Sydney and the world over, many years later he was being widely praised for having provided Australia's first city with some excellent examples of Georgian architecture.

It was Macquarie who established a desig-nated street width (with footpaths) and who demolished any buildings which stood in their way. He also renamed the streets which had previously been called rows and sometimes bore several names along their length. The obelisk he erected in Macquarie Place is still the point from which all road distances from Sydney are measured. The hospital he had built on the street that bears his name later became the core of the State Parliament House.

Francis Greenway was transported in 1814 for forgery, but his real talent was architecture. Under the patronage of Macquarie, he designed some 40 buildings; those that survive are regarded as exceptional examples of Georgian Colonial architecture. They include St James's Church in the City, St Matthew's Church at Windsor and St Luke's in Liverpool. Governor Macquarie pardoned Greenway after his achievement in designing Hyde Park Barracks, but Greenway's fortunes declined after Macquarie departed: Commissioner Bigge considered his work "too grand for an infant colony".

Indeed, Australia should be grateful to Lachlan Macquarie for its name. In 1817 he first used the word "Australia" in viceregal correspondence, thus giving official recognition to a word mooted by the explorer Matthew Flinders from the previously used Terra Australis, meaning "south land".

In the countryside to the northwest of Sydney are "Macquarie's Five Towns". The Hawkesbury River was the granary for the colony at this time, but periodic flooding caused great damage, so Governor Macquarie established townships on the high ground. Some have since declined, but Richmond and Windsor are substantial communities proud of the appellation as Macquarie towns.

The first in a long line of Sydney entrepreneurs was John Macarthur, an officer on the Second Fleet which arrived in 1790. He, along with his wife Elizabeth, was responsible for kickstarting the Australian wool industry: she ran the business details while he went around the colony stirring up trouble for anyone who threatened his industrial interests.

Convicts and free men

As for the convicts, most came from the lower classes of England, and their crimes were overwhelmingly offences against property. Men outnumbered women by four to one. On arrival in the colony they were not restrained, since the hostile environment was no doubt thought to be a sufficient barrier to prevent escapees. Some continued with their life of crime. Many others saw the window of opportunity.

First Fleeter James Ruse grew the first wheat crop in the colony, and was rewarded with the first grant of land. Mary Reiby arrived in 1792, aged 15. She married a free settler, was later widowed, then set about turning the wine business she inherited from her husband into a thriving empire.

FREE SETTLEMENT

In 1832 free settlers were offered assisted passage by the English government to the new colony; some 70,000 took up the offer over the next 10 years, swelling the population of Sydney.

with them western diseases. Smallpox killed half their population before the colony was two years old, and within 50 years of white settlement fewer than 300 Aborigines remained in the region (compared with 3,000 when the First Fleet arrived).

Up to 1840, when transportation to NSW ceased, a total of 83,000 convicts had been

The population of Sydney increased rapidly as the convict numbers were boosted by the arrival of free settlers. From the 1,000 inhabitants of the first days, there were 6,156 in 1810 and 10,815 in 1828. There was pressure to expand, but it took 24 years to cross the Blue Mountains to the western pastures. In 1820 Sydney covered 2.5 sq km (1 sq mile).

The Aborigines of Sydney were victims of the expansion of the colony and the mere presence of the European settlers, who brought

sent to the state. Few returned home at the end of their sentences. The system of parole known as "ticket-of-leave" ensured that most had begun making a home in the colony before their sentences expired, and had little reason to go back.

In a typically analytical view, Charles Darwin, later the author of *The Origin of Species*, visited Sydney in 1836 and wrote: "As a real system of reform it has failed, as perhaps would every other plan; but as a means of making men outwardly honest – of converting vagabonds most useless in one hemisphere into active citizens of another, and thus giving birth to a new and splendid country – a

LEFT: Governor Lachlan Macquarie laid the city's foundations. **ABOVE:** Aborigines in Sydney's newly built streets in the early 19th century.

grand centre of civilisation – it has succeeded to a degree perhaps unparalleled in history."

This was a time of rapidly expanding commercial life, and the first of the wealthy merchants' mansions of the eastern suburbs were built in Potts Point and Darling Point. Other suburbs started to spring up with subdivisions at Paddington, Redfern, Pyrmont, Woolloomooloo, Newtown, Surry Hills and Glebe.

Municipal advances

The first street in Australia was the bullock track that became George Street, and the first road leading out of Sydney was built to the early settlement of Parramatta in 1794. That

one from the Botany Swamps. This, in turn, was superseded by a weir on the Nepean River built during the 1880s. With the water supply sorted out, Sydney town was finally declared as the City of Sydney in July 1842.

The gold rush

In the words of W.C. Wentworth, an eminent early explorer and politician, gold discoveries "precipitated Australia into nationhood". The first publicised gold discovery in Australia was made in 1851 near Bathurst, to the west of the Blue Mountains, by E.H. Hargraves. He was a prospector who had recently returned from the Californian gold fields claiming that

road was extended to Windsor in the same year. (Today's car-yard-lined Parramatta Road follows roughly the same route.) A coach service to Parramatta and beyond followed. Parramatta was also the first place linked to Sydney by rail, in 1855. Six years later a horse-drawn tram started service along Pitt Street between Sydney Cove and the railway terminus, and steam trams came into operation in 1879 for the International Exhibition.

Not surprisingly, by 1820 the Tank Stream had become inadequate for Sydney's irrigation needs. To improve the situation, a tunnel from the Lachlan Swamps (now Centennial Park) was constructed in 1837, but later replaced by

they had reminded him of parts of NSW.

Despite general ridicule, he proceeded from Sydney to Bathurst with an acquaintance and announced that they were standing on gold. His first panful of dirt duly produced gold and he declared, "Here it is. This is a memorable day in the history of New South Wales. I shall be a baronet, and you will be knighted, and my old horse will be stuffed, put in a glass case, and sent to the British Museum!" It was indeed a memorable day for NSW, but for the rest he was wrong – the remainder of Hargraves's life was uneventful until he died in Sydney in 1891.

Gold had been found in NSW previously, but the authorities suppressed the news because it was considered too dangerous to start a gold rush in a penal colony. By 1851, however, transportation had ceased and the colony needed new immigrants. Hargraves's discovery was publicised, and the ensuing rush boosted the fortunes of Sydney and the whole colony. Sydney's population nearly doubled in 10 years (54,000 in 1851, 96,000 in 1861). It also hastened some degree of self-government.

A less beneficial effect for Sydney of gold discoveries in Australia was that the sustained gold rush of Victoria pushed this latter colony into pre-eminence. Melbourne now became the major city and was the first with a population of almost half a million.

It was fitting that Sydney's weather on the morning of 1 January 1901 was hot and cloudy with the clouds parting mid-morning – a typical Sydney summer's day. For this was the day that the Commonwealth of Australia came into existence. Thousands of people poured into Centennial Park to watch the swearing in of Australia's first Governor General, Lord Hopeton, who read messages of congratulations from Queen Victoria and others. There were choirs and artillery salutes and endless crowds of cheering people. This was a vibrant city now with an established literary and arts movement; existence was no longer merely life

home of the Australian parliament after Federation in 1901.

A national image

In the second half of the 19th century an Australian heritage developed. At the time of the 1861 census, more than half the population had been born in the United Kingdom. By 1871, about 60 percent had been born in Australia, and by Federation in 1901 the figure had risen to 82 percent. By the first year of the new century, Sydney had become a big city

LEFT: Sydney was a thriving port by 1850.
ABOVE: busy Pitt Street in 1895.

CONSTRUCTING A GRAND CITY

"The overflow of bricks and mortar has spread like a lava flow," was how one observer described Sydney's ever-increasing suburban sprawl. The main city streets had been paved with wooden blocks by 1885, finally removing the horrid dust pall which had long plagued the city. Buildings fitting the grand image of a Victorian British city were being built, including the Town Hall (1889), the Customs House (1887) and the Art Gallery, which was begun in the 1880s.

In 1895, Samuel Clements (better known as Mark Twain) visited Sydney and aptly declared it "an English city with American trimmings".

then death in a colonial backwater. Sydney had come a long way from the time when a group of convicts sat at Sydney Cove watching the hoisting of the Union Flag over the new colony before the military officers retired to a celebratory feast of maggoty meat.

However, not everything was rosy around the time of Federation. Sydney and NSW, like the other five Australian colonies, had experienced a major depression in 1892 as the result of heavy speculation, a run of bad seasons, a drop in wool and wheat prices, and reluctance in the London markets to lend to the colonial governments after the labour strikes of 1890–91. The colonies largely traded themselves out of trouble by

expanding the areas under wheat. Since the first days of Sydney's settlement, the city has been economically dependent on the primary industries in the hinterlands.

A more immediate problem was an outbreak of bubonic plague in 1900, which killed 112 people in Sydney as it spread through the Pacific ports. But the direct result was that the Sydney Cove slums had an overdue clean-up.

Technology and conflict

The first years of the new century were ones of excitement. In 1909, Australia's first flight took place at Narrabeen Beach where G.A. Taylor flew a motorless aircraft. This was fol-

lowed by a motor-propelled flight by Colin Defries at Victoria Park Racecourse.

By 1912, Australia had its first air race: inevitably between Sydney and Parramatta. Early aviators received a heroes' welcome when they touched down at the field which was later to be named Kingsford Smith Airport after Australia's greatest aviator. The all-Australian Thomson motor car made its appearance in 1900, the Pyrmont Bridge was opened in 1902 and body surfing became popular.

On 18 August 1914, the Australian Naval and Military Expeditionary Force left Sydney Harbour for German New Guinea, becoming the first allied Australian troops to join Britain in World War I. During the next four years, 60,000 of the 330,000 Australians who served overseas were killed. News of the long-awaited Armistice arrived at the offices of the *Sydney Morning Herald* at 7pm on 11 November 1918. By 8pm the city's streets were full of Sydneysiders celebrating (in the words of the newspaper) "that the menace of Prussianism was swept away".

The postwar period was a time of innovation. Sydney's underground railway opened in 1926 and the England–Australia Telephone Service commenced in 1930, putting Sydney in direct voice contact with London. But soon after, the main topic of conversation was the Great Depression. The debate on how to tackle the daunting and debilitating level of unemployment developed into a class war: the Labor government of Premier Jack Lang against the right-wing New Guard.

It was under the shadow of political turmoil that one of the city's most distinct features, the Sydney Harbour Bridge, opened in March 1932. Just as the structure has become an enduring part of the city landscape, the opening ceremony has become part of its history. Before Jack Lang could ceremonially cut the ribbon, Captain de Groot of the paramilitary New Guard rode up and slashed the ribbon with his sword, declaring the bridge open on behalf of "the decent and loyal citizens of NSW". The ribbon was retied and the official ceremony continued.

A long-term benefit of the Depression was the construction of several major roads in Sydney. These included the Wakehurst Parkway and the highway to Epping. The opening of the

Harbour Bridge in 1932 precipitated the development of the northern suburbs, now linked directly to the city by road and rail. In 1921, there were 30,000 cars registered in NSW; by 1961 this figure had risen to more than 625,000.

A casualty of the reign of the motor car was the Sydney tram. Although the expression "shoot through like a Bondi tram" is still used, the last tram finished its run in 1961. Old tram rails still occasionally surface at the bottom of deep potholes on some suburban streets.

It wasn't only the car population that grew dramatically. From half a million at the turn of the 20th century, Sydney's population passed the 1 million mark before 1931 and 2 million

many servicemen that poured into the city – a six-year period when the whole world seemed to come to Sydney.

Postwar immigration

After the war, the stream of new arrivals continued as many left Europe seeking a new life. Over 75 percent of Sydney's population growth between 1947 and 1971 came from immigrants and the children they then had in Australia. (Even so, Sydney took second place to Melbourne as the destination of immigrants.) In 1958, the dictation test set in 1901 for immigrants wishing to enter Australia was abolished, and for the first time

before 1961. Over 4 million people now live in the city – about 22 percent of Australians.

The widespread construction of tall apartment blocks started in Sydney in the 1920s and 1930s. Although fought by resident groups and some councils since then, the proliferation has continued. A shift in housing occurred during World War II: after three Japanese midget submarines torpedoed a ferry in the harbour, the value of waterfront homes fell instantly. Another effect of the war was the

LEFT: brave bathers frolic in the surf at Bondi Beach in 1911. **ABOVE:** Sydney Harbour Bridge was begun in 1923 and completed in 1932.

people of all races were welcomed. This influx changed Sydney from an insular colonial outpost to one of the world's most cosmopolitan cities. In the 1970s, immigrants from Southeast Asia joined their European forerunners. The range of restaurants is just one indication of the changes that were wrought. Far more fundamental (and beneficial) were the multicultural attitudes injected into Sydney by the new international arrivals.

The high life

In the 1960s, the centralised shopping patterns changed as the city's big department stores established branches in shopping centres in the suburbs. In contrast, the city centre was moving upwards.

One of the tallest buildings in Sydney before World War II was the 11-storey Australasian Temperance and General Mutual Life Assurance Company building. In 1961, the AMP insurance company finished its 26-storey building on Circular Quay. Crowds flocked to marvel at the view from the top which today is hindered by the taller buildings around it. By 1968, the vogue rooftop was the 50-storey tower of Australia Square. The highest construction in Sydney so far is the AMP Tower on top of Centrepoint, but proposals to exceed it are in the pipeline.

After the soul-searching Vietnam Moratorium marches of the 1960s, Sydney appeared to slip into social somnolence in the 1970s. There was a moment of fervour in 1975, when Labor Prime Minister Gough Whitlam was dismissed and people took to the streets in a display of solidarity similar to the one over Premier Lang's dismissal, also by the representative of the Crown, over 40 years earlier. But it was short-lived. Instead came the 1980s and the age of the yuppie, when lifestyle sections became obligatory in every newspaper.

So it was with some surprise that Sydney woke on 26 January 1988 to the dawn of the third century of white settlement. Everyone expected the Bicentenary to be a great party, an expression of joy about living in a city blessed with both a waterfront and the climate to revel in it. The event was all that and more.

Sydneysiders found themselves at a turning point in history. The cultural disregard which had characterised Australia for the past 200 years was receding. Sydney is still a long distance from the rest of the world but it is now self-sufficient – in 1986 the Proclamation of Australia Act finally broke the last legal ties with Britain.

Into the 21st century

Inflation and record interest rates soon dampened the afterglow of the Bicentenary. Sydney's property boom collapsed in 1989, ushering in what the federal treasurer described as "the recession we had to have". Bankrupt developers left the city dotted with excavations filled with water and rubbish.

But, ever resilient, Sydney was back on track with the announcement in September 1993 that it would host the 2000 Olympic Games. The state government immediately began committing public money, A\$3.2 billion in total, to the main Olympic venues including the Athletes' Village. Millions more were earmarked for public works projects, particularly in the area of roads and transport. The end result? A spectacular international festival of sport that did wonders for Sydney's image and Australia's tourism industry.

Sydney's population reached 4 million in 1998 and now stands at around 4.2 million. Much of the increase during the 1990s came from overseas migration but this has now dwindled. An ageing population, later marriages and fewer children, combined with traffic congestion, has seen a trend in inner-city apartment living. The city and suburbs are becoming more cosmopolitan, particularly with the proliferation of restaurants and cafés.

Olympic Games money and euphoria drove Sydney into the third millennium. Advantages of climate and location, supported by political and financial stability, should ensure the city's future as a commercial centre in the South Pacific, and as a major tourist destination in the 21st century. ❏

LEFT: opening ceremony of the 2000 Olympic Games.

Politics Sydney-style

Politics in New South Wales was never a profession for the wealthy and cultured gentleman, but rather a leg-up for ambitious men born into modest circumstances. Henry Parkes was born into a poor family in Warwickshire in 1816, and arrived in Sydney in 1839. He was premier four times, and he is best known for his advocacy of federation, which would see all the states of Australia come together as a nation. Aged 79, he married the nursemaid to the children from his second marriage despite a warning from a friend that "her sexual instincts may be strong". Parkes died six months later of heart failure.

Jack Lang, the "Big Fella", was a Labor premier during the 1920s and 1930s. A devout Catholic from a poor family and an anti-capitalist, he kept a mistress at Burwood and enjoyed modest wealth. In 1932, the Conservative federal government took over the financial powers of his administration, so Lang ordered NSW public servants not to pay funds into the federal treasury.

Sir Robert Askin, the son of a tram driver, was the Conservative premier of NSW from 1965 to 1975. He died in 1981, leaving an estate of nearly A$2 million. Soon after, the *National Times* claimed that the owners of the illegal gaming clubs and bookmakers that flourished in Sydney paid Askin and senior police officers thousands of dollars a week in bribes. He was also accused of selling knighthoods at A$60,000 per title.

Neville Wran, a highly successful Labor premier of the 1980s, found himself fighting corruption allegations while still in office, as did his Conservative successor Nick Greiner. Both men were exonerated. Happily, the worst thing they have to say about the current NSW premier, Bob Carr, is that he is overly intellectual.

Apart from its colourful coterie of NSW premiers, Sydney is also home to many current and former national politicians. Gough and Margaret Whitlam, were

Australia's "First Couple" between 1972 and 1975. Now in their eighties, they remain gregarious participants of Sydney's social scene, and among the many indefatigable Sydneysiders who would go to the opening of an envelope if asked.

Bob Hawke, Labor prime minister from 1983 to 1991, hails originally from Melbourne. On being unceremoniously booted from office by his own party, Hawke moved to Sydney, stayed in the suite of a five-star hotel, renovated a harbourside mansion, divorced his wife and married his somewhat younger biographer. His usurper Paul Keating, prime minister between 1991

and 1996, was born in Sydney – but certainly not where he now resides. Keating created a good deal of gossip when he bought a A$2.3-million house in one of Sydney's most exclusive streets, rather than in his electorate in the outer suburbs.

The present prime minister and Liberal (read conservative) John Howard is from Sydney, and downright refuses to move to the national capital, Canberra, as he is supposed to do. Instead, Howard and his family reside at the prime ministerial Sydney residence, Kirribilli House, a Victorian Gothic mansion with rolling green lawns and sublime harbour frontage. ❏

RIGHT: Sydneysider John Howard.

Decisive Dates

C.45,000 BC The first Aboriginal people arrive in the Sydney area; they live by hunting and fishing, and paint elaborate rock art.

1770 Captain James Cook lands at Botany Bay and raises the Union Flag, claiming the east coast of Australia for the British Crown.

1788 The First Fleet arrives from England with 1,030 people, including 736 convicts under the command of Arthur Phillip. The prison camp of New South Wales is set up in Sydney Cove.

1789 First convict is hanged for murdering a fellow-prisoner. Skirmishes with Aborigines, Bennelong captured as mediator.

1790 Ill-equipped Second Fleet arrives; the colony nearly succumbs to starvation.

1793 Free settlers arrive in the colony; ex-convict James Ruse begins the first farm in Parramatta.

1797 The first Merino sheep brought to Australia from South Africa, starting the wool trade.

1802 After four convicts are killed by Aborigines, a party is sent out to "punish the natives". White settlement of Australia is pushed forward with "a line of blood".

1803 The *Sydney Gazette*, Australia's first broadsheet newspaper, is published.

1804 Irish convicts revolt in Castle Hill Reserve. The uprising is crushed, and nine leaders are hanged.

1808 Soldiers rebel against the heavy-handed Governor William Bligh in the so-called "Rum Rebellion" (rum being the colony's main unit of currency).

1810–21 Governor Lachlan Macquarie begins to transform Sydney from a convict camp into an outpost of the British Empire. Ex-forger and architect Francis Greenway begins designing public buildings.

1815 Explorers Blaxland, Wentworth and Lawson find a way through the Blue Mountains, heralding Sydney's commercial expansion as a port.

1836 Visiting Sydney on the *Beagle*, Charles Darwin is fascinated by Australian flora and fauna, and predicts grand things for British settlement. Free settlers begin to arrive in large numbers.

1840 Following pressure from free settlers, the transportation of convicts to Sydney is abolished.

1851 Gold discovered near Bathurst in the Blue Mountains, starting Australia's first gold rush. Fears of Russian invasion: Fort Denison built in Sydney Harbour.

1855 The first railway, between Sydney and Parramatta, begins operation.

1868 Attempted assassination of the Duke of Edinburgh while on a royal visit.

1880 The Garden Palace, in the Botanic Gardens, hosts the southern hemisphere's first International Exhibition. *Sydney Bulletin* magazine heralds a literary boom.

1891 Australian Impressionists of the Heidelberg school, Arthur Streeton and Tom Roberts, set up artists' colony in Mosman.

1900 Bubonic plague causes large areas of Sydney's Rocks area to be razed.

1901 Federation: states join together to become the Commonwealth of Australia. Melbourne is the temporary capital, but Sydney insists that a new capital, Canberra, be built halfway between the two cities.

1902 Women win the right to vote in New South Wales. Thanks to union movement, Sydney workers attain higher living standards than British or American equivalents.

1914 Sydneysiders enlist en masse to fight in World War I, in which Australia suffers the highest per capita casualties of any allied nation.

1919 Spanish influenza epidemic kills more people in Sydney than four years of war.

1930 Donald Bradman scores 452 not out, a record score in first-class cricket, at the Sydney Cricket Ground.

1932 Sydney Harbour Bridge opens. Premier Jack Lang dismissed for threatening to default on war debt payments to Britain. Relations with Britain further damaged by England cricketers' bodyline bowling tactics, which aimed directly at batsmen.

1935 Luna Park, Sydney's harbourside entertainment centre, opens its gates.

1939 Sydneysiders enlist en masse again to fight in Europe during World War II.

1942 Japanese advance in the Pacific: Australian forces recalled from Europe. Three midget submarines cause havoc in Sydney Harbour, torpedoing a ferry on which troops are sleeping; 19 troops are killed.

1945 To celebrate the return to peace, the first Sydney to Hobart sailing race is held.

1951 Australia signs ANZUS defence treaty, aligning itself more closely with the USA.

1954 Outpourings of support as Queen Elizabeth II visits Sydney.

1956 Television comes to Sydney, and with it American cultural influences.

1958 Work begins on the Sydney Opera House.

1961 The last trams are removed from Sydney's streets.

1965 The first Australian troops are sent to Vietnam; skyscrapers begin to change Sydney's skyline.

1967 Australian Aborigines are allowed to vote for the first time.

1973 Sydney Opera House opens. With the demise of the White Australia policy, Asian immigration begins to change the face of Sydney. "Green bans" imposed by building unions save key historical districts from demolition.

1978 The first Gay and Lesbian Mardi Gras parade staged in Darlinghurst.

1980s Sydney takes over Melbourne's role as the financial capital of Australia.

1988 Sydney is the focus of celebrations for the Australian Bicentenary; Aboriginal activists lead protests against 200 years of white "invasion", demanding native land rights.

1993 Sydney wins bid to hold the 2000 Olympics. Massive public building begins, followed by a real estate frenzy.

1997 The last Easter Show is held in Randwick; site is developed as Rupert Murdoch's Fox film studio.

1999 The NSW Labor government wins easy re-election (giving it a historic third term). Massive New Year's Eve fireworks display over

Sydney Harbour sees in the millennium.

2000 Sydney hosts the Olympic Games.

2001 Australian Centenary of Federation Day Parade held in Sydney.

2002 Construction begins on the Cross City Tunnel. Sydney hosts the 6th International Gay Games.

2003 Bob Carr's NSW Labor Government re-elected for historic third term. A $60-million City Gateways project announced, to upgrade and beautify the city's main entry points. Sydney hosts the Rugby World Cup Final (England beat Australia 20–17).

2005 Completion date for City Gateways and Cross City Tunnel. ❏

LEFT: ships approach 19th-century Sydney.
RIGHT: Luna Park, Sydney's harbourside funfair, opened its doors in 1935.

SYDNEYSIDERS

It was the world's most picturesque penal colony.
But successive generations replaced brutality
with a famously relaxed attitude, and subsequent
waves of immigration have produced a multicultural
city containing people from all over the world

Sydneysiders, as they like to be called, are most commonly described as "easygoing", in the same way that New Yorkers are "brash", Parisians are "arrogant" and Romans are "mad". And if you have to choose one word for an umbrella description of 4 million people, "easygoing" is probably not a bad one to settle for.

Go into the most expensive restaurant in Sydney and you'll probably spot a man without a tie. Take a stroll through an inner-city suburb and you'll see casual groupings of café dwellers perched on tiny stools alongside busy roads, yelling at one another in order to be heard over the street noise. Go anywhere near a beachside suburb in summer and the dominant garb is a wet swimming costume and bare feet. In Sydney you sit up front in the taxi, and the driver talks to you the whole way.

Formality, whether it's a waiter shaking out your napkin, or a shop-girl showing you the latest young designer trends, always seems like a parody. Business meetings begin with a joke or quick round-up of the weekend cricket scores. Builders call their wealthy clients "mate", as they shake their heads over a difficult job before they put the price up. And wasn't it a Sydneysider, the then Prime Minister of Australia Paul Keating, who put his hand in the small of the Queen's back to steer her forward, creating a tabloid furore about the familiarity towards a Royal personage?

But despite this "no worries" approach to life's complexities, Sydneysiders play hard, and there is no way that this city could have become what it has in 200 years without the

formidable will of its people. Sydney was a penal colony on the outer rim of nowhere. It was an infamously brutal place, but also a clean slate. The prejudices of the old class system seemed absurd when set against the common discomfort and despair, and the eternal need for food and shelter.

It was a place where, overwhelmingly, ability was more important than just about anything else. The early Sydneysiders not only learnt to make do in the most rudimentary of circumstances, but also put their collective shoulder to the bulwark and pushed and struggled their way out of the mire and misery of their beginnings.

Successive waves of immigrants have arrived, adding layers of complexity to the question of what the Sydney character actually is. But what they have not done is to dilute the essence of the city's determination. Indeed, their own fierce ambition for escape and renewal has only served to fuel that which already exists. An easygoing attitude is to Sydney what good manners were to 18th-century England: the acceptable front, the filter through which the business of life is conducted. But what really gets Sydneysiders out of bed in the mornings is their ambition, impatience, curiosity, energy and the belief that it can always be done better.

are a professional couple or a single person, you'll probably enjoy life in a terraced house or modern apartment in the fastest growing residential area of Sydney, the inner city.

But if you're spot-on average, a low- to middle-income family with a couple of kids, home will be Sydney's demographic heartland, the western suburbs. And, like the majority of the population, you may take a trip to the city centre and see its postcard images only once every few months.

Multicultural Sydney

As one of the prime destinations for immigrants, together with Melbourne, Sydney is

Demographics

If you live in Sydney, it is likely your household will have an average weekly income of between A$600 and A$700. You will have a one in six or seven chance of being tertiary educated and a one in four chance of being born overseas. If you are rich or well-off you will live in the eastern suburbs or the North Shore; if you are one half of a young, middle-class couple with a good income, you will probably have just bought a house in the inner west; and if you

home to representatives of no fewer than 180 nationalities. English is definitely the main language, but Italian and Spanish, Chinese and Arabic, and a host of other major and a few more obscure languages are spoken daily at work and at home.

To be sure, the cultural mix (and political power) in Australia has, until recent times, been dominated by the broadly defined Anglo-Saxon and Anglo-Celtic cultures, but the modern nation of Australia has to a large degree been multicultural and multiracial since the very first flotilla of British and European colonialists arrived. New arrivals on the First Fleet overwhelmingly consisted of convict citizens

PRECEDING PAGES: at Royal Easter Show, Olympic Park.
LEFT: cold beer aids the "no worries" attitude.
ABOVE: exhibitor at the Museum of Contemporary Art.

from England, but also included the Irish, former slaves from Africa and those of Jewish faith. The Second and Third Fleets brought people from still broader cultural horizons, and this population laid the groundwork of the pot-pourri of peoples who would come to be known as "Australian".

Fifty-six percent of the 160,000 convicts who came to Australia were English. English migrants continued to drift steadily to Australian shores, with big influxes in the 1920s and post-World War II. Around 1 million Australians are probably English-born.

After the English, the most substantial grouping is Irish: 23 percent of all convicts were of Irish stock. Further large numbers immigrated in the late 19th century as a result of the Great Potato Famine. Seven million Australians now claim Irish heritage. Politically, Australia's powerful union movement began with the Irish Catholics, and even today they can be said to be well represented in the lively arena of left-wing politics.

The gold-rush years of the 1850s saw an immense leap in new arrivals and significant numbers of Italians and Chinese, but the real changes to Australia's predominantly "Anglo" stock didn't come until the major immigration programmes of the 1950s and 1960s, and the enormous intake of immigrants from South-

SYDNEY'S CHANGING FACES

To trace the history of a small inner-suburb block and its neighbourhood, as Nadia Wheatley and Donna Rawlins did in the 1980s children's book *My Place*, is to realise the diversity of the city's people. Beginning as an Aboriginal camp in 1788, this block has included, in sequence, an English settler, his family and their descendants; a ticket-of-leave man (a pardoned convict) and his family; the family of an American gold miner; a Chinese market gardener; a German family called Müller (renamed Miller by 1918); a cell of the Labor Party; a city banker and family; World War I veterans; a large Irish family; Greeks, Italians, Lebanese immigrants and an Egyptian family.

east Asia from the 1970s, as well as people from the Middle East. The result of these immigrations has been a huge shift in demographics, with the old, broadly defined cultures having to digest a loss of cultural domination and a gain of immense energy, entrepreneurialism and cosmopolitanism.

The influence of the Italians on the life of the city is profound. Whenever a Sydneysider sits down to a perfectly made espresso, they can thank post-World War II immigration for their luck, not to mention food, the arts, business and politics, indeed a whole range of areas to which this phenomenally successful group has contributed. Half a million Italians came to Australia, with the greatest number coming to Sydney. The Italian community based itself around Leichhardt, which is still the best place to go for a knockout Italian meal.

Following the horrors of World War II, Australia had one of the most relaxed immigration policies in the world, and was an obvious choice for many of the Jewish survivors of the Holocaust, as well as other refugees from war-torn Eastern Europe.

The Asian inheritance

An estimated 115,000 Sydneysiders have Chinese as their first language. The first Chinese emigrated to Australia in the last years of the

Vietnamese represent the latest mass-immigration project, and because Cabramatta has a drug problem, this particular Asian community is readily vilified by direct attack or by implication. The fact of the matter is that if there were a way of measuring achievement against hardship, these people who arrived in leaky, unstable boats with their lives torn asunder by war would probably count as the city's most successful community.

Some of the first Japanese to come ashore in Australia were distinctly unwelcome, arriving as they did in enemy submarines in Sydney Harbour during World War II. In recent years, however, this unhappy past has been

18th century, but the big influxes came with the discovery of gold. The commercial and social heartland for the Chinese is Chinatown, with big residential communities in Burwood in the inner west and Chatswood on the North Shore.

From 1975 some 140,000 Vietnamese came to Australia, most of them refugees from the Vietnam War. In Sydney they settled in the western suburbs, many of them around Cabramatta, which is probably the most intensely non-Anglo pocket of Sydney. Because the

forgotten and Japanese schools are as prolific in the city as the Japanese restaurants.

Other groups

The other significant cultural communities of Sydney are the Lebanese (105,000 speakers of Arabic), Greek (although many more went to Melbourne, which is now one of the largest Greek cities in the world), Indonesians (although, again, larger communities exist in Darwin, which is nearer to the Asian island country than it is to its own capital), Turkish, South Americans (particularly from Chile and Argentina), South Africans and, the nearest of neighbours, the New Zealanders, who have

LEFT: schoolchildren on the way home by ferry.
ABOVE: ferries are also used for commuting to work.

quite a colony at Bondi. And, of course, the indigenous people of Australia, the Aborigines, still have a place in the country, and, after years of repression, are beginning to make their mark in their land of birth.

Today it is not just a case of being one race or another – it has been estimated that half of all Sydneysiders are of mixed race, and half of those are a mix of three races or more.

Heroes and villains

In his book *The Fatal Shore*, Robert Hughes said Sydney was destined to be both tainted and ennobled by its beginnings as a penal settlement. This statement can be tested by a look at both

sides of what the city's famous larrikin streak and irreverence for authority has produced.

For Sydneysiders, the abuse of power is no surprise. The city has had its fair share of gangs, thugs and debauchery, including the infamous 1920s madams, Kate Leigh and Tilly Devine. When Justice James Wood, heading up a royal commission on the police force in the 1990s, found that police corruption was "systemic and entrenched", Sydney said, "Yes, and what else is new?" The line between the crooks and the enforcers has always been a very thin one. Known crime figures have gone about their business, unheeded, for decades; politicians have used

their positions to further their own interests and the police have basically run their own show in the way that suits them best.

Just as the first convicts looked at their captors' controlling systems and wondered why they were the ones in chains, later Sydneysiders have decided that if "everyone else is doing it, why shouldn't I?" On a more positive note, however, these days Sydney is so paranoid about damaging allegations that it tends to keep its power bases, at least in the public sector, fairly well swept.

This Sydney trick of pushing the limits has also produced some exceptional individuals who have turned it to the public good. Jack Mundey was a union leader in the 1970s, who initiated the "green bans", whereby unionists would refuse to work on sites that threatened historic or environmentally sensitive areas of the city. Juanita Nielsen was an heiress and a journalist campaigning for the same cause, particularly in preservation of the Potts Point terrace houses *(see page 162)*. She disappeared in July 1975, and was most likely murdered. The efforts of these courageous people saved the last swathes of what are today Sydney's most notable districts.

Pioneers have also appeared in the field of medicine, with people such as heart transplant surgeon Victor Chang, and eye doctor to the Third World, Fred Hollows. Then there are the sporting heroes, people such as Kay Cottee, the first woman to sail solo around the world, and Dawn Fraser, who won Olympic gold at three games but was barred from the fourth for improper behaviour. Dawn Fraser could, in fact, serve as a kind of parable for the character of Sydney: three parts exceptional, fully armed with a determination to see it done, and one part unpredictable, never knowing what the next move might be.

Most Sydneysiders are now tired of the "convict" tag, particularly since so few of them now have any kind of convict heritage, but the unruly character has persisted in the city to a more positive end – a flouting of authority and an independence of spirit, which may go against the traditional grain of the so-called "motherland", but certainly gets things done. ❑

LEFT: Chinese Australians in Sydney's Chinatown.

The First Sydneysiders

I t is thought that all Aboriginal Australians originally hailed from Asia, crossing over from New Guinea around 50,000 BC, when there was still a land bridge. (Tasmania and New Guinea were not separated from the mainland until 12,000 BC, when sea levels rose after the last ice age.)

Aboriginal people probably settled in the Sydney area around 40,000 BC. When the First Fleet arrived, three groups occupied the region: the Eora people lived around the harbour, the Duruk to the north and the Dharawal to the south. They pursued a nomadic existence, living in tight territorial groups, with respected elders but no leader; order was provided by family ties, language and rituals.

There were probably some 1,500 Eora living in the vicinity of Sydney, surviving on shellfish, bush food and animals. They sheltered in harbourside caves and were superbly adapted to their land and its conditions, preserving whatever they could – unlike their colonisers.

The Eora people greeted the Europeans calmly at first, but nothing in their existence could prepare them for the future. Governor Phillip was under orders to treat the "natives" with kindness, and he dealt severely with anyone he suspected of maltreatment. But the British settlers could not understand the Aborigines' nomadic lifestyle or the profound connection they had to their tribal lands. It seemed that they came and went without reason across the sparse landscape. The island of Australia was conveniently declared a *terra nullius* ("no-one's land") – effectively an uninhabited void that Europeans could occupy without further thought.

The results were devastating. As white settlers arrived by the boatload, Aboriginal communities were systematically pushed from their homes, leading to the disruption and destruction of their traditional culture and communal life. Massacres of the

RIGHT: intermingling at a Corroboree.

indigenous people became common, and introduced diseases such as smallpox killed off many more. In 1788, there were possibly more than 300,000 Aborigines in Australia; by 1900, there were 60,000.

No descendants of the Eora people remain but Sydney has an Aboriginal population of some 35,000 drawn from other parts of Australia. The original tribes survive only in Aboriginal names such as Bondi, Woolloomooloo and Parramatta.

It was not until the 1970s that Aborigines began to campaign for civil rights and the government began to listen. The Department of Aboriginal Affairs was

established in 1972, followed by the Aboriginal Development Commission in 1980.

The 1990s were a decade of attempted reconciliation between white Australians and the Aborigines. A High Court decision in June 1992 declared that, contrary to the legal position that had been upheld for the past two centuries, Australia was in fact an occupied country when the British arrived. This decision has had enormous implications for the seeking and granting of Aboriginal land rights, an issue which, more than any other, will determine whether or not the concept of reconciliation can be fully realised. ❏

CREATIVE SYDNEY

The early colonials were too busy with survival to devote much time to culture, but for the past 100 years or more Sydneysiders have made their mark in literature, the visual arts and film

The Europeans who arrived in Australia in 1788 had no idea what to make of this new country. They had no way of framing the vast sweep of the continent, no points of reference back to the compact, picturesque island that they had left behind, in most cases for ever. Their early paintings of animals showed strange mythical beasts, kangaroos that looked like half-horses, tiny marsupials that looked like ship rats. The landscapes similarly made little sense. The essential features, the scale and the shape were right – but the imagination that rendered them was distinctly European, filtering any possibility of visual truth.

The writers, too, struggled for context. Faced with a beautiful wilderness one First Fleet correspondent could only see the absence of his own familiar landscape: "This is the poorest country in the world… overrun with large trees, not one acre of clear ground to be seen."

By the time this alien world did start to make some kind of sense, it was largely because of interpretations by artists and writers, who "framed" the new landscape for the benefit of the public, even if at times it took the public 40 or 50 years to grasp the image.

Until recently, Sydney has never had much of a reputation for culture. Quite simply, there were too many other things to do, too many hardships to overcome. The writers, painters and other artists who did pursue creative prac-

tices were isolated twice over – from their own community, and from the cultural activity of the rest of the world. Even today, the tradition of fleeing abroad to find a more appreciative audience remains quite strong. But isolation has not been all bad, and has produced some fascinating adaptations. Australian culture is judged these days not for how well it measures up to other cultures, but for how well it stands individually and alone.

The printed page

Literature in Australia once meant literary works from Britain, but in recent years Australians have developed a growing reputation

LEFT: the Sydney Symphony Orchestra at the Opera House. **RIGHT:** award-winning author Peter Carey.

for being readers and book buyers of American authors, other post-colonials and, increasingly, work by a home-grown stable of writers.

Australia in the 19th century was a rural society; the industrialisation of Sydney did not really begin until the 1870s. Novelists wrote about the bush rather than the city, so the only real 19th-century writing about Sydney is in travel books, such as Backhouse's *A Narrative of a Visit to the Australian Colonies* (1843), and Trollope's *Australia and New Zealand* (1876).

It wasn't until the early 20th century that Sydney writers began looking to their urban environment for inspiration. Louis Stone's

Jonah (1909), a naturalistic account of the career of a larrikin from the slums, was the first novel of any literary merit set in urban Sydney. Christina Stead's early novels, *Seven Poor Men of Sydney* (1934) and *For Love Alone* (1944) evoke Sydney during the 1920s and 1930s.

Kylie Tennant's *Foveaux* (1939) is set in Surry Hills, then Sydney's most notorious slum, on the cusp of World War II. Ruth Park's *Harp in the South* (1948) and its sequel, *Poor Man's Orange* (1949), offer a more vivid, if at times sentimental account of impoverished Irish family life in Surry Hills.

Patrick White's *Riders in the Chariot*

(1961) and *The Solid Mandala* (1966) are set in Sydney's northwestern suburbs, but the focus is more on character than landscape. Sydney is a more palpable presence in *The Vivisector* (1970). Written after White moved from Castle Hill to Centennial Park in 1964, it is about the life of a Surry Hills painter who later lives and works in the city.

Contemporary writers include Peter Corris (born 1942), whose fictional detective Cliff Hardy trawls through the seedier streets of the city, and Peter Carey, who was born in 1943 in Melbourne, but has featured a refracted Sydney in a selection of his prize-winning novels. His *True History of the Kelly Gang*, based on the life of Australia's favourite outlaw, won the 2001 Booker Prize.

Two of Sydney's most famous novelists are Thomas Keneally and Bryce Courtenay. Both have made their name casting their net further than the bounds of Sydney life. Keneally's most famous book is *Schindler's Ark* (1982), a harrowing tale of the wartime Holocaust in Europe, and a Booker Prize-winner, while Courtenay's *The Power of One* is set against the drama of South Africa's apartheid system. Both have also been made into internationally successful films.

Early visual art

The first artists of Sydney were not European at all, but rather the Eora people, who carved images of humans, animals and Dreamtime figures into the sandstone of the area, and made drawings and stencils from ochre. There are some 5,500 rock-art sites in the Sydney region, including those that record colonisation. Although some of the early colonists were fascinated by the artwork, the more common view was that it was crude and inferior.

The first European drawings and watercolours of Sydney were by amateur artists who arrived on the First Fleet. George Raper, a midshipman on the *Supply*, and the anonymous "Port Jackson Painter" recorded the Aborigines, Australian landscape, flora and fauna, and later the progress of settlement.

The arrival of Conrad Martens in 1835 marked the beginning of professional landscape painting in Sydney. He remained in the city until his death in 1878, painting many large oils and watercolours of Sydney, particularly its harbour and foreshores. *Elizabeth Bay and Elizabeth House* (1839), *View of Darlinghurst, Woolloomooloo Bay on Left* (1843) and *Campbell's Wharf, Circular Quay, from Dawes Point* (1855) are among the finest examples.

Joseph Fowles, George Peacock and Samuel Elyard also painted views of Sydney in the Romantic tradition until the 1870s. Landscapes of the interior by Louis Buvelot, William Pigunit and Eugene von Guerard, however, attracted the most interest and the commissions.

Buvelot's *plein air* techniques inspired the

but Sydney's younger artists were seeking new inspiration. Dorrit Black, Roy De Maistre and Roland Wakelin began under Impressionist influences but by the 1930s were working in abstract, cubist, constructivist and even vorticist styles. Dorrit Black moved from the Impressionistic *Boatshed, Neutral Bay* (1920) to the cubist-constructivist *The Bridge* (1930). Grace Cossington Smith's *The Bridge In-Curve* (1930) shows vorticist influences. De Maistre's *Old Cremorne Wharf* (1918) reflects Monet, while *Dry Dock (The Rocks, Sydney)* (c.1929) features geometric outlines and flat colours characteristic of German modernists.

Heidelberg school, a group of painters who brought Impressionism to Australia in the 1880s. Tom Roberts, Julian Ashton, Charles Condor, Arthur Streeton and Sydney Long were among its members who worked in the city. Examples of their work include Roberts's *The Camp at Sirius Cove* (1899) and *Mosman's Bay* (1894); Streeton's *McMahon's Point* (1890) and *The Railway Station, Redfern* (1893); and Condor's *Departure of the SS Orient* (1888).

Impressionism lingered after World War I

Postwar Moderns

Since 1945, abstract and other modernist styles have overshadowed landscape painting. Still, Sydney has been favoured more than any other Australian city by the work of four painters who interpreted its moods and contradictions. Sali Herman painted the narrow lanes and crumbling terraces of 19th-century Sydney: *McElhone Stairs* (1944) and *Near the Docks* (1949) are two of his best-known paintings. Geoffrey Smart, by contrast, paints the expressways, glass and concrete of the late 20th century in the urban realism style. *Cahill Expressway* (1962) and *Central Station* (1974), with their architectural outlines and

LEFT: author Thomas Keneally in his study.
ABOVE: *The Blue Mountains*, by Conrad Martens.

GALLERIES AND PERFORMING ARTS

In the *Activities* section of *Travel Tips*, starting on page 221, you'll find a detailed listing of many of Sydney's art galleries, followed on page 222 by a round-up of the city's theatre, opera and dance companies, and the venues where they perform.

flat blocks of colour, suggest the alienation of the individual in an impersonal city.

Lloyd Rees's career spanned three-quarters of the 20th century, during which time he produced paintings and pencil drawings of Sydney's buildings and landscapes. In his last years, he painted a series of Turner-esque

landscapes of the harbour. *Three Boats, Lane Cove River* (1979) in the Art Gallery of New South Wales (AGNSW) captures the heat and colours of the harbour better than the work of almost any other artist.

Brett Whiteley is probably Sydney's most famous painter of the last 30 years. Sensual, expressionist canvases like *Balcony 2* (1975) and *Balmoral* (1975–78) depict a Sydney landscape of intense but fleeting pleasures. Much of his work can be seen at his studio in Surry Hills *(see page 124)* and at the AGNSW.

Globalisation has brought down the borders in recent years, and a wash of international trends and themes are spilling over onto Aus-

tralia's shores. If contemporary artists, children of the 1960s and 1970s, touch on Australian themes at all, it's likely to be the dominance of suburbia in Australian life. The Museum of Contemporary Art (MCA) in The Rocks has a strong collection of modern Australian work, typified by the Loti and Victor Smorgon Collection, over 150 works from the 1980s and 1990s by Australian artists spanning several generations.

But the most dynamic work these days is that by indigenous artists – it has taken 200 years for the colonists to reach into their imaginations and start seeing its possibilities, which is what initially they so steadfastly

refused to do. The AGNSW has the largest collection in Australia of works in traditional and contemporary styles, and the MCA's permanent exhibits include the Maningrida and Ramingining collections, both containing stunning examples of work being produced by Aboriginal artists.

Australian cinema

You don't have to wait to come to Australia to see an Australian film – these days they are everywhere. Australia was one of the pioneers of cinema, producing films, or parts thereof, in the late 19th century. The local industry pottered along for about 70 years until the

1960s and 1970s, when there was a sudden explosion of output, or a renaissance as it was generously called. It was prompted by the setting up of the Australian Film, Television and Radio School and the introduction of tax breaks for investment in the local product.

Sydney and Melbourne have long competed for dominance in this industry, and it is usually Melbourne that does slightly better, particularly from a critical perspective. However, the setting up of Fox Studios at Darling Harbour means that Sydney will probably now gain the upper hand, if only commercially – particularly since Hollywood film director George Lucas chose Sydney as a base for film-

Desert (1994); and a deceptively simple tale of one girl's dream to get married in *Muriel's Wedding* (1994).

Not all Sydney *auteurs* stay at home to make their movies. After creating two pieces of classic Australian cinema – *Picnic at Hanging Rock* (1975) and *Gallipoli* (1981) – Sydney-born Peter Weir headed for Hollywood, to direct a string of commercially and critically successful movies, from *Witness* (1985), through *Dead Poets Society* (1989) and *The Truman Show* (1998) to the swashbuckling seafaring adventure *Master and Commander* (2003), starring his compatriot Russell Crowe.

ing large sections of two *Star Wars* films, *The Phantom Menace* (1999) and *Attack of the Clones* (2002).

Some of the better-known films shot partly or completely in Sydney include action fantasy *Mad Max 3: Beyond Thunderdome* (1985); a tongue-in-cheek look at the world of dance and a more serious look at racial prejudice in *Strictly Ballroom* (1992); the tale of three drag artists on tour across the Outback in *The Adventures of Priscilla, Queen of the*

One of the most popular dates on the Sydney calendar for film buffs is the annual Sydney Film Festival, which occupies two weeks in the middle of June. Hollywood blockbusters, low-budget gems and artist retrospectives are among the events on offer.

Fans not just of films but of cinemas themselves should pay a visit to the venerable State Theatre on Market Street (also the main venue for the Sydney Film Festival). Opened in 1929, its baroque interior, featuring an original Wurlitzer organ that still rises from below the stage before each performance, is a beautiful remnant from the cinema industry's golden age. ❑

LEFT: Sydney's most commercial artist, Ken Done, and his *Chinaman's Beach*. **ABOVE:** the Bangarra Dance Theatre combine Aboriginal and Western traditions.

SPORTING SYDNEY

The spectacular setting and amenable climate encourage exercise. But sport also has an important social function for Sydneysiders

L ike the rest of Australia, Sydney is addicted to sport – although the obsession is not as pathological as it is in Melbourne (the country's self-styled sporting capital), where sport is the most seriously discussed issue on any given day. In fact, when Melbourne hosted a Rugby League event, a game native to Sydney and alien to Melbourne, the highest attendance figure was recorded for any such match held in Australia. In terms of sport, Melbournians will watch anything, anytime, anywhere. Sydneysiders are perhaps a little bit more relaxed. They love the big one-off events, they loved the idea of staging the Olympics (although they grumbled a lot about the logistics), they love their home-grown rugby and they love a summer's day spent at a cricket match. But most of all Sydneysiders love the social and communal possibilities that sport brings with it – the chance for a big event, preferably with fireworks, a good time and a bit of an argument. They recognise that sport is, by nature, a diversion, particularly in a city as beautiful and energetic as this one.

The Home Code – Rugby League

Rugby League, "the toughest game on earth", is what people generally mean when they talk about "football" in Sydney. It is a large-scale physical game, a war between teams comprising 13 muscle-clad players apiece.

Rugby League began in 1907 after a dispute in the amateur rugby union over the payment

of expenses. A group of players left the game and set up a new code, calling it "league"; the players of the original code had to make do with the term "union". (Much the same had happened in England 12 years earlier.) The game took off immediately in Sydney, with the South Sydney Club winning the first premiership in 1908.

For many years the competition was strictly local, but in the 1980s Rugby League became a national affair, drawing in clubs from Queensland, regional NSW and Canberra, as well as losing local favourites such as Newtown, the oldest club in the League. The new national profile made the game a target and, in 1996,

LEFT: the NSW Waratahs (in blue) vs. the Queensland Reds. **RIGHT:** a dedicated fan of the Sydney Roosters.

A BRUTAL GAME

Australian novelist Patrick White described rugby as "thugs writhing in the mud and bashing the hell out of one another in the name of sport".

media baron Rupert Murdoch attempted to "buy" the game and the valuable broadcasting rights that went with it. The official body, the Australian Football League (ARL), went into battle with the billionaire titan and the result was a split league. The ARL kept 12 teams, while 10 went over to the new competition called Super League. Needless to say the fans were not happy, and displayed deep apathy

towards both competitions. Recognising the possibility of a "divide and lose everything" scenario, the two sides came together in 1998, putting an unwieldy 20 teams into competition under the banner of the National Rugby League; the number of teams was changed to 14 in 2000, then to 15 the following year.

The rough and tumble of rugby makes it a terrific spectator sport. Games are played from March to September. There are a number of venues around town, but the home ground of the Sydney Roosters – NSW's most successful team in recent years – and the   South Sydney Rabbitohs is the Aussie Stadium, built in 1988 in Moore Park. The Penrith Panthers play at

Penrith Stadium. Tickets to most of the season's games are inexpensive and easily procured.

Some of the most fierce and exciting matches are played in the State of Origin series, where players discard club allegiances to play for their home state. Look out for games at the Telstra Stadium in Olympic Park from May to July each year.

Rugby Union and Aussie Rules

Rugby Union takes a fairly quiet course through the Sydney football scene. Born of the English public-school rugby code, it was first played in the colony in 1829, and remained strictly an amateur sport up until 1996, when the game was commercialised at the top level. The Wallabies are Australia's international team, playing around six home games a year – but a lot more than that in 2003, when Australia hosted the Rugby World Cup. The Wallabies were beaten 20–17 by England in the final, played at the Aussie Stadium.

The New South Wales Waratahs play in the Super 12, an international provincial series that consists of five teams from New Zealand, four from South Africa and three from Australia. The Waratahs play their home games at the Aussie Stadium.

Australian Rules Football is Melbourne's version of the game; the one that paralyses the southern city for the final few weeks of the season in September. When there was talk in 1998 of scheduling a federal election one week after the Grand Final, great minds went to work on the question of whether or not football fever might prove too much of a distraction to the voters. And the prevaricating was not that absurd, for the truth of the matter is that many Australians don't care much about politics, unless a political decision is made that affects their footy. Like League, Aussie Rules went national in the 1980s, and Sydney, somewhat spellbound by this strange code, agreed to take on the old South Melbourne team as their official home team. The result is the Sydney Swans, a fairly successful side. They play their home games at the Sydney Cricket Ground, and occasionally at the Telstra Stadium, from March through to August or September. Watch a game if you can – there is no other code like it in the world.

Soccer

Soccer is played by 400 million people world-wide. In Australia, while it has nothing like the profile of the other codes, it enjoys the highest participation rate, with some 100,000 players in Sydney alone taking to the field each weekend. When multicultural TV station SBS (fondly known as "Soccer Bloody Soccer") broadcasts the World Cup games, its normally low ratings go through the roof.

The Ericsson Cup, the national league competition, is played from October to May. Several Sydney clubs are involved and games are played at venues across town, with finals at Sydney Football Stadium, Centennial Park.

series (where the players sensibly wear traditional and cooling white) and World Series one-day matches (in brightly coloured nylon uniforms for the benefit of the cameras).

For a decade or more, Australia has been the dominant team in both the one-day and five-day versions of the game. Outstanding New South Wales players who have represented their country in recent years include Mark and Steve Waugh, Brett Lee, Glenn McGrath, Michael Bevan, Michael Slater and Stuart MacGill.

Tickets are readily available for most of the local matches, but book ahead for the World Series matches, which are by far the most popu-

Cricket

Like many former outposts of the British Empire, Australia looks on cricket as one of the compensations for years of colonial rule.

The first official match was played in Sydney in 1804 (it's hard to imagine why it took so long), on a site that would later become Hyde Park. Sydney Cricket Ground saw its first action in 1854, with a match between locals and Victorians. Cricket today is played at state level in the Sheffield Shield Competition, and at international level in Test Cricket

lar. A traditional way to watch a match is on the "outer", the area where the cheapest tickets are sold. It's also a good way to catch the sun while shouting sport for your chosen team.

Basketball

Basketball dominates the winter indoor activity in the country, with Sydney being handsomely represented in the National Basketball League by the Sydney Kings. To borrow a cliché, the game has gone ahead in leaps and bounds in Australia since the national league was launched in the late 1970s.

The Kings and their arch rivals West Sydney Razorbacks both play at the Sydney

LEFT: the Sydney Swans (in red and white) fly the flag for Aussie Rules. **ABOVE:** Sydney Cricket Ground.

Entertainment Centre and the State Sports Centre in Olympic Park, where they do battle with sides from all other major cities, as well as each other. Although Australia's semi-professional league is still dominated by imported American players, the national team has enjoyed a strong standing within the world's top 10 since its creation.

Horse racing

No aspect of Sydney life has more intrigue, drama or colourful characters than the world of horse racing. Australians, they say, will bet on two flies crawling up a wall; Sydney has turned that national passion into a way of life.

Randwick, headquarters of the Australian Jockey Club (AJC). Not to be missed during the Carnival is the Golden Slipper at Rosehill. It may only be a 6-furlong (1,200-metre) sprint for two-year-old colts and fillies, but with prize money of A$2 million on offer, it stops the nation during its 70-second run. At Randwick at Easter, catch the 2-mile (3.2-km) Sydney Cup and the 1½-mile (2.4-km) AJC Derby.

Of course, you don't have to make it to the track to watch the action. Satellite TV in pubs and clubs covers metropolitan and provincial race meetings. You can bet in almost any number of combinations at a branch of the Totalizator Agency Board (TAB).

The action takes place on tracks in the suburbs of Canterbury (King Street), Royal Randwick (Alison Road), Rosehill (James Ruse Drive) and the suburban Warwick Farm (Hume Highway). They all rate among the best racecourses in the world in terms of the comforts they afford to the average racegoer: there are ample parking facilities, but the tracks are also accessible by public transport.

Sydney races all year round, with major midweek and Saturday afternoon meetings. The biggest dates in the calendar feature in March and April when the Autumn Carnival draws Australasia's finest horseflesh to the Sydney Turf Club's Rosehill course and Royal

If you have any cash to spare, save it for the greyhounds at Wentworth Park or the harness racing ("the trots") at Harold Park, Glebe, in the evening. In terms of esteem both rank behind the sport of kings. But what they lack in social status they match in gambling action.

Sailing

Sydney Harbour provides superb sailing for all levels, from professional racers to amateur weekend sailors. The big event of the year is the Sydney to Hobart Yacht Race, which starts in the harbour on Boxing Day. This is one of the city's favourite celebrations, attracting hordes of Christmas-fatigued residents carrying picnics of leftovers to whatever bit of the craggy foreshore offers a view of the billowing sails of the million-dollar boats as they whisk through the heads and out to the Tasman Sea.

Boat racing takes place right through the summer, and the best way to take a look is to hop aboard a Manly Ferry in the early evening. By far the most impressive of these races are those held for the 18-footer-class yachts, which skim, scud and scurry their way across the foam-tipped harbour waters with amazing speed. The Sydney Flying Squadron, which organises some of the races, offers tag-along ferry trips for spectators, leaving from the clubhouse in Milson's Point.

Surf carnivals

Between October and March, so-called surf carnivals are held almost every weekend up and down Sydney's beautiful coastline.

As well as providing the chance to watch professional surfers ride the waves with apparent ease, these are great family days out, with daredevil life-saving displays, Iron Man competitions and boat races all part of the fun.

Since the carnivals obviously depend on the wave conditions, many locations are not finalised until the day of the event. If you want to catch a local carnival, tune in to local radio stations on a Saturday morning to get the correct venue information.

Swimming

It's actually quite hard *not* to swim in a city like Sydney, surrounded as it is by water on all sides and basking in a climate that can be called Mediterranean one week, subtropical the next. Lap swimmers head for the Andrew (Boy) Charlton Pool in the Domain or the North Sydney Pool, both with salt water and harbour frontage. During Sydney's brief winter, the North Sydney Pool is tucked away under a huge balloon, to protect swimmers from the odd cold nip in the air.

The Sydney International Aquatic Centre at Olympic Park has raised the stakes considerably in terms of what Sydneysiders may expect from an indoor facility. Gone are the

WINTER SKIING

Skiing may not be a sport usually associated with sun-drenched Australia, but just over 200 km (125 miles) south of Sydney are the beautiful Snowy Mountains, with well-organised resorts and slopes to suit skiers of all abilities.

days of cloudy water, mouldy tiles and bathhouse temperatures. This sleek glass-encased facility has two Olympic-sized pools, a tropical-inspired leisure pool complete with rapids, and temperature and hygiene controls to rival those on a NASA spaceship.

A quintessentially Sydney experience is

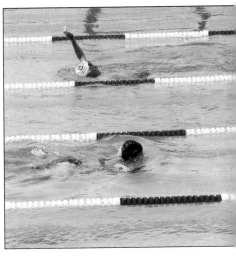

sea-bath swimming. Out of favour for some time, the chlorine-fatigued are returning to have another look at these naturally filled marvels, perched along the edges of the suburban coastlines. The Bondi Icebergs is a Sydney institution as well as a pool, the place where the grand old men (and women) of the city strip down to their bathers in the middle of winter, and jump into an ice-filled pool to mark the start of the winter swimming season. Around the corner, Bronte offers another possibility. Down the coast at Coogee, female swimmers can visit a pleasing anachronism, the Women's Baths, while those of both sexes can lap it up at Wiley's Sea Baths.

LEFT: winning by three lengths at Royal Randwick.
RIGHT: swimming lengths in the "Boy" Charlton Pool.

WHERE TO WATCH AND PLAY

For details of the city's sports venues and information on playing tennis or golf, running or swimming while in Sydney, see the Sports section of Travel Tips, starting on page 229.

Jogging, walking and cycling

The ultimate jog in Sydney is the course of the City to Surf fun run, a 14-km (8½-mile) route along which more than 40,000 mad and merry men and women set out, each August, for the ultimate prize of having their name printed in the *Sydney Morning Herald* – provided, of

course, that they finish the race. Those who feel tired at the mere thought of such a run can select a choice spot from which to watch what is an amazing spectacle.

Less ambitious joggers, and cyclists as well, should head for Centennial Park for a gentle plod or pedal around this superb innercity parkland, which, at the 2000 Olympics, was the site of the hugely popular marathon and various road-cycling events. Bicycles can be hired at Centennial Park, as well as horses for the equestrian in need of a gallop.

The Domain is a spectacularly beautiful jogging location, as are Bondi Beach and the parkland around the lower North Shore, where you might just spot the prime minister, John Howard, stepping out from Kirribilli House for his regular morning constitutional.

Golf

Australia has the most golf courses in the world per head of population – there are around 100 courses in Sydney alone. Many of the private clubs have reciprocal membership arrangements with overseas clubs, so enquire at home before you leave.

If you have no club membership but still fancy a putt, the public courses are plentiful, cheap and very good. Suggestions include Moore Park, for its proximity to the city, and Long Reef, for the fact that it sits out on a finger surrounded by ocean on three sides – the ocean gales cause no end of problems, but with those views, anything is tolerable. The cost of 18 holes ranges from around A$10 to A$80.

The top championship golf courses hosting major tournaments are the Royal Sydney Golf Course, the city's most exclusive; the Lakes; the Australian; and the New South Wales Golf Course, on the cliffs of La Perouse, which, according to golfing legend Greg Norman, could easily become – perhaps with a little work – one of the top 10 golf courses in the world. The New South Wales Golf Association is as good a starting point as any for golfers in need of advice (tel: 9505 9105; website: www.nswga.com.au).

Tennis

Australia's main tennis tournament, the Australian Open, is staged in Melbourne, but visitors to Sydney might be able to catch some warm-up games at the Adidas International Tennis Tournament, held in mid-January at the NSW Tennis Centre in Olympic Park.

Those who want a bit of a hit should try the picturesque clay courts at Rushcutters Bay or the synthetic grass surfaces at Primrose Park Terrace in Cremorne on the lower North Shore. Tennis is cheap in Sydney compared to courts in Europe or the US; expect to pay between A$10 and A$15 for a game. Many courts are also floodlit for those wishing to play after dark. Contact Tennis New South Wales with course or event queries. ❑

LEFT: a clifftop chip at the New South Wales Golf Course.

A Sporting Spectacular

The Sydney 2000 Olympic Games were the biggest event ever held in Australia: some 10,000 athletes from 200 countries, 5,000 officials, 1,500 media representatives and several million visitors descended on the city. To accommodate the event, the old industrial site of Homebush Bay was given a thorough makeover, transforming it into Olympic Park *(see page 167)*.

Its most prominent sporting venues were the 110,000-seat Stadium Australia – the largest stadium in Olympic history, now called the Telstra Stadium and used by the various football codes and for large-scale concerts – and the Sydney International Athletics Centre, designed for preliminary competitions and as a warm-up venue for the competing athletes. The International Aquatic Centre was built to Olympic standards, with 10 competition lanes, waveproofing and rigid temperature controls. But it was planned with post-Olympics use in mind and includes leisure facilities such as a hydro-slide, a rapids pool and a training pool for Sydney's dedicated lap-swimmers.

The nearby Multi-Use Arena can accommodate 15,000 spectators for sporting events, primarily artistic gymnastics and basketball, and the 30-hectare (75-acre) Sydney Showground, newly relocated in Homebush Bay from its old site near Moore Park, accommodates baseball, handball and badminton, among other sports.

Among the many other sporting facilities at Homebush Bay are the State Sports Centre, the Tennis Centre, Golf Driving Range and the (Field) Hockey Centre.

Other Sydney areas were also upgraded to host Olympic events and to accommodate the vast number of visitors. A new train line was built from the airport to the city, and cruise ships were moored around the harbour for fear the city would be unable to provide sufficient hotel accommodation for the heavy influx of visitors.

With all of this accomplished, the

Games kicked off in truly spectacular fashion with the opening ceremony at Olympic Park, which climaxed with Australian Aboriginal sprint champion Cathy Freeman ascending an escalator-like catwalk to light a huge Olympic torch. As she did so, fireworks exploded over Sydney Harbour.

Sydney lived and breathed sport for the entire two weeks of the Games and even those with little interest in sporting events found themselves drawn into the spirit.

For those unable to attend the sporting events in person, seven vast television screens were installed around the city centre to relay live action from 7am to 11pm

daily, and bars were set up in Martin Place to cater to the public partying and general revelry that accompanied the adrenalin of the sporting events.

After the closing ceremony at Olympic Park – and another fireworks display – the President of the International Olympic Committee, Juan Antonio Samaranch, declared the 2000 Olympics "the best Games ever".

Sydney continued its post-Olympics sports mania with the Paralympic Games, held later in 2000, and involving some 4,000 physically handicapped athletes participating in 18 sports, using the same venues used for the Olympics proper. ❏

RIGHT: Aboriginal athlete Cathy Freeman prepares to light the Olympic flame.

EATING OUT IN SYDNEY

Few cities in the world can match Sydney's range of restaurants, its variety of cuisines, reflecting the city's multicultural make-up, or its dramatic and picturesque locations for eating

In range, quality and value, Sydney offers some of the best dining in the world. Successive waves of immigrants have introduced many different national styles of cooking, putting to good use the incredible diversity and quality of Australia's natural produce, particularly seafood. Although Sydney likes to pride itself on its sophisticated atmosphere, and certainly has a variety of excellent "exclusive" dining options, in keeping with the generally informal Australian character, good food at cheap prices is relatively easy to find. Add to this the unrivalled settings that Sydney's harbour and beaches offer, and you have a combination that is hard to beat.

Modern Australian cuisine

Sydney's first ethnic restaurants were opened by immigrants to serve food based closely on their native cuisine to fellow immigrants. But the one major obstacle they faced was the lack of local and seasonal produce straight from the field and forest that gives the great international cuisines of the world their unique character. On the other hand, they were able to call on a wider range of fresh produce that was available most of the year round.

Both foreign and then Australian chefs began applying Asian and European cooking techniques to fresh local ingredients to produce food with different flavours and textures. The Australian climate, lifestyle and concerns with diet demanded food that was fresh, light, low in fat, not too fussy in its presentation, and within a reasonable budget.

The elaborate "architecture" and sauces of French haute cuisine and heavy Italian pastas have yielded to Asian cooking techniques based on steaming and stir-frying, and readily available fresh produce such as fruits, vegetables and red meat.

What is now described as "Modern Australian" cooking is a fusion of the world's great traditional cuisines, particularly French, Italian, Chinese, Japanese, Vietnamese and Thai. Modern Australian restaurants generally lean towards one particular ethnic tradition, while, in turn, the ethnic restaurants often adapt the ingredients and techniques of the modern Australian chefs.

Top of the range

At the top of the range in Sydney's restaurants, judged purely in terms of the quality and originality of the food, is Tetsuya's, in Kent Street, where the food is neither Japanese, French nor Australian, but a haute cuisine combination of all three, prepared with refined taste. The only dining option is a *dégustation* menu, and the waiter's description of any particular dish (there are 15 of them) takes longer to hear, in most cases, than it does to eat. It is hard to imagine dining in a top restaurant in a city like Paris or London for the same amount. A wine list is offered but BYO (bring your own alcohol) is permitted.

Rockpool in The Rocks is Modern Australian cuisine with a seafood emphasis, and the menu is an example of the Modern Australian fusion of styles. At the MG Garage, also Modern Australian, you can sit at a table next to a shiny MG sports car while enjoying a salad of snails, pig's trotters, pig's ears and purslane.

The open kitchen at Bel Mondo in The Rocks is on a raised dais from which the chef conducts the almost operatic proceedings. The food is rooted in Bel Mondo's Italian heritage, but these days chef Neil Pass gives it an inspired Modern Australian slant.

The Quay in the Overseas Passenger Ter-

Claude's at Paddington, described as French, also offers a fixed-price menu at A$100 but no wine list. The food at the Darley Street Thai in Kings Cross, described as a "symphony" of textures and flavours, is so exotic that the waiters have to explain the menu to diners before they order.

At the next level are the glamour-driven restaurants catering for the beautiful and the successful in theatrical settings. The food is usually excellent – not as imaginative as Claude's or Tetsuya's but a little cheaper.

minal – the *Sydney Morning Herald*'s Restaurant of the Year in 2003 – has a panoramic view of the Opera House.

The Forty One – now on the 42nd floor of the Chifley Tower – offers diners a panorama which stretches from Manly to Botany Bay. The excellent wine list offers such rarities as a Margaux 1945 at just under A$5,000 or a Petrus 1989 at $5,250, should you wish to indulge in these to accompany your delicious roast rack of venison.

Banc, appropriately in the middle of Sydney's banking district, serves French/European food and wines in an art deco setting. The expensively tailored diners seem unaware

LEFT: traditional fish and chips at Doyles.
ABOVE: steamed pigfish, oriental-style.

or unconcerned that expense-account lunches are no longer tax deductible.

Many of Sydney's discerning diners are more interested in good food and wine than glitzy settings. The city's best Italian restaurant, Buon Ricordo, has no views but a comfortable, relaxed atmosphere and impeccable service. The style of cooking is Neapolitan with local innovations, and the cellar offers a range of Australian and Italian wines. The Cicada occupies a spacious Victorian mansion at Potts Point. The food was French to begin with, but Italian, Middle Eastern and Asian influences have since crept in. The wine cellar is extensive.

Food with a view

Sydney offers a range of restaurants where the food and wine can be (but is not always) less important than the setting. If you literally want to scale the heights, try the revolving Summit on top of Australia Square, decorated in a neo-space-age style, complete with a cocktail bar, tinkling piano and buffet. The Japanese Restaurant on 36, serving sublime food on top of the Shangri-La Hotel in The Rocks, also offers vistas of urban Sydney.

Many restaurants are sensibly located to take advantage of Sydney's endless views of beaches, harbour and the nearby Blue Mountains. Bondi and Manly beaches are lined with

restaurants and cafés in every style and price range. Jonah's, above Palm Beach, has a Modern Australian menu as well as six rooms attached for those unable or unwilling to drive back to the city. The Beach Road Restaurant at the Palm Beach golf course serves Modern Australian food in a wonderfully relaxed, subtropical garden atmosphere.

On the harbour at Glebe, the Boathouse on Blackwattle Bay serves some of Sydney's best fish dishes in a converted boathouse. Other good fish restaurants with harbour views are the perennially popular Doyles on the Beach at Watson's Bay and the Pier at Rose Bay. The cathedral-like setting of the top-class Guillaume at Bennelong, located in the Opera House complex, serves fashionable Modern Australian food on three levels, all with stunning wrap-around views of the maritime bustle of Circular Quay.

For a change of scenery, go to the Mount Tomah Botanic Gardens restaurant in the heart of the Blue Mountains National Park, where you can gaze across endless hazy, grey-green mountain vistas while enjoying Modern Australian food of a quality not normally to be expected in such an out-of-the-way location. Further west, at Blackheath, Cleopatra serves classic southern French dishes, such as daube of beef and roasted guinea fowl with walnut wine sauce. Nearby Vulcan's operates around a wood-fired baker's oven, offering innovative Modern Australian food prepared with the freshest ingredients.

European cuisines

Sydney's hundreds of ethnic restaurants offer constantly changing variety, originality and, above all, value for money. French cuisine may have inspired much of the Modern Australian cooking but in its purest form continues to attract its own following. Banc and EST in the City, and Quay on Circular Quay West set the standard, while more modest establishments such as Café Sel et Poivre in Darlinghurst and La Toque in East Sydney prove that authentic French cuisine need not be prohibitively expensive.

The Italians largely dominated Sydney's ethnic food scene until the Asian invasion began in the late 1970s. Leichhardt in the inner west, the centre of Sydney's Italian community, offers many Italian restaurants. Frattini and La Perla are among the best. Beppi's has been in East Sydney for longer than most other restaurants in Sydney and, in both food and decor, has resisted the fads of the passing years. At Machiavelli, a long-time favourite with politicians, located in a city basement, the antipasto and salads are set out on a rustic table in the middle of the restaurant.

Lebanese restaurants were popular in the 1970s but have since dwindled slightly in the face of competition from the Asians. Cadmus at Opera Quays, one of Sydney's most expensive restaurants, draws on Leba-

which mainly uses seafood, kebabs and sausage cooked on the barbecue, is represented by the Balkan Continental and Balkan Seafood at Taylor Square.

Sydney's Little Spain is in Liverpool Street west of George Street. At Casa Asturiana select from a range of appetising tapas and enjoy a glass of Spanish wine while they prepare you the best seafood paella outside Valencia.

Latin America has also now gained a culinary foothold in Sydney. The unusual Casapueblo restaurant at Redfern, owned by immigrants from Uruguay, serves regional seafood, chicken and vegetarian dishes.

nese traditions. Al Mustafa in Surry Hills serves good traditional Lebanese fare at low prices. El Manara and La Roche at Lakemba cater for the large local Muslim population, offering the cheapest, freshest and most authentic Lebanese food outside Beirut.

German and Austrian cooking is most readily available at Una's, a moderately priced restaurant-cum-café in Kings Cross. A devoted clientele has enjoyed the schnitzels, stuffed beef rolls, noodles, dumplings and cakes for more than 25 years. Balkan cooking,

LEFT: dining al fresco in the Italian Forum, Leichhardt.
ABOVE: harbour views from the Park Hyatt restaurant.

Asian cuisine

Chinatown's dozens of restaurants provide meeting places for the large Chinese community living in nearby high-rise units.

The Golden Century, perhaps the best and certainly one of the most popular, is bustling day and night until very late. Live lobsters, abalone, crab, trout and barramundi fill its fish tanks. The Kam Fook in Market City is Sydney's biggest restaurant, seating 800 diners, and the staff communicate by walkie-talkie. Despite its size, apparent confusion and waiters who seem unable to speak English, it successfully serves great roast duck and other Cantonese dishes. But it is just one of dozens of good-value Chinese restaurants in the area.

Yum cha is served in big restaurants in Chinatown and the suburbs. Similar to dim sum in Britain, this is a very cheap and popular way of meeting friends. Diners can choose from up to 250 dishes consisting of small servings of dumplings, won tons, noodles and vegetables from circulating trolleys.

Dixon Street in the heart of Chinatown has three Asian food halls. Based on Singapore's famous open hawkers' centres, each has a dozen or so independently leased stalls serving a range of Chinese, Malaysian, Vietnamese, Indonesian and Japanese dishes. A basic but sustaining meal for two generally

in Sydney with the waves of Japanese tourists and business travellers in the 1980s. Most are located in the city and on the lower north shore. Some, like the Yamato Steakhouse at Potts Point, cater almost exclusively for a Japanese clientele. The trendy sushi bars springing up around the city and inner suburbs offer quick, tasty, sustaining and cheap lunches and snacks. No visitor to Sydney should miss the cornucopia of the seas on display at the Fish Market at Pyrmont (*see page 127*) or Sydney's freshest sushi and sashimi at the Fish Markets Sushi Bar.

Indian restaurants, despite the absence of many Indian immigrants, have become estab-

should not cost more than A$20 or so.

Thai restaurants are usually modestly priced and unpretentious, and rely more on a non-Asian clientele than their Chinese counterparts. The Sailor's Thai in The Rocks offers a modified version of the Darley Street Thai's menu downstairs, while the upstairs noodle bar has views of Circular Quay. The Arun Thai in Macleay Street is in the style of an 18th-century Thai nobleman's house. The walls are panelled in Tasmanian oak, and the cabinets and comfortable armchairs crafted from teak. Spice Market in Double Bay is another top Thai restaurant for visitors staying east of the city.

Japanese restaurants and sushi bars arrived

lished across suburban Sydney since the 1980s. The highly regarded Oh Calcutta! in Kings Cross has evolved an eclectic menu by fusing north and south Indian techniques with those of Pakistan and Afghanistan, while using the best Australian produce. Zaafran in Darling Harbour serves sophisticated Indian cuisine in a harbourside setting.

Café life

Sydney has hundreds of cafés, more and more with outdoor tables on the pavement, offering very good espresso coffee, together with food ranging from snacks (such as an Aussie favourite, deep-fried potato served with soured cream and chilli sauce), sandwiches and pastas to three-course meals.

In the city centre, the Hyde Park Café behind the Museum Station, the outdoor Paradiso in Macquarie Place, the Bar Coluzzi in Elizabeth Street, the Pavilion on the Park in the Domain opposite the Art Gallery of NSW, and the Italian café Bambini on Castlereagh and Elizabeth streets, can all supply a caffeine fix in agreeable surroundings.

In the suburbs, the cafés tend to cluster: the best-known strips are, in Kings Cross, Victoria Street between Craigend and Liverpool streets, and the corner of Macleay Street and Challis Avenue; in East Sydney, Stanley Street; in Paddington, along Oxford Street; in Newtown, King Street between Missenden Road and the Newtown Station; in Double Bay, Knox and Bay streets; and in Leichhardt, Norton Street. Also try the ever-popular Bar Coluzzi at the Cross, Luigi Brothers in Double Bay, Bar Italia at Leichhardt, and Sean's Panorama at Bondi, if you'd like a spot of sea air with your caffeine.

Bars and nightclubs

After a slap-up meal in Sydney, it wouldn't be an unknown occurrence for slightly less than sated diners to go in search of "one for the road". However, be warned: Australia has some of the toughest drink-driving laws in the world, and ignorance is not a defence. Sydney also has some strange licensing laws that basically require patrons to have food with their alcohol in all places other than pubs.

The upshot of this has been that many of the old, tiled, male-only bastions of the past have been given designer revamps, and can now look like anything from a European café to a New York nightclub.

But there is still some tradition to be found, and those seeking a historic drink should head for the Hero of Waterloo or the Lord Nelson Brewery Hotel, Sydney's oldest hotels dating back to 1842, both located in The Rocks. In the city, drop into Customs House Bar, popular with the Friday night crowd, or in Paddington, settle down on the veranda of the Royal Hotel, a three-storey Victorian pub with some

impressively ornate architectural detailing.

Those seeking a little elegance in their surrounds should try Wine Banc in Martin Place, Horizons Bar at the Shangri-La Hotel in The Rocks, and for the ultimate in luxury drinking, the Krug Room at the Restaurant Forty One, where prices start at around A$15 for a glass of bubbly. Most visitors are happy to pay the prices for the view alone.

The young of body (and older imposters) should try East Village, a seriously cool outfit in one of the city's many revamped pubs; the Grand Pacific Blue Room in Paddington, a dancing, schmoozing and drinking venue for the grown-up children of the wealthy Eastern

Suburbs; and the Slip Inn in the City, a venue offering the works, including pool tables and a pretty courtyard (or beer garden as they were known before we started sipping cool, crisp Sémillon in them). The Soho Lounge in Potts Point is one of the oldest pubs of a new generation of watering holes with street cred, and offers more relaxed dancing and drinking without the prospect of a coterie of impossibly well-dressed patrons.

For local colour and some of the best views in Sydney, you can't go past the Bondi Icebergs. You'll pay a A$5 membership, but be served drinks at about a quarter of the price of those in fancier establishments. ❏

LEFT: serving varieties of yum cha in Chinatown.
RIGHT: there's no shortage of traditional pubs.

PLACES

A detailed guide to the city with the principal sites
clearly cross-referenced by number to the maps

Sydney covers an expansive 1,580 sq km (610 sq miles), so don't feel obliged to try to see everything during your stay. There are only a few Sydney taxi drivers who've achieved that – and even they have trouble finding their way home. For most visitors, the starting points are the City and The Rocks, adjacent areas that combine Sydney's history and its classic views. Walk across the "old coathanger", Sydney Harbour Bridge, and from its eastern walkways you will see the city at its prettiest: the waterfront dwellings and parks; the yacht races; the ferries; the architectural jumble that surrounds Circular Quay. Descend from the bridge into that scramble and observe the dubious architectural practice of "facade-ism" where, literally, only the shell of history is preserved to make way for more modern interiors.

After ticking off the quintessential Sydney sights – the Opera House, the Botanic Gardens, Darling Harbour – take time to explore the less renowned aspects of city life. In the Kings Cross district, enjoy the decorous rows of terrace houses, many of which were once brothels but have now been converted into elegant restaurants, then enjoy a genuine Italian coffee in trendy Darlinghurst. When you need to get away from the madding throng, Sydney has many parks, ranging from the tiny to the venerable and vast Centennial Park with its ponds, palms and lawns. Or pick up some souvenirs or a collector's gem in the lively markets of Paddington.

It takes very little effort to reach rural life from Sydney. Only a short drive from the city centre are the historic colonial towns on the Hawkesbury River, the cool climate of the Southern Highlands villages (a relief in summer), and the spectacular valleys, eucalyptus forests and rock formations of the Blue Mountains. And, of course, there is the coastline, with that most famous of Australian locations, Bondi Beach.

Enjoy the harbour, by all means – most Sydneysiders do. But there is far more to the city than its picture-postcard image. Expand your horizons, and you won't be disappointed.   ❏

PRECEDING PAGES: harbour lights – The Rocks and City skyscrapers twinkle after dark; a harbour ferry leaves Circular Quay.
LEFT: the Royal Botanic Gardens with the Central Business District beyond.

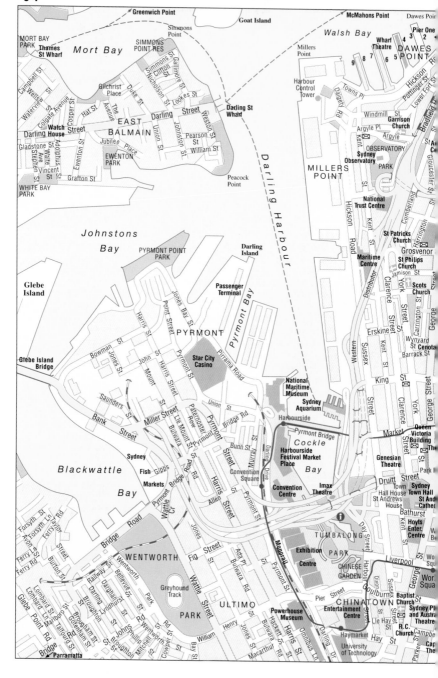

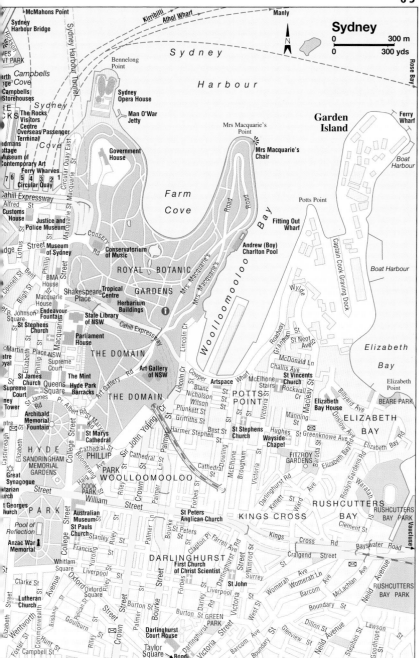

Sydney

0   300 m
0   300 yds

Sydney Harbour

Kirribilli   Athol Wharf   Manly

Rose Bay

McMahons Point
Sydney Harbour Bridge
VES NT PARK
Campbells Cove
Campbells Storehouses
Sydney
The Rocks
Visitors Centre
Overseas Passenger Terminal
Museum of Contemporary Art
Ferry Wharves
7 6 5 4 3 2 1
Circular Quay
Cahill Expressway
Alfred St
Customs House
Justice and Police Museum
Museum of Sydney
Conservatorium of Music
BMA House
Shakespeare Place
Tropical Centre
Macquarie House
Endeavour Fountain
State Library of NSW
St Stephens Church
Parliament House
Supreme Court
St James Church
The Mint
Hyde Park Barracks
Art Gallery of NSW
Archibald Memorial Fountain
St Marys Cathedral
Great Synagogue
St Georges Church
Pool of Reflection
Anzac War Memorial
Australian Museum
St Pauls Church
Lutheran Church
Darlinghurst Court House

Bennelong Point
Sydney Opera House
Man O'War Jetty
Government House

Sydney Harbour

Farm Cove

Mrs Macquarie's Point
Mrs Macquarie's Chair

Garden Island
Ferry Wharf
Boat Harbour

Potts Point
Fitting Out Wharf
Andrew (Boy) Charlton Pool

Captain Cook Graving Dock
Boat Harbour

Elizabeth Bay

Elizabeth Point
BEARE PARK

ROYAL BOTANIC GARDENS
Herbarium Buildings
Conservatorium Rd

THE DOMAIN
Lincoln Cr
Cahill Expressway
Supreme Court
Queens Square
St James Rd
Sydney Tower

HYDE PARK
SANDRINGHAM MEMORIAL GARDENS

Woolloomooloo Bay
Artspace
McElhone Stairs
St Vincents Church
Rockwall

POTTS POINT
Wylde
Roadway
St Neot Ave
McDonald Ln
Challis Ave
Cowper
Blanc
Nicholson
Wilson
Plunkett St
Griffiths St
Harmer Stephen St
Best St
St Stephens Church
Wayside Chapel
Hughes St
Greenknowe Ave
Manning St
Baroda
Elizabeth Bay House
Onslow Ave
Roslyn Gardens Rd
Waratah

ELIZABETH BAY
Elizabeth Bay Rd
FITZROY GARDENS
Billyard Ave
Macleay St

WOOLLOOMOOLOO
Cathedral St
McElhone
Brougham
Forbes
Victoria
Dowling
Crown
Palmer
Riley
Bourke
William Street
Cook Park

St Peters Anglican Church
KINGS CROSS
Kings Cross Rd
Darlinghurst Rd
Kellett
Ward
Roslyn
Clement St
RUSHCUTTERS BAY
Bayswater Road
RUSHCUTTERS BAY PARK
Vaucluse
Lawson
Goodhope
Stephen

PARK
DARLINGHURST
First Church of Christ Scientist
St John
GREEN PARK
Darlinghurst Court House
Taylor Square
Bondi

Whitlam Square
Clarke St
Oxford Street
Oxford Square
Liverpool St
Burton St
Stanley St
Francis St
Yurong St
Palmer Ln
Darley St
West St
Surrey
Kings Cross Rd
Cralgend Street
Craigend
Womerah Ave
Womerah Ln
Barcom Ave
McLachlan Ave
Boundary St
Dillon St
Glenview St
Neild Avenue

Wentworth Ave
Commonwealth St
Brisbane
Goulburn
Pelican
Campbell St
Hunt St
Foster St
Riley
Crown
Bourke
Palmer
Forbes
Darley
Victoria
Barcom

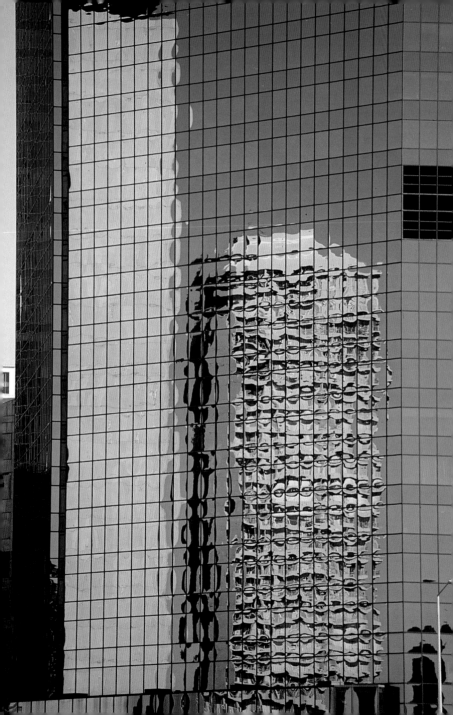

THE CITY

Sydney's commercial and business centre is a fascinating blend of colonial buildings, Victorian and modern shopping precincts and peaceful parks, all within easy walking distance of one another

Map on page 68

The first glimpse of Sydney for most visitors is through an aircraft window while descending into Kingsford Smith Airport. Coming in from the north, the flightpath of the international jets passes over the bush landscape and houses of the northern suburbs, and then the overwhelmingly beautiful harbour. For tired travellers, the view is a refreshing tonic, rekindling enthusiasm.

Looking east, the arc of the Sydney Harbour Bridge points towards the dense cluster of skyscrapers that forms the city centre. On the waterfront, the soaring sails of the Opera House, the huge shells that share top billing with Uluru (Ayers Rock) as the best-known symbols of Australia, glint in the sunlight. However, the city centre looks far too small to be Australia's premier metropolis.

The lure of the beach

Once within it, however, the city takes on its rightful perspective as a bustling, outgoing hive of activity. In summer, the concrete skyscrapers swelter under the combined effects of heat and carbon monoxide. This is when city workers are most colourfully dressed – as if, at any minute, there could be a mass exodus to the beach. Indeed, between October and March this impression often turns into reality as soon as the shops and offices close up for the day.

"It will be a nice city when they finish building it," was the much-quoted response of one visitor to Sydney some years ago. During the 1980s Sydney underwent a decade of incredible development that left many Sydneysiders in the 1990s feeling disorientated. However, the surge of construction turned a previously uninspired colonial outpost into the vibrant commercial centre of the southern hemisphere. The

LEFT: towering glass mountains soar above the city.
BELOW: a harbour ferry approaches Circular Quay.

The City and the Rocks

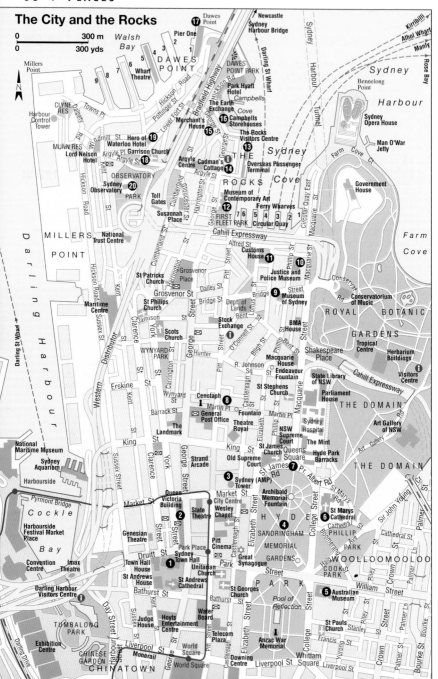

expansion – mostly upward – has continued into the 21st century.

Just as Sydney's urban sprawl pushed the fringes of the suburbs first to the edges of the Cumberland Plains and then into them, the city centre continues to expand where it can. The harbour was a barrier until North Sydney exploded into the city's second business district; the Botanic Gardens and Domain remain the boundaries to the northeast.

The formerly run-down southern area of the city towards Broadway and Central Station has been successfully revitalised by modern offices and hotels. And in the west, the derelict train yards and warehouses of Darling Harbour and Ultimo were cleared in the major urban renewal scheme which produced the glittering visitor-orientated complex that now stands there.

Around George Street

Even so, the heart of the city, combining colonial history with modern commercialism, is a compact area easily covered on foot – which is fortunate, since driving and parking can be a nightmare of one-way streets, dead-ends and no standing/loading zones. A good starting point is the **Sydney Town Hall ❶**, on the corner of George and Park streets, opposite the stately Queen Victoria Building.

The startling mixture of styles reflects the several architects who worked on the town hall before the building was opened in 1869, and on extensions thereafter. Irrespective of aesthetics, it is an imposing building. Inside is a blend of marble, crystal and the restored six-keyboard, 8,500-pipe Grand Organ in Centennial Hall, the bad acoustics of which are rued by every concert-goer. This aside, the town hall is now a regular venue for classical music concerts, as well as state balls.

Tours of the interior are available

(tel: 9231 4629). If you want to arrange a rendezvous, meeting on the town hall steps, under the clock, is a Sydney tradition. Heading south from the town hall takes you to the cinema strip of George Street. Going north you are faced with the striking **Queen Victoria Building ❷**, QVB for short *(see page 73)*.

Continuing along George Street towards the harbour, the city's main shopping area is on the right. One soon memorises the litany of main streets: George, Pitt (a pedestrian mall between Market and King streets), Castlereagh and Elizabeth forming a democratic mix of monarchs and British prime ministers running north–south, and Park, Market, King, Martin Place, Hunter, and Bridge as the shorter cross streets, east–west. These become a ready grid reference so it's difficult to get lost for long.

To leave town, Park Street leads to Kings Cross and the Eastern Suburbs, George Street leads to all points south and west, and heading north on almost any road will lead to the Sydney Harbour Bridge.

Map on page 68

TIP

The City's shopping areas include Pitt Street Mall for fashion and art, and Mid City Centre for music and gifts. The MLC Centre caters for those with designer tastes.

BELOW:
Queen Victoria sits outside "her" building.

The Anzac War Memorial in Hyde Park.

BELOW: the AMP Tower is Sydney's highest lookout.

Sydney panorama

A visit to the **Sydney Tower** ❸ (sometimes still described as the AMP Tower) is arguably the best and most interesting way to gain an orientation of central Sydney (open daily 9am–10.30pm; entrance fee). The city is all laid out at one's feet like a three-dimensional street map, beneath the southern hemisphere's tallest building (which contains the southern hemisphere's highest revolving restaurant).

For those who just can't contemplate eating somewhere that moves, there are many good restaurants cafés at ground level in the City.

Around Hyde Park

Continuing east along Market Street and to the right of Elizabeth Street is **Hyde Park** ❹, a welcome haven of greenery in the heart of the city. Created in 1810, a stroll around its carefully landscaped paths reveals a number of references to Sydney's history.

The **Anzac War Memorial**, built in 1934 in the art deco style fashionable at the time, commemorates the lives of all Australians who have died for their country. At the northern curve of the park are the carefully preserved **Hyde Park Barracks** (open daily 10am–5pm; entrance fee). Commissioned by Governor Macquarie in 1819 to provide accommodation for convicts working in the city, it was designed by architect Francis Greenway, himself an ex-convict *(see page 20)*. From the late 1840s, after transportation of convicts from Britain had ceased, the barracks were used as a lodging house for single women and orphaned girls. In 1979 extensive restoration commenced, and now the museum gives an insight into the social history of the state, including reconstructed convict quarters and an exhibition detailing the work of Greenway.

On the eastern edge of Hyde Park is the country's oldest museum, aptly called the **Australian Museum** ❺ and housed in an impressive Georgian sandstone building at 6 College Street (open daily 9.30am–5pm; entrance fee). Located here is the country's largest collection of natural history exhibits, from prehistoric times to the modern-day environment, and an excellent "Aboriginal Australia" display – by far the most illuminating in the city. An Indonesia Gallery also pays tribute to Australia's closest neighbours across the Pacific Ocean, and a popular gallery with children allows them to bring in insects and pieces of rock for identification by the museum's experts.

Around Queen's Square

A brief walk northwards up College Street, and right into Cathedral Street, brings you to **St Mary's Cathedral** ❻ (open Sun–Fri 6.30am–6.30pm, Sat 8am–6.30pm). Australia's first Catholic place of worship was begun in 1821 and

Map
on page
68

opened in 1882, although the building was not finally completed until 1928, and the towering sandstone spires seen at the southern end of the cathedral, intended to be part of the building's original design, were not added until the late 1990s.

One of the most impressive features is the cathedral's crypt, whose mosaic flooring took some 15 years to finish. Today, St Mary's is also a popular venue for musical concerts.

Not all the marvellous buildings of convict architect Francis Greenway are still standing, but at **Queen's Square** ❼ there are two more excellent examples – the **NSW Supreme Court** and **St James's Church**, both in the Colonial Georgian style. The latter, Sydney's oldest church, built in 1820, includes marble tablets commemorating the Victorian explorers who failed to return from Australia's harsh interior.

An overview of these buildings and the harbour can be obtained from the cafeteria of the modern law courts opposite: it's on the 14th level and is open to the public. Phillip Street, in the morning before court starts and in the afternoons after sittings, is a mass of black-caped barristers wearing the formal, tightly-woven wigs with tassels at the back.

Macquarie Street to Martin Place

At Nos. 135–137 Macquarie Street stands the pinnacle of Sydney's art deco buildings, the BMA (British Medical Association) House, built in 1930. The facade of this building is truly wonderful and well worth a look. Note details such as the carved stone koalas.

Towards the southern end of Macquarie Street, opposite the top of the Botanic Gardens, is the old State Library, housed in one of the most impressive buildings in Sydney. It is commonly referred to as the **Mitchell Library**, although that is just one wing of the complex, and houses documents and maps preserved from the files of the First Fleeters. The main reading room is a large airy hall, naturally lit by a

Hyde Park Barracks, now a museum.

BELOW: the Archibald Fountain in Hyde Park commemorates the alliance of Australia and France in World War I.

Map
on page
68

TIP

Duty-free shopping in central Sydney (as well as at the airport) can save you money on jewellery, clothing, cameras, wine, etc. Look for the duty-free shops, and be prepared to show your passport and onward flight ticket.

BELOW: there's no escaping the Justice and Police Museum.

vast skylight. The modern structure of the 1988 State Library next door, connected by a glass walkway, is also very accessible, with a plethora of material on Australian history in the Reference Library, public and exhibition areas and a good café. Most sections of the library are open to the public Mon–Fri 9am–9pm, Sat–Sun 11am–5pm.

Martin Place ❽ is a wide pedestrianised mall that runs between George and Elizabeth streets. A visitors' information stand is located here, as is the **General Post Office** (GPO), easily recognised by its clock tower. At the western end of the mall, on the corner of George Street, is the Martin Place **Cenotaph**, the focus of annual war memorial services on Anzac Day. Concerts and other entertainments regularly take place in the amphitheatre in Martin Place during workday lunchtimes.

Around the Quay

At the northern end of Phillip Street, at the base of the modern Governor Phillip Tower, is the **Museum of**

Sydney ❾ (open daily 9.30am–5pm; entrance fee). Situated on the site of the city's first Government House, the museum, which opened in 1995, focuses on the city's history from its Aboriginal beginnings to its colonial era and up to the present day. Ancient hunting tools detail the lives of Sydney's first inhabitants, the Eora Aborigines, while videos and other multimedia devices chronicle the 18th-century European settlement of Australia's east coast. The original Government House is no longer in existence, but its foundations and a piece of its original sandstone wall are on display in the museum.

A short walk away is another fascinating museum detailing Sydney's past. The **Justice and Police Museum ❿** (open Sat–Sun 10am–5pm; January Sat–Thur 10am–5pm; entrance fee), housed in the former 19th-century police buildings, relives the various crimes and punishments of Sydneysiders during the Victorian era. A recreated courtroom, disciplinary instruments, prison uniforms and old photographs and artefacts illustrate the harsh meting out of justice during that austere time.

The only colonial building in the north of the city centre is **Customs House ⓫**. This is supposedly the historic site where the Union Flag was flown for the first time in Sydney Cove in 1788. The building is closed to the public, but for passersby notable external features of this 1885 building are the intricately carved stone coat of arms over the entrance and the unamused Queen Victoria visage above the entrance door. A popular café at the front of the building offers comfy seating shaded by large umbrellas and an opportunity to watch locals and visitors alike rushing through the busy Circular Quay bus and ferry terminal. ❏

Victorian Shopping Arcades

One of the least expected and therefore all the more enchanting aspects of Sydney's abundant retail industry is the survival of its ornate Victorian shopping arcades, which are reminiscent of wealthy 19th-century Europe. The most important of these are the Strand Arcade and the Queen Victoria Building (QVB).

From the moment it opened in 1892, the Strand Arcade was described as the very latest in shopping-centre design. A century on, after two Depressions and two World Wars, it is still a vital and unique part of Sydney life. Almost destroyed in a catastrophic fire in 1976, the tiered mezzanines of this iron-and-glass damsel connecting George and Pitt streets between King and Market streets were completely restored, while carefully preserving the individual character of English architect John Spencer's 1890s design. Attention to detail was of paramount importance – even the patterns on the shop windows match those of the floor tiles.

Today jewellers, watchmakers, leading fashion designers and craftsmen ply their trade side-by-side with purveyors of speciality chocolates and nuts, old-style coffee houses and gift and souvenir shops. Many of the shops are Sydney landmarks, and one of the most popular is the Strand Hatters, which sells traditional Australian Outback Akubra hats – without the corks. For light refreshments, visit Harris Coffee & Tea, on the ground floor near the Pitt Street entrance, as it has been since 1892.

The Queen Victoria Building is the Cinderella story of all Sydney architecture. Occupying a complete city block beside the town hall on George Street, the QVB opened in 1898 as a produce market, designed by City Architect George McRae. Yet for much of the mid-20th century it was regarded as a white elephant, and was due for demolition until Sydney started to get smart about its own heritage. (This said, it was purchased for restoration by a Malaysian firm.)

By the time the QVB closed for restoration in 1980 it consisted of offices and low-rent shops running perpetual "closing down" sales. Six years and A$75 million later, after one of the finest refurbishing programmes ever seen in the city, the QVB re-emerged as it is today: tiered galleries of upmarket shops in a building worth a visit if only for its beautiful stained-glass windows, wrought-iron details and Romanesque-style arches.

The attention to detail, both old and new, is evident everywhere in this fine building – not only in its stained glass, but also in the elegant shop fronts, polished timbers and patterned floor tiles. The quality of the setting is echoed in the nearly 200 shops and boutiques it houses, with retail stock covering the spectrum of fashion, footwear, jewellery, leather goods, antiques and crafts. French fashion designer Pierre Cardin has referred to the QVB as the "most beautiful shopping centre in the world".

On the lowest level are the "Eat Street" restaurants and cafés, which cater for rushed food-on-the-go or leisurely sit-down meals. There is also an overrated, kitsch-encrusted "Royal Clock" cluttering the ceiling that many stop to admire.   ❑

RIGHT: restored to its original glory, the wrought-iron-and-glass Strand Arcade.

RESTAURANTS, CAFÉS & BARS

Restaurants

Athenian
71 York Street
Tel: 9262 2624
Open: L & D daily. **$$**
Popular Greek and seafood restaurant in the city centre. Favoured for its good food, service and ambience.

Banc
53 Martin Place
Tel: 9233 5300
Open: L & D Mon–Fri, D Sat. **$$$**
French cuisine with the chance to rub shoulders with the bankers and barristers of Sydney. Reflects the desire among professional Sydneysiders looking for a more upmarket wining and dining experience.

Beppi's
Cnr Yurong/Liverpool Streets
Tel: 9360 4558
Open: L & D Mon–Sat. **$$$**
This upmarket restaurant, popular with the media, is the finest in Sydney's Little Italy. Opened in 1956 by Beppi Polese and family-run to this day. Traditional Italian cuisine.

Bodhi on the Park **$$**
Cook and Phillip Park, College Street
Tel: 9360 2523
Open: 11am–10pm daily; yum cha until 5pm daily. **$$**
Chinese vegetarian and yum cha cuisine in an outdoor setting. Licensed. The ambience, setting and food allegedly outshines the service on most days.

Capitan Torres
73 Liverpool Street
Tel: 9267 3787
Open: L & D daily. **$$**
Located in the Spanish Quarter near the George Street cinema strip. Licensed. A maritime theme colours the decor and the menu; seafood is a speciality of this long-standing Spanish restaurant. Daily for lunch and dinner.

Est
Establishment Hotel, 252 George Street
Tel: 9240 3010
Open: L daily, D Mon–Sat. **$$$**
French/European cuisine in classy surroundings, with an adjoining sushi restaurant, cigar bar and an elegantly retro downstairs bar on street level.

Forty One
Chifley Tower, Chifley Square
Tel: 9221 2500
Open: L & D Mon–Fri, D Sat, L Sun. **$$$$**
This restaurant recently moved up to level 42 of the tower (it was previously on level 41), but it is still called Forty One. Serves Modern Australian cuisine lifted to dizzying heights. Located at the top of an office tower in the city's financial district, this was to be the penthouse for one of Australia's richest men. Now it provides luxury dining with views as far as the city outskirts.

Hyde Park Barracks Café
Queen Square, Macquarie Street
Tel: 9223 1155
Open: 10am–4pm Mon–Fri, 11am–3pm Sat–Sun. **$$**
Over the road from Hyde Park, this large café displays a historic, colonial feel thanks to the architecture and surroundings. Modern Australian cuisine. Fully licensed.

Machiavelli
123 Clarence Street
Tel: 9299 3748
Open: L & D Mon–Fri. **$$**
In the centre of town. The massive antipasto offering is the city's best. Attracts a business crowd during the week.

PRICE CATEGORIES

Price indications are for a three-course meal for one, including half a bottle of house wine, coffee and service.
$ = under A$50
$$ = A$50–75
$$$ = A$75–115
$$$$ = over A$115
Abbreviations:
L = lunch, D = dinner.

LEFT: fine wines and fine dining at Est.

The Summit
Level 47, Australia Square,
264 George Street
Tel: 9247 9777
Open: L & D Sun–Fri, D only
Sat. $$$
Situated in the financial
district, this high-rise
restaurant offers truly
panoramic views of the
city and harbour. Buffet
and cocktail bar. Modern
Australian cuisine in
modern surroundings.

Sydney Tower Restaurant
100 Market Street
Tel: 8223 3800
Open: L & D daily. $$
(buffet) $$$ (à la carte D
Tues–Sat)
The revolving restaurant
in Sydney Tower is per-
haps the best spot to
both eat and sightsee
at the same time. The
views are especially
beautiful around sunset
and dusk. The econom-
ical lunchtime buffet is
popular with groups of
local office workers
during the week.

Tetsuya's
529 Kent Street
Tel: 9267 2900
Open: L Fri–Sat, D Tues–Sat.
$$$$
Drawing on Japanese and
French cuisine, this is
regarded as one of the
city's top gourmet experi-
ences. Average dinner
A$170 (six courses).

RIGHT: wok-fried scallops and prawns.

Cafés

Borders
Skygarden, Pitt Street Mall
Situated inside the large
Borders bookstore, this
outlet offers a vast array
of coffee styles. The
management doesn't
mind if you grab a maga-
zine or two from the well-
stocked store's racks to
read while you sample
the coffee.

Gloria Jean's Coffees
Cnr Pitt and Park streets
Next door to the recently
opened Galeries Victoria
shopping centre. For a
wide choice of coffee
and comfy armchairs.

Starbucks
Cnr Elizabeth and Park
streets
Typical Starbucks in a
good location. Has out-
door seating, big, comfy
armchairs indoors and
huge windows with views
across to Hyde Park.

Bars

Bar Broadway
2 Broadway
Opposite the UTS Univer-
sity, this modern bar is
open 24 hours. Large
upstairs venue hosts
music acts. Downstairs
is for pool tables, music
videos and sports tele-
casts on the many TVs
around the bar.

Century Tavern
Liverpool Street, corner
George Street
An upstairs bar, tucked
away overlooking
George Street. Dark,
low-key decor. Attracts
mixed alternative-music
crowd and city office
workers.

Cheers Bar and Grill
561 George Street
American-style pub in the
Spanish Quarter and
George Street cinema
district. Open late.

Civic Hotel
Cnr Goulburn and Pitt
streets
Has an attractive, retro
50s style, complete with
dim lighting and spot-
lights. One of Sydney's
many recently "yuppi-
fied" watering holes.

Scruffy Murphy's
43–49 Goulburn Street
Situated near to Hay-
market, Central Station
and the George Street
cinema strip, this large
pub packs them in all
week. A mix of local
office workers and
tourists crowd in, day
and night, to this Irish-
flavoured pub. The
crowd spills out onto
Goulburn Street.

Three Wise Monkeys
555 George Street
A pub in the thick of
things on one of Syd-
ney's busiest intersec-
tions. Attracts young
locals and fashion-
conscious international
backpackers.

ARCHITECTURE: THE COLONIAL AGE

Many of Sydney's early colonial buildings were torn down before conservation became the vogue, but a few treasures have endured

It is a strange irony that most of the convicts transported to Australia in the early days of the colony were convicted for crimes against property, for on their arrival in Sydney they were the labour force employed to build the city's first homes. These were crude affairs, not only due to the unskilled workmanship, but because materials were scarce and architectural expertise almost non-existent.

When Lachlan Macquarie arrived in 1810 as the new governor of New South Wales, it was to change the face of the city. His vision was to turn Sydney into a city as grand as its European counterparts, and commissioned impressive public buildings in the classic Georgian style. As more free settlers began to arrive, bringing with them both wealth and European ideals, they began to create opulent mansions.

ABOVE: Sydney's earliest terrace houses were reflections of the Georgian style seen in urban England. They fronted directly onto the street, leaving no room for verandas or any other protection against the sweltering Antipodean weather. But from the 1840s to the end of the Victorian era, houses came to be set back from the street, and verandas (single, double and occasionally triple) became an essential feature of terraces, with thin classical columns and decorative iron filigree.

RIGHT: Sydney's Victorian shopping arcades were temples to late-19th-century consumerism, shrines to the new affluence of the colony. The Queen Victoria Building, which was designed by George McRae and completed in 1898, emphasised the cathedral-like effect with a series of domes and domelets, Byzantine arches, rich plaster ornamentation, extensive wood panelling and sumptuous stained-glass windows.

ABOVE: Hyde Park Barracks, erected to house more than 600 convicts, was designed by Francis Greenway *(top)* – a former convict himself – and completed in 1819. Although Greenway's work was declared by some as "too grand for an infant colony", he was responsible for around 40 of Sydney's finest Georgian Colonial buildings under the patronage of the visionary Governor Lachlan Macquarie.

ELEGANCE AND INNOVATION IN THE STRAND ARCADE

The commercial prosperity of late-19th-century Sydney was reflected in the building of several grand shopping arcades *(see page 73)*. Perhaps the grandest of all was the Strand Arcade, occupying a whole block between George and Pitt streets. When English architect John Spencer unveiled his ambitious plans for the building in the mid-1880s he received a standing ovation. The arcade was to be 104 metres (340 ft) long and three storeys high. Magnificent cedar staircases at each end led to the second- and third-floor galleries, which were linked by a central bridge.

It was one of the first Victorian buildings to be designed for the harsh Australian climate. The glass roof was specially tinted to reduce glare, and the access gallery of the top floor was projected to shade the lower levels. In 1892, the *Sydney Mail* wrote: "The style of architecture is an adaptation of several favourite continental designs, the object being to combine strength with elegance." Spencer's design was indeed elegant – delicate ironwork supporting the galleries and railings, marble columns, finely carved cedar balustrades and shopfronts, and a richly-tiled floor.

The innovative lighting system combined gas and electricity in fittings designed by the architect, some of which still exist; two huge central chandeliers each used 50 gas jets and 50 electric lamps. There were also two Victorian state-of-the-art hydraulic lifts, and even the toilets were ahead of their time ("The sanitary appliances have received every attention," said the *Sydney Mail*).

BELOW: The classically elegant Art Gallery of New South Wales, built between 1896 and 1909, is one of Sydney's most distinctive landmarks, reflecting 19th-century notions of the cultural role of a gallery as a temple to art and civilising values. It is the work of the Government Architect, Walter Liberty Vernon, who secured the prestigious commission over the less conventional architect John Horbury Hunt. Hunt's eclectic and controversial designs – widely ridiculed by the Sydney press and public – included a heavy gothic structure with a blind arcade of pointed arches winding round the building, and even a Byzantine/Islamic hybrid with Moorish arches and a series of domes. They were all rejected in favour of Vernon's chaste, classical building, which features a Grecian portico with Ionic columns.

ARCHITECTURE: THE 20TH CENTURY AND BEYOND

The eye-catching Opera House achieved instant worldwide recognition, but many other innovative buildings have transformed the cityscape

Sydney is justly famous for its masterpiece 20th-century building, the Sydney Opera House *(see page 94)*, but some of its other modern architecture is a hotchpotch. This is partly explained by the city's former obsession with property speculation – during the 1960s, the low-scale Victorian city landscape was ripped apart by multiple eruptions of high-rises in the Central Business District, and many of the buildings bear the mark of an enthusiasm for money-making rather than great design and sympathetic civic planning. However, when Sydney *does* get it right, the result is some of the finest modern city architecture in the world, with many buildings that complement and enhance the cityscape.

ABOVE: The postwar Sydney school of architecture, a reaction against the alienating effects of modernism, gradually evolved an "organic" style in which buildings respond to the natural lines of the landscape. It is perhaps Australia's first genuinely home-grown architectural style. The National Maritime Museum, designed by Philip Cox and opened in 1991, is a good example, with its billowing "sails" curving over Darling Harbour.

RIGHT: During the 1950s, Sydney's most innovative architecture, such as this modernist house on the Northside, sprang up not in the commercial city centre but in the rapidly expanding affluent suburbs. Rose Seidler House in Wahroonga, created for his parents by Harry Seidler between 1948 and 1952, has a minimal colour scheme, open planning, and innovative labour-saving devices. It is now managed by the Historic Houses Trust and open to the public.

RIGHT: The city's most prominent landmark, the Sydney Tower (which has also been known as Centrepoint Tower and the AMP Tower) was designed by architect Donald Crone and is Australia's tallest building at 320 metres (1,050 ft). Work on the Centrepoint shop and office complex below began in 1970, and the tower was finally opened in 1981, to serve as both a communications tower and a tourist facility. The turret at the top is equivalent in size to a nine-storey building and is serviced by three high-speed elevators. Its observation platforms and restaurants can accommodate nearly 1,000 people. Fifty-six steel cables stabilise the tower.

ART DECO IN APARTMENT BLOCKS, CINEMAS – AND PUBS

BELOW: When the city decided to build a new Exhibition Centre beside Darling Harbour as part of the 1988 Bicentenary celebrations, they again turned to Philip Cox. His design is a blend of glass, steel and maritime imagery: its most distinctive feature are the giant steel masts and stays, which both support the load of the vast structure and recall the rigging of a sailing ship. The building, covering 25,000 sq metres (270,000 sq ft), stretches in staggered formation along the western side of the Darling Harbour Park, with the eastern face glazed to provide natural lighting.

In the 1930s an art deco trend was spearheaded by Sydney architects Emil Sodersten and John Crust. Apartment blocks are Sydney's most prevalent manifestations of the style. Most of the best preserved and historically significant examples are concentrated in the inner-city precincts of Potts Point and Elizabeth Bay, which probably contain the highest density of art deco architecture in the southern hemisphere.

The Metro (formerly Minerva) Theatre in Orwell Street was commissioned by MGM to be the showcase cinema in the rapidly burgeoning suburb of Potts Point. The initial sketches were by Bruce Dellitt, the designer of the art deco Anzac War Memorial and the Archibald Fountain in Hyde Park, but the commission was completed in 1939 by cinema architects Guy Crick and Bruce Furse. The adjacent Minerva Café, which also contained flats and office space, was designed by Reginald Magoffin, in similar art deco style.

A uniquely Australian phenomenon of the 1930s was the appearance of striking art deco hotels and pubs, which served as three-dimensional advertisements for the breweries who built them. Good surviving examples include the Criterion Hotel in Park Street, the Piccadilly Hotel in Potts Point and the Hotel Hollywood in Surry Hills.

THE ROCKS

Long disregarded by Sydneysiders as a deprived area, The Rocks is now a tribute to the architectural vision and survival instinct of Australia's first European inhabitants

The Rocks is the site of the first white settlement in Australia. Located on the west side of Circular Quay, it offers a rare sight of the city landscape with a few golden-coloured sandstone buildings set against the brilliance of the harbour on one side, and the clutter of high-rise buildings on the other. For most of its life it has been known as one of Sydney's worst areas; now, somewhat typical of this city, it is as much a source of pride as it once was of derision.

Its history could be said to illustrate one important theme in the broader story of Sydney: a collective desire of the inhabitants to escape from the memory of the colony's beginnings, or, as commentator Robert Hughes remarked, "to edit from their mental record [the fact] that white settlement of this country had occurred in order to create an enormous jail, the jail of infinite space, for people who were perceived as members of a criminal class".

To this end The Rocks, birthplace of white Australia, has been variously ignored, vilified, and very nearly destroyed several times.

Sydney's first colony

The First Fleet established the new colony at The Rocks, Sydney Cove, on 26 January 1788, six days after landing in Botany Bay. Captain (later Governor) Arthur Phillip decided on this location because it had a freshwater stream on the edge of what he came to describe as the "finest harbour in the world".

Development, by necessity, was swift, and within weeks the first huts of cabbage-tree palm and mud were being built among the raggedy tents. Streets, hastily hacked out of the rock face by convict labour, were soon curving up the hillside. Lining them were warehouses, cottages,

Map on page 68

LEFT: sightseeing in Sydney's oldest quarter. **BELOW:** traditional skills.

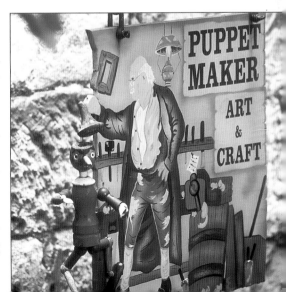

offices and stores built to no particular design.

Interestingly, given that this was a convict colony, no prison was constructed here for the first 30 years. It was not until 1819, with the erection of the Hyde Park Barracks on the other side of the city, that there was a night-time lock-down for convicts (until then the landscape was thought a sufficient deterrent to escape).

Free-roaming convicts didn't exactly help boost the area's reputation. A few free men built substantial houses here, but most colonists went elsewhere, anxious to escape from a place which, in terms of filth, crime and poverty, soon rivalled the worst of what late-18th-century London had to offer.

By the 1820s and 1830s, The Rocks was the preserve of seamen, prostitutes, criminals and the disadvantaged. A commissioner sent to the colony to make a report remarked, "The Rocks is a place distinguished for the practice of every debauchery and villainy," and by the 1870s and 1880s gangs of hoodlums and street fighters ("pushes" as they were called) virtually owned the streets.

Bubonic plague broke out in the early part of the 20th century, sealing the area's fate as Sydney's worst suburb. To try to contain the plague the government demolished substantial sections of the area. The Great Wall, still standing, was built to keep rats and their plague-bearing fleas confined to the riff-raff zones of the waterfront area.

In the 1920s another large section of the district was demolished to make way for the new bridge, and with it 800 homes of some of the poorest people in Sydney.

The greatest threat to The Rocks, however, came as recently as the 1960s. The Sydney government, still uncertain of what it was and convinced that no one would want to look at what it had been, embraced plans to destroy the neighbourhood for a development of hotels, shops and plazas. Conservationists and unions launched an enormous and ultimately effective campaign to save what remained.

A street performer on Circular Quay.

BELOW: the modern scupture is a memorial to the first settlers.

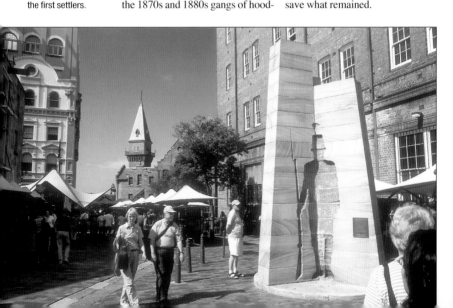

The Rocks today preserves many old buildings if not the old working-class character that defined the district for so many years. Some who remember the old Rocks are dismayed by the chic flavour the area has acquired through attempts to populate it with tourists. But this is no historic theme park, and even the most ardent purist would agree that the influx of shops, galleries and restaurants is a small price to pay for the preservation of European Australia's most significant historic site.

Circular Quay and beyond

Sydney is a city of the water and Circular Quay is its symbolic gateway, the place of arrival and departure. The promenade that links the Quay with Bennelong Point and The Rocks is a hugely popular quarter of the city, and on weekends it is full to bursting with buskers, strollers, joggers and hawkers. The Writers Walk which encircles the Quay honours famous Australian writers with plaques that bear brief descriptions of their careers and the impact of their works. On the Quay's western flank, First Fleet Park is a good place to relax while taking in the view, and it is also home to numerous public performances and events, particularly during festival times.

Just beyond the park is the **Museum of Contemporary Art (MCA)** ⓬ (open daily; tel: 9241 5892 for exhibition details). The museum is housed in the old Maritime Services Board building, which was begun in 1939 but not completed until 1952 because of World War II. Its art deco style and carefully chosen building materials were designed to complement the functionalist style of Circular Quay Railway Station.

The museum moved to its current premises in 1991, with the objective of providing access to the best and latest works and trends in contemporary art from around the world. It has its own collection of works by luminaries such as Warhol, Hockney and Christo, as well as contemporary Australian artists. The highly regarded **MCA Café** looks across the water to the Opera House.

Just past the MCA is the **Overseas**

Map on page 68

Why is Circular Quay not round? It was once called Semicircular Quay, which well described its original shape. This was shortened to Circular Quay, and the name stuck even after reconstruction made it rectangular.

BELOW: Aborigines entertain on Circular Quay.

Passenger Terminal. Where once the leg-ironed convicts and distempered officers struggled ashore, today's arrivals usually glide effortlessly from luxurious quarters to awaiting taxis and tourist entertainments.

The Rocks East

The area to the east of the Bradfield Highway is where much of the tourist and commercial activity of The Rocks takes place. Here you will find cafés, restaurants and dozens of little shops and galleries dealing in Australiana. On weekends and school holidays there is nearly always some form of street entertainment, and the large open-air weekend markets are great fun.

There are many sites of interest in The Rocks, and a visit to the **The Rocks Visitors' Centre** ⓭ on George Street is recommended for an introductory overview (open daily; tel: 9240 8788). In among the brochures, maps and books you will find excellent displays on The Rocks, including artefacts from local archaeological digs. Pick up a

Home-made confectionery on sale at the Rocks weekend market.

BELOW: Campbells Storehouses are now restaurants.

self-guide historic walk brochure, or join a walking tour of the area.

The centre is housed in the old Sailor's Home, which was built in 1864 as alternative accommodation for sailors to the brothels and dangerous inns. The Rocks by this stage had gained international notoriety as a location for "leisure that was even more perilous than the sea".

Cadman's Cottage ⓮, on the southern side of the Sailor's Home, is the oldest extant residence in Australia. It was built in 1815 to house the crews of the governor's boats. The convict John Cadman, transported in 1798 for horse-stealing, was pardoned in 1821 and was appointed coxswain of government boats. He resided in this building with his family until 1846. The cottage was originally on the waterfront, but the 1840s reclamation of land left it high and dry. It later became part of the Sailor's Home as an annexe for ships' officers, and today the small stone building houses the Sydney Harbour National Park Information Centre (open Mon–Fri 9.30am–4.30pm, Sat–Sun 10am–4.30pm; *see page 150*).

Suez Canal lies beyond this foreshore area at the back of George Street. The lane was created in the 1840s and was probably first known as the "Sewers Canal", of which no further explanation is needed.

Susannah Place, in Gloucester Street, is an interesting terrace of four Irish-style houses built in 1844 and privately occupied until 1990. These solid houses were constructed for the free-settling couple Edward and Mary Riley, who arrived in from Ireland in 1838 with their niece Susannah.

The buildings have particular significance today for their preservation of early fire insulation, drainage, ventilation and sanitary systems, as well as for the extent to which they display the various ren-

ovations made by the different generations of occupants. The terrace is now run as a museum (open Sat–Sun 10am–5pm, daily during Jan; tel: 9241 1893; entrance fee).

Argyle Cut was built to link Darling Harbour with The Rocks. The early authorities used convict labour on the Cut, each equipped with a small hammer and chisel to hack through the solid rock. Work progressed slowly until the convict transports ceased in the late 1840s. Free settlers were then employed and, in a surprising move, made use of explosives. The Argyle Stores were built between 1826 and the 1880s and are now home to a department store.

Heading towards the bridge along George Street, at No. 43 is the **Merchant's House** ⓯, which was built in 1842 for plumbers and glaziers Martyn and Coombes, and designed by John Bibb, a practitioner in the Greek Revival architectural style. This abode was home to the Royal Indian Navy in 1942, and run as a boarding house until the 1980s. It is currently closed to the public.

Campbells Cove

Campbells Cove, a sub-cove of Sydney Cove, is the site of the magnificent architectural landmark **Campbells Storehouses** ⓰, named after Australia's first real waterfront entrepreneur, Robert Campbell. He bought the land here in 1799, and 40 years and much prosperity later built the storehouses that exist to this day. Their construction began in 1839, and they were originally a series of two-storeyed stone buildings; the government added a third storey after buying them in 1890.

The complex is now home to popular outdoor restaurants with maritime themes, colonial-influenced decor and incomparable harbour views. The weekend trade is particularly healthy.

Nestled into the northern crook of the cove is the **Park Hyatt Hotel**. The bar and restaurant has fine views of Sydney Cove and the Opera House. The Rocks offer several accommodation options including the **Observatory Hotel**, designed by prominent local architect Phillip Cox and featuring a near replica of

Map on page 68

Atherdon Street, near the Merchant's House, is Sydney's shortest street. You can see the cliff face of sandstone at the end of the thoroughfare, an indication of the geological form that gave the area its name.

BELOW: Cadman's Cottage, Australia's oldest house.

Building the Coathanger

The Sydney Harbour Bridge was an engineering feat of massive proportions when it was built between 1923 and 1932; and it remains so to this day, as the second-longest single-span bridge (short of first place by a mere 63 centimetres) to be trudged by weary mankind.

It was designed and supervised by the government's Chief Engineer, Dr John Bradfield, who also oversaw the development of Sydney's electric railway system.

The span, at 503 metres (1,650 ft) in length, was built from both shores simultaneously, sunk into 12 metres (40 ft) of sandstone foundation either side. Once the two ends met, the deck was built from the centre out, 59 metres (195 ft) above sea level. Hinges at either end of the arch were added to allow movement in the wind and compensate for the expansion of the steel in extreme heat.

When the last bolt had been riveted into place, Bradfield tested the structure by having 96 locomotive engines distributed across the bridge – the equivalent of 5,900 motor cars.

The politics of the "coathanger" (as it

was nicknamed early on) were always controversial. Thirteen men died during the construction work, hundreds of families were evicted from the areas needed by the bridge and given no compensation, and country people saw the project as a blood-sucking venture, a case of the city robbing the "bush" to fund the project.

Given the mood of the times, it is perhaps not surprising that at the opening ceremony, just as Premier Jack Lang was about to cut the ribbon, a man on horseback, Francis de Groot, armed with a sword, rode forth and slashed the ribbon before the premier could exercise his representative snip.

De Groot, owner of a furniture factory and member of the right-wing New Guard, detested the premier and his socialist government, and felt the bridge should be opened by a member of the local "aristocracy" or the royal family.

The total cost of the construction eventually reached £6.2 million. The loan that financed it was paid off by toll fees – but not until 1988. (The toll is still levied, and pays for bridge maintenance and the Sydney Harbour Tunnel.) Today the bridge serves more than 150,000 vehicles each day as they journey between the city centre and Sydney's north shore and northern suburbs.

The bridge requires constant maintenance. Every 10 years, a team of painters who have just finished coating the bridge with 30,000 litres (6,600 gallons) of paint – enough to cover approximately 60 football fields – are forced to start all over again from the other end.

At the time of construction, planners were considering decorating the bridge an eye-catching golden colour but, fearing that this might make the structure too visible a target should war break out again, it was painted in the much more muted shade of dark grey seen today. This dull coloration may be partly responsible for the bridge's other unofficial name amongst Sydney-siders, the "Meccano set". ❑

LEFT: the bridge took 1,400 workers nine years to build, and cost £6.2 million (US$10 million).

the famous Elizabeth Bay House staircase *(see page 114)*, and the **Russell Hotel**, offering boutique-style accommodation in 19th-century surrounds.

Dawes Point offers a stunning view of the underside of the Sydney Harbour Bridge, the Opera House and the Sydney ferries on the harbour. It gets its name from artillery engineer Lieutenant William Dawes, an officer with a love of amateur astronomy who came out on the First Fleet's lead ship, *Sirius*. Under direction from the British Board of Longitude, Dawes established Australia's first observatory here in 1788. Dawes Point Battery was the nation's first fortified position, established by Governor Phillip in 1791. It was demolished in 1925 to make way for the bridge.

Millers Point

The Rocks area has been virtually cut in half by the Bradfield Highway, the traffic feed for the Harbour Bridge. The area to the west of the Bradfield is a far quieter spot than its eastern counterpart – many of the buildings here are still private residences. The main draw for visitors is the chance to visit one of the historic pubs that raise a storm on Friday and Saturday nights.

The area can be reached by walking around the foreshore of Dawes Point or through the Argyle Cut. A quiet stroll through this area, by day or night, is always a pleasant experience.

Beyond the Cut is **Argyle Place**, the oldest surviving urban space in Sydney. The whole area known as Millers Point is strewn with superb terraces surviving from the Georgian and Victorian eras. The **Garrison Church** is a monument to early regimental worship. It was designed by Henry Ginn in 1840 and built by convict labour, with additions made in 1878.

The **Lord Nelson Hotel** claims to be the oldest hotel in Sydney, and is certainly one of the few remaining of the very first 37 licensed premises. It has been in business since 1842 and serves its own strong brews, best consumed while examining the picturesque interiors and

Map on page 68

TIP

The Harbour Bridge Pylon Lookout (open daily; entrance fee) gives superb bird's-eye views of the harbour – if you can manage the 200 steps. If you're feeling adventurous, you should don overalls and do the Bridge Climb. Tours leave hourly, dawn to dusk daily, from the base of the Bridge's southeastern pylon at Dawe's Point (tel: 8274 7777; entrance fee).

BELOW: lunch German-style at a Rocks bierkeller.

Map
on page
68

*Entertainment at
The Rocks includes
oompah bands.*

BELOW: the bar of
the Australian Hotel.

absorbing the old-world atmosphere.

The **Hero of Waterloo Hotel**  is close by and neck-and-neck with the Lord Nelson for the title of oldest hotel. However, where the Hero is today very populated on weekends, in the old days it was used by short-staffed sea captains as a means of depopulating The Rocks of seaworthy men. The legend goes that after a few too many, unsuspecting luggers were hit over the back of the head and bundled down a tunnel to a most uncertain life at sea.

The wharves and the Observatory

A conveniently secretive place to transport these early victims may have been at the foreshore of the site now known as the **Walsh Bay Finger Wharves**. Prior to development, the Walsh Bay foreshore was characterised by precipitous cliffs, and ships at anchor could only be serviced by small boats. In the early 1800s, roads were cut into the rock and wharves developed. However, the plague of the 1900s was traced back to ships stationed there, and the

entire existing infrastructure was demolished, with the finger wharves being subsequently developed.

Like the deep-sea finger wharf at Woolloomooloo *(see page 112)*, their construction pushed the engineering know-how of the pre-World War I period to the limits. The majestic wharves are today no longer used for shipping.

Pier Four and **Pier Five** are the home of several artistic performance companies, including the Sydney Theatre Company, The Sydney Dance Company and Bangarra, the Aboriginal and Torres Strait Islander dance group *(see page 223)*. The **Wharf Restaurant** at the end of Pier Four has beautiful harbour views. Pier One is a shopping centre.

Another sterling view is to be found at the **Sydney Observatory** ❷⓿ (open daily 10am–5pm; free), a direct offspring of the astronomical and timekeeping efforts of Lieutenant Dawes. The Observatory was established in 1858, and today serves as an interactive museum of astronomy, with educational programmes and evening viewings through the telescope (every night; booking essential, tel: 9217 0485; entrance fee). The first ever photographs of the southern skies were taken from here in the 1880s.

Observatory Hill is the highest point in the city, and for this reason also had grain-grinding windmills in the colony's early days. Looking north from the hilltop, visitors are treated to a spectacular view along the Bradfield Highway as it leads onto the Harbour Bridge. To the left, below the Bridge, is tree-lined Lower Fort Street, noted for its stately, multi-storey terrace houses.

The **National Trust Centre** (open Tues–Fri 10am–2pm, Sat–Sun noon–5pm; tel: 9258 0123) is also on the hill, and houses the S.H. Ervin Art Gallery, which focuses on themes of Australian history. ❑

RESTAURANTS & BARS

Restaurants

Bel Mondo
Level 3, Argyle Department Store, 12–24 Argyle Street
Tel: 9241 3700
Open: L Mon–Fri, D daily. $$$
Exceptional Italian food in one of Sydney's best dining precincts. Admire the historic colonial decor, redolent of an Outback shearing shed.

Japanese Restaurant on 36
Level 36, Shangri-La Hotel, 176 Cumberland Street
Tel: 9250 6123
Open: L Mon–Fri, D daily. $$$
One of the city's top Japanese restaurants, on the 36th floor, with some of the best high-rise views in the city. A cheaper sushi bar is attached.

MCA Café
140 George Street
Tel: 9241 4253
Open: L only. $$
Part of the Museum of Contemporary Art on Circular Quay West, more a restaurant than a café, but one with a relaxed feel. Enjoy the great coffee and views of the Opera House.

Quay
Overseas Passenger Terminal, Circular Quay West
Tel: 9251 5600
www.quay.com.au
Open: L Tues–Fri, D daily.
$$$$

The pâté here was pronounced "too good for the general public", such is the standard of the French cuisine on offer. Chef Peter Gilmore keeps up the fantastic standards of his predecessor Guillaume Brahimi (now at the Opera House). The superb views of the harbour match the cuisine.

Rockpool
107 George Street
Tel: 9252 1888
Open: D Tues–Sat. $$$$
The first fine-dining restaurant in The Rocks (1989) underwent a radical renovation in 2002. The decor and ambience reach the same heights as the Modern Australian food prepared by celebrity chef Neil Perry.

The Rocks Teppanyaki
176 Cumberland Street
Tel: 9250 6020
Open: L Mon–Fri, D Mon–Sat. $$
Situated in the northern end of The Rocks, an area popular with Japanese visitors. Known for its specialty Japanese grills.

Sailor's Thai
106 George Street
Tel: 9251 2466
Open: L Mon–Fri, D Mon–Sat. $$$
Excellent modern Thai in the oldest part of

Sydney. A favourite among the many Thai restaurants that have been popular in Sydney for years.

Bars

The Australian Hotel
100–102 Cumberland Street
The outdoor seating at the Australian gives a prime view along the Bradfield Highway as it heads north onto the Harbour Bridge. A little removed from the main tourist districts of The Rocks, but a popular spot for locals and visitors alike.

Fortune of War
137 George Street
You're right to expect a heritage feel in a pub situated on Australia's oldest roadway. In business since 1839 and still going strong.

Hero of Waterloo
81–83 Lower Fort Street
A truly historic Rocks pub and a local landmark. If you want to experience a "true blue" Australian hotel, this much-loved and historic watering hole is a prime choice.

Lord Nelson Hotel
19 Kent Street
Competes with the Hero of Waterloo for title of Sydney's oldest pub, and is imbued with a colonial

19th-century feel. Several beers are brewed in-house for that unique Lord Nelson experience.

Mercantile Hotel
25–27 George Street
An Irish pub almost in the shadow of the Harbour Bridge. The Rocks markets stall-holders' wares are directly adjacent (weekends only). Outdoor seating is also available for people-watchers.

Palisade Hotel
35 Bettington Street
Away from the main tourist thoroughfares of The Rocks, the Palisade is worth a visit just to admire its architecture. The building has a towering, spire-like design overlooking Walsh Bay at the back of The Rocks district. The restored, quaint terrace houses of The Rocks district's residential area fill the surrounding streets.

PRICE CATEGORIES

Price indications are for a three-course meal for one, including half a bottle of house wine, coffee and service.
$ = under A$50
$$ = A$50–75
$$$ = A$75–115
$$$$ = over A$115
Abbreviations:
L = lunch, D = dinner.

THE DOMAIN TO THE OPERA HOUSE

The site of early European settlement, this district has a remarkable history. In addition to some well-preserved colonial sights, you will also find one of Australia's most enduring modern icons

S et beside the picturesque Sydney Harbour, the area comprising The Domain and the Royal Botanic Gardens through to the Sydney Opera House is a treasure trove of colonial history and landscaped beauty, dotted with superlative architecture. It has been an immensely popular location since its establishment by Governor Macquarie in 1816, for its numerous and free outdoor activities as well as its inspiring views. Without a doubt, the area is one of Sydney's greatest assets, and has served to keep otherwise unchecked harbourside development at bay. The areas around Woolloomooloo Bay, Farm Cove and Bennelong Point are of the utmost significance in Australian history. It was on and around these sites, combined with Sydney Cove and The Rocks, that the European settlers first camped and tilled the earth of their early farms.

Civic protest

The Domain ❶ is a large public garden stretching from St Mary's Cathedral *(see page 70)*, past Woolloomooloo to Mrs Macquarie's Chair. Its position near the harbour, combined with its history as a location for successive generations of public meetings and civic protest, compensate for its very average

botanical features. In 1917, enormous crowds met here to defeat Prime Minister Billy Hughes's attempts to introduce conscription, and in 1931, more than 100,000 people turned out to give the governor an ear-bashing for his dismissal of Premier Jack Lang.

The Domain's western edge is bordered by the old colonial precincts of administration that include Sydney Hospital, Parliament House, the Mint and the State Library of NSW *(see page 71)*.

Map on page 92

LEFT: the Choragic Monument (1870) in the Royal Botanic Gardens. **BELOW:** tropical succulents in the Gardens.

Admission is free to Parliament House and the Mint Mon–Fri (closed weekends). When the NSW state legislature is not sitting there are free guided tours of Parliament House several times a day. Booking essential; tel: 9230 2637 for details.

Nearer the eastern boundary, on Art Gallery Road, is the **Art Gallery of New South Wales ❷** (open daily; tel: 9225 1744). The gallery was established in 1874 and in 1885 moved to the present building, designed by John Horbury Hunt. The Academic Classical facade is the result of a series of stylistic prevarications. Hunt's building was eventually considered unsuitable, so another was built in 1897, with additions between 1904 and 1909 by NSW Government Architect W.L. Vernon, including a sandstone entrance.

Extensions added in 1971 almost doubled the available exhibition space and the Cook Bicentenary Wing, added in 1988, uses natural light and exterior views to help combat exhibition fatigue. The result is a well-proportioned, dramatic structure.

The gallery holds a number of major collections of Australia's finest works, European works from the 19th century, the largest permanent exhibition of Aboriginal art in the world, a rich field of Pacific and Asian work, and an international collection of contemporary paintings, including some by the great artists of the 20th century. There is also a gallery dedicated to photography.

Further down Art Gallery Road, over the Cahill Expressway, is the **Andrew (Boy) Charlton Pool** (tel: 9358 6686 to check seasonal opening hours). The "Boy Charlton", recently upgraded and modernised, is just one of Sydney's numerous and astonishingly scenic outdoor salt-water pools, with views towards the naval docks and the old immigration wharves at Woolloomooloo. Even if you don't like swimming, take your bathing suit and "dag around", as they say, just to soak up the ambience of the local characters, the harbour and the sun.

BELOW: the "Boy" Charlton salt-water swimming pool.

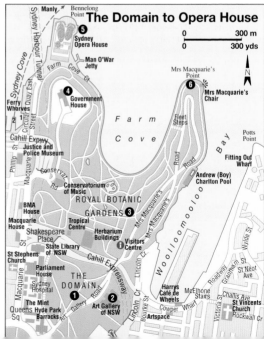

The Domain to Opera House

Botanic Gardens

The **Royal Botanic Gardens ③** (open daily; tel: 9231 8111; free) occupy almost 30 hectares (75 acres), and, combined with the Domain and Government House, were once part of the Governor's Domain established by Lachlan Macquarie. The site of the current gardens was home to the colony's first farm, established by Governor Phillip in 1788 (Farm Cove), the Governor's kitchen garden shortly after, and then, with the establishment of the Botanic Gardens in 1816 and the appointment of botanist Charles Fraser, Australia's first scientific institution.

The attractions of the Botanic Gardens today, quite apart from their history, are manifold. The **National Herbarium** is a major research institution and holds about one million specimens, including some of those collected in 1770 by Captain Cook's botanist, Joseph Banks. **Palm Grove** is one of the oldest and most loved sections of the gardens. Established in 1851, it is home to over 140 types of palm, including the cabbage tree palm, a Sydney native, and many strange and exotic-looking sibling specimens. Palm Grove also has some of Australia's oldest cultivated trees from the colonial period, the most prominent of which is a Queensland kauri, the tallest tree in the gardens, planted in 1853. Next to Palm Grove is the **First Farm**, the first land cultivated by the early colony. There are floral displays here relating to the early farm, as well as numerous plants dating back to the 19th and early 20th century. The **Herb Garden** is a small wonderland of aromas and herbal species and information.

The **Tropical Centre** (entrance fee) is a complex contained in two glasshouses shaped as a pyramid and an arc. The pyramid holds Australian tropical plants, including living specimens from the monsoonal woodlands of the tropical north, and the arc provides a botanic tour through lowland rainforests and high-altitude tropical zones from around the world. The **Palace Garden** features ornamental flower-

Mrs Macquarie's Folly in the Royal Botanic Gardens.

BELOW: keeping the Gardens green.

The Building of the Opera House

Statistics relating to the design and construction of the Sydney Opera House are remarkable. The entire arts complex covers 1.8 hectares (4½ acres); the roof, comprised of 2,194 pre-cast concrete sections, weighs a total of 158,000 tonnes and is braced by 350 km (220 miles) of tensioned cables. More than 6,200 sq metres (66,740 sq ft) of tinted French glass enclose its interiors, where concrete spandrels rise dramatically out of the floor and arc up towards the zenith of the sails.

Beyond the glass walls, the harbour shimmers back at visitors. Pink aggregate granite covers the walls, stairs and floors; native brush box and white birch plywood are used liberally in the interior. This mass of detail, the solid permanence of the building and its status as an icon make it hard to believe that this was a building that nearly never was.

When the Danish architect Jørn Utzon won the international competition to design the Opera House in 1957, he did so almost by accident. The majority of the assessment committee had already dismissed his ambitious sketches when they were retrieved from the reject pile by a late-arriving judge, US architect Eero Saarinen. He went on to sway the committee to the visionary nature of Utzon's design.

Upon winning the commission, Utzon wanted sufficient time to develop the advanced technology required to build the revolutionary sail-like structures, which at that stage had no precedent in structural engineering. But the state pressurised him into starting the building process a full two years early, beginning in 1959.

As the building work progressed in fits and starts, and as the problems that Utzon had attempted to avoid arose during the actual construction, costs escalated, eventually by more than 1,000 percent on the original A$7 million budget. By the time of its opening in 1973, the project had soaked up no less than A$102 million.

Happily, this sum was mostly paid for by punters taking a wager on the Opera House Lottery (a very Australian solution for funding major public works), but the then premier-to-be Robert Askin couldn't resist using the project as a political football, preying on community fears about the unusual design and supposed mismanagement occasioned by the building's soaring finances. Askin was elected in 1965 and soon withheld progress payments to force Utzon to reduce costs. Utzon refused to see his design mutilated and, in 1966, he resigned, incurring street marches, resignations, and career shifts among the Australian architectural community in protest at his treatment.

But despite the politics, enough of Utzon's genius eventually got through to leave the World Heritage-nominated Sydney Opera House that exists today. That Australia came by one of the finest international buildings of the modern era almost by accident is a remarkable tale in itself.

The Opera House has earned itself international esteem (voted first of the Seven Wonders of the 20th century by readers of *The Times* in 1991) and has been nominated for UNESCO World Heritage listing. On home ground, it has become a definitive national icon. ❑

LEFT: Utzon's unmistakable "sails".

beds, statues and memorials. It occupies the former site of the Garden Palace, a Victorian Academic Classical structure built for the 1880 Great International Exhibition but destroyed by fire in 1882.

In addition to a number of other fine displays, the Botanic Gardens are also home to a quite wonderful array of native Australian wildlife, including white cockatoos, superb blue wrens, tawny frogmouths, brush-tailed possums and fruit bats, to name but a few. There is a "trackless train" that runs through the gardens on regular guided tours, leaving from the entrance near the Opera House.

Government House

Around the curve of Farm Cove and just set back from Bennelong Point is **Government House ④** (open Fri–Sat 10am–3pm; grounds open daily; tel: 9931 5200; free), which was designed by the London-based architect to King William IV, Edward Blore, and erected between 1837 and 1845. Built in the form of a mock castle, with crenellated

skyline and interiors of a baroque intensity, its advanced blend of Gothic Revival and Regency styles was an architectural trendsetter in the colony for decades after it was completed. Government House remained the residence for the State Governor of NSW until very recently, but the building, with its fascinating collection of 19th-century furnishings and state rooms, is now fully open to the public.

Sydney Opera House

It is one of the quirks of history that out of a site that bears tales of such misery and difficulty arose one of the most truly inspired architectural works of the 20th century, the **Sydney Opera House ⑤** (open daily, some areas accessible by tour only; tel: 9250 7870; fee for tours).

Danish architect Jørn Utzon was born in 1918 and studied at the Copenhagen Academy of Arts. He designed the Sydney Opera House in 1957. Built over 14 years from 1959 until its opening in 1973, its world-famous arcs have been variously described as akin to a cluster of

Map on page 92

Water lilies in the Royal Botanic Gardens.

BELOW: Government House, built of local sandstone.

TIP

On Sundays, there is free outdoor entertainment at the Opera House, ranging from street theatre to jazz bands.

seashells, billowing sails, or a gaggle of nuns embedded in rock. In architectural terms, it has echoes of the Gothic cathedral style combined with a modernist symphony of organically inspired geometric forms.

One of the major achievements of Utzon's design is its harmonic relationship to the surrounds, prompting one commentator to suggest that it's as if the harbour itself had been created and filled simply to complement the building.

Despite it not quite being the building that Utzon wanted *(see page 94)*, the Opera House has earned itself international esteem (voted first of the Seven Wonders of the 20th Century by readers of *The Times*), and has been nominated for World Heritage listing. On home ground, it has become a definitive national icon.

There are four main venues within the Opera House. The Concert Hall is the largest, seating 2,690 people, with a roof-vault of 67 metres (220 ft). It also has the largest mechanical tracker action

organ in the world, with no less than 10,500 pipes. The stage curtain in the Opera Theatre, which seats 1,547, was designed by John Coburn. Its warm abstraction has earned it the name "Curtain of the Sun". The ceiling of the Drama Theatre is comprised of refrigerated aluminium panels, which create an even temperature. It seats 544, and also has a Coburn-designed woven stage curtain, its darker hues prompting the name "Curtain of the Moon". The Playhouse is a smaller venue of 398 seats. There is also a reception hall, and bars and restaurants with spectacular views.

The Opera House's first performance in 1973 was Australian Opera's production of Prokofiev's *War and Peace*. Since then, the pace has accelerated to 3,000 events and performances each year and an annual audience of around 2 million people, thus making it the busiest performing arts centre in the world. It houses all forms of the performing arts, including opera, theatre, ballet, music, as well as exhibitions and film screenings.

BELOW: inscription marking the completion of Mrs Macquarie's Road.

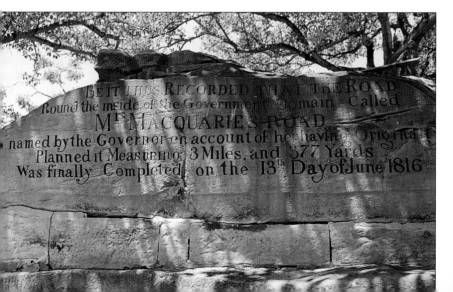

Bennelong Point

Bennelong Point is named after an 18th-century Aborigine who was forcibly abducted from Manly by Governor Phillip in 1789 and was later the first Aborigine to learn English. Phillip's intention was to take Bennelong and one of his compatriots to England, to introduce them to white civilisation. Bennelong escaped, but later returned to Sydney Cove and was given residence in a hut on the point named after him. He voluntarily accompanied the governor to England in 1792, where he remained for three years. Shunned by his own people on his return, and rejected by the whites, he lived a lonely existence until he was killed in a tribal conflict in 1813.

In recent years there has been an ironic twist to the development of Bennelong Point. Whereas Utzon's initial design for the Opera House was thwarted by costs and political interference, the recent building of an elite apartment block near by is the gravest insult yet to the integrity of the Opera House's design and its relationship with its surroundings.

The block has been dubbed the "Toaster" by art critic Robert Hughes, and Utzon himself declared it a "development which completely ruins" the connection of the Opera House to the Botanic Gardens and the ferry harbour of Sydney Cove.

Mrs Macquarie's Point

On the eastern edge of the Royal Botanic Gardens is Mrs Macquarie's Road, built on the request of Governor Macquarie's wife for a scenic route around the spit of land between Farm Cove and Woolloomooloo Bay.

The road leads to Mrs Macquarie's Chair, a sitting-place carved into the sandstone at **Mrs Macquarie's Point ❻**, where this grand lady regularly took time to enjoy the view. And what a view! From here the present-day viewer can take in the Opera House, the Harbour Bridge, Kirribilli House on the North Shore, Pinchgut Island and the wharves of Woolloomooloo. Above Mrs Macquarie's Chair is an inscription commemorating the completion of the road. ❑

The "wedding cake" lighthouse in Sydney Harbour.

RESTAURANTS & BARS

Art Gallery of NSW
Art Gallery Road
Tel: 9225 1744
Open: restaurant L daily. **$$**
Café L daily, D Wed. **$**
Coffee and snack outlets are in short supply in this area. Luckily, the Art Gallery offers a comfy upstairs restaurant and deli-café for gallery visitors and passers-by. Both get busy at weekends. Café opens Wed evening in conjunction with the gallery's Art After Hours programme.

Cadmus
Opera Quays, Level 10, 1–3 Macquarie Street
Tel: 9252 6800
Open: L Mon–Fri, D daily.
$$$$
Perhaps Sydney's most ambitious restaurant: no expense spared on the decor – and menu prices. The food is Lebanese/ Eastern Mediterranean with a Pacific slant. The views are stunning.

Guillaume at Bennelong
Sydney Opera House,
Bennelong Point
Tel: 9241 1999
Open: L Thur–Fri, D Mon– Sat. **$$$**
Award-winning restaurant where chef Guillaume Brahimi delivers exquisite French fare to match the exquisite surroundings. Service is unobtrusively excellent and prices are reasonable for the quality (apart from the excellent but pricey wine list).

Opera Quays
East Circular Quay
Situated below the controversial "Toaster" apartment block, Opera Quays has a selection of food and drink places, at a range of prices, mostly with outdoor seating. The Dendy Cinema is a licensed movie house: sample classic Aussie beers and wines while you watch a film.

● ● ● ● ● ● ● ● ● ● ● ● ●
Price indications are for a three-course meal for one, including half a bottle of house wine, coffee and service.
$ = under A$50
$$ = A$50–75
$$$ = A$75–115
$$$$ = over A$115
Abbreviations: L = lunch, D = dinner.

Map on page 92

DARLING HARBOUR AND CHINATOWN

This redevelopment of 19th-century industrial warehouses and Chinese ghettos has successfully turned the city's harbour district into a popular centre for entertainment, shopping and nightlife

E very city, it seems, has to have its urban slum, a grimy collection of derelict factories growing old disgracefully, and for many years Darling Harbour fulfilled the role as Sydney's dirty sink. It's strange how fate elevates some areas and devalues others: Darling Harbour could have been the fashionable focal point of Sydney from colonial beginnings – its shipping potential was definitely better than that of Sydney Cove. But instead it had to wait until the late 1980s before becoming an attraction rather than an eyesore.

Cockle Bay

Darling Harbour was the lynch-pin in Sydney's reputation as a major seaport for more than 100 years. However, it was a slow starter and an early finisher. Its deepwater anchorages were not developed in the first 22 years of white settlement because the ridge between it and Sydney Cove was too steep for on-land cart traffic.

Instead, the shores of the narrow bay were convenient places to collect reeds for roof-thatch cockles. Hence it was known as Cockle Bay, until it was renamed in honour of NSW Governor Ralph Darling during his term in office between 1825 and 1831. The inner harbour area is still called Cockle Bay.

The development of Darling Harbour as a wharf and industrial area was similar to many others throughout the Western world. The first steam mill in Australia opened here in 1815, kickstarting the country's industrial age and quickly replacing the windmills; sawmills, shipbuilding, soapworks and slaughterhouses followed.

This was also the site of the 1870s factory that turned out the zinc-galvanised, corrugated-iron roofing sheets which became an integral part

Map on page 102

PRECEDING PAGES: the City, with Darling Harbour beyond. **LEFT:** the tranquil Chinese Friendship Garden. **BELOW:** a Chinese Australian shops in Paddy's Markets.

TIP

Visit Darling Harbour around the Chinese New Year (usually mid-February) and catch the Dragon Boat races in Cockle Bay, in which more than 2,000 take part.

BELOW: the Monorail has run from the city to Darling Harbour since 1988.

of the Australian landscape. It still is today: corrugated roofing bedecks the new Darling Harbour buildings, as the wheel comes full circle.

The first step in the establishment of a Sydney landmark was taken in 1858 when a private toll bridge across Darling Harbour from Pyrmont to the city was opened. The charge for pedestrians was two pence each way, but they could bring their sheep or pigs for a farthing a head. By the 1880s the old wooden bridge had outlived its usefulness, and the government bought it and abolished the toll, later replacing the whole structure.

When the **Pyrmont Bridge** that still stands today was opened in 1902, it was a mechanical wonder. Its 800-tonne, 70-metre (230-ft) swing span was operated by electricity, and the machinery required to open it pushed the limits of contemporary engineering.

However, decentralisation ensured

that the city would turn its back on this industrial quagmire of rail yards, wharves and factories. By the 1970s, these metallic slums were just an unsightly hole in the landscape to be ignored while crossing Pyrmont Bridge. So eventually a consortium of government and private enterprise tore down the whole lot and rebuilt the area from scratch, using the waterway as a central theme.

Controversial novelty

There are as many elements to Darling Harbour as there were detractors during its creation. After decades of trying to curb illegal gambling, the state government finally provided the city with a giant legal casino. Many regard the result, Star City, which displays interiors redolent of the Australian landscape, with resigned bemusement. The Monorail is regarded by many citizens as an unattractive abomination,

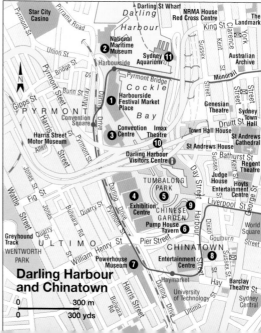

Darling Harbour and Chinatown

and its every breakdown and financial loss is eagerly reported in the press. The back row of the Entertainment Centre is said to provide the same vantage point as watching the event on a small television screen; the Convention Centre was unconventionally late in coming on line; shoppers did not want to make the journey to Darling Harbour to visit retailers who already had outlets in the city centre… The list of complaints goes on and on.

But it is hard to deny the overall success of Darling Harbour. A 54-hectare (133-acre) dump has been revitalised into a place of parks and people, of entertainment and education. The **Monorail**, despite its questionable aesthetic appeal, provides a practical means of getting around and is particularly popular with children; buy a day ticket to avoid the high cost of one-trip fares (tel: 9552 2288).

The **Darling Harbour Visitors' Centre** is located near the Imax Theatre. Here you can get advice about composite tickets for a variety of attractions (tel: 9286 0111).

The Harbourside

If it can be said that there was a model for today's Darling Harbour development, it would be Fishermen's Wharf in San Francisco. In keeping with this, the **Harbourside Festival Market Place ❶** is an enormous speciality shopping centre with more than 200 shops and many food outlets, offering a range of cuisines reflecting the diversity of Australia's cultural base.

Known as "the largest island, the smallest continent", Australia has largely defined itself by its boundaries – the girth of ocean which separates it from its neighbours. So it's surprising that it took so long for the importance of the ocean to be recognised in a **National Maritime Museum ❷**. Beneath the thematic sail-like roofs are displays dealing with all facets of Australia's relationship with the sea (open daily 9.30am–5pm; tel: 9552 7777; entrance fee).

No one can accuse the Darling Harbour **Convention Centre ❸** of being merely conventional. This seven-storey spiral edifice can seat

Darling Harbour's Convention Centre.

Map on page 102

BELOW: submarine and patrol boat side by side at the National Maritime Museum.

Enter the Dragon

S ydney's first Chinatown was in The Rocks *(see page 81)*. Its beginnings can be traced to the dozen or so indentured coolies, brought from Amoy in 1848 and 1849, who worked as labourers for Robert Towns's wharf. In the 1850s thousands of free Chinese immigrants in search of riches landed in Sydney on their way to the newly discovered goldfields of NSW and Victoria.

As gold petered out in the mid-1860s, Chinese miners drifted back to Sydney to work as cabinet-makers, tailors, cooks and grocers. Rising rents in The Rocks forced the poorer Chinese to rent houses and rooms in Campbell and Hay streets at the city's southern end, near the cattle markets. The Chinese soon became Sydney's most identifiable, residentially segregated and persecuted ethnic minority.

The European newspapers periodically railed against the filth and degradation of Chinatown, particularly the lodging houses. They blamed the Chinese for a smallpox outbreak in 1881 and the plague epidemic of 1900. Allegations that Chinese gambling and opium dens were corrupting the police and young white girls resulted in a Royal Commis-sion in the 1890s. The report concluded that the poorest Chinese lived in squalor that was no worse than that of the European poor, and that concerns about Chinese vice and corruption were wildly exaggerated.

When the Central Markets were built on the swampy upper reaches of Darling Harbour in the 1920s, Chinese traders and fruit and vegetable providers moved into Dixon Street, one of a maze of narrow, winding streets on the markets' eastern fringe. Chinese shops, restaurants, clubs and gambling dens followed. Over the next 30 years, Dixon Street became the commercial and social hub for Sydney's Chinese community.

With the dismantling of the "White Australia policy" in the 1970s, which finally permitted citizenship to non-European immigrants, Chinese arrivals from Malaysia, Hong Kong and Singapore began settling in Sydney. In contrast to their predecessors who came in search of employment and political stability, many now came equipped with substantial capital to invest. Many went straight to the suburbs of Canterbury, Fairfield, Parramatta and Strathfield, to elegant Chatswood and to the North Shore. Others, however, more accustomed to the excitement and intensity of the inner-city life they had left behind, preferred the new high-rise apartment blocks overlooking Darling Harbour.

Sydney's Chinatown district today officially extends from Liverpool Street south to Thomas Street, and from Harbour Street west to Pitt Street. But the short, bustling stretch of Dixon Street from Goulburn to Hay streets still remains the symbolic heart of Chinatown and its popular tourist centre.

The transformation of Dixon Street into a tourist attraction began in 1971, when the Sydney City Council established a Chinese Committee. The street was closed to traffic in 1979, paved and ornately decorated with ceremonial gateways, planter boxes with native Chinese plants, and an octagonal pavilion. Popular restaurants with plate-glass and marble facades occupy Dixon Street's shopfronts, alongside oriental banks and currency exchanges, jewellers, and souvenir and craft shops. ❑

LEFT: Chinese Australians in Chinatown.

3,500 delegates, making it the largest conference centre in Australia. The long-awaited **Star City Casino** is not just for gamblers. Anyone can come and be amazed at the extraordinary design features that include re-creations of tropical rainforest and Outback desert, fountains of coloured water, and Hollywood-style staircases. Practical features include a 2,000-seat lyric theatre, a nightclub, restaurants and, of course, banks of "pokies" (brightly-lit coin-fed gambling machines) and acres of gaming tables (tel: 9777 9000).

The **Convention and Exhibition Centre ❹** was sorely needed by Sydney for trade shows and public displays. Its sprawling roof, supported by steel masts and stays that resemble the rigging of a ship, covers an indoor area the size of five football fields, but all the goals here are commercial. It has 27,200 sq metres (6½ acres) of exhibition space, and the convention rooms can cope with gatherings from 50 to 3,500.

There is also an appealing concentration of museums and other public entertainment complexes in the area. The **Entertainment Centre** straddles the division between Darling Harbour and Chinatown. Many of the world's biggest stars have performed at the "Ent Cent" and many more will probably continue to do so – as long as Sydney's summer is contemporaneous with northern hemisphere winters.

Park and Powerhouse

In the heart of the Darling Harbour redevelopment, **Tumbalong Park ❺** is 5 hectares (12 acres) of parkland designed using eucalyptus and other native Australian foliage, incorporated with fountains and an urban stream, with tree-lined walks radiating into the middle distance. There is both a children's play-

ground and an amphitheatre for open-air drama performances and free weekend concerts.

There was a strange kind of logic at work when it was decided that the old **Pump House Tavern ❻** should be developed as a boutique brewery. The Pump House Tavern originally provided the hydraulic pressure for the lifts of Sydney; for years it provided home-brewed beer, giving, as it were, a different kind of lift to the city's lifestyle. The future of the building is now in doubt.

One part of the whole redevelopment which is now above criticism is the **Powerhouse Museum ❼** (open daily 10am–5pm; tel: 9217 0111; entrance fee). It wasn't always this way, but the disputes that flared throughout its design and construction have faded as its merits are recognised. It is now considered the finest celebration of Australian arts, science and social history, presented in dynamic displays and novel contexts such as "hands-on", interactive and audiovisual presentations which encourage full visitor participation.

Map on page 102

TIP

The Teahouse in the Chinese Garden serves traditional Chinese tea and sweets.

BELOW: the Twin Pavilion in the Chinese Garden.

Map on page 102

The Imax: Sydney's biggest screen.

BELOW: the Emperor's Garden in Chinatown.

Chinatown

Moving away from the harbour towards the city centre is **Chinatown ⑧**, which stretches from Harris Street to Castlereagh Street. Like the rest of the area, it has emerged from its run-down past into a brightly decorated, bustling area, adorned with Chinese gateways and oriental street lamps. Traditional Asian grocers, medical practitioners and restaurants serve the locals and enchant the visitors.

Another cultural link between Australia and the Orient is forged by the **Chinese Garden of Friendship ⑨** (open daily 9.30am–5pm; tel: 9281 6863; entrance fee), built as a bicentennial gift in 1988 by the government of China's Guangdong Province. Two carved dragons represent the sister cities of Guandong and Sydney. Within the garden walls is a peaceful refuge of lakes covered with lotus flowers, waterfalls and perfect Chinese landscaping. The Twin Pavilion, a classical Chinese pagoda, has woodcarvings of waratahs, the state flower of New South Wales.

The children's harbour

The **Panasonic Imax Theatre ⑩** has an eight-storey-high screen and a regular programme of adventure and children's movies in 2D and 3D format. From the right viewing position, the clarity of the images is sensationally lifelike; if you want to save your eyesight, however, arrive early to get a seat at the back of the auditorium (tel: 9281 3300; entrance fee).

The **Sydney Aquarium ⑪**, on the city side of the water's edge and shaped like a breaking wave, contains a good cross section of the incredible range of fish that inhabit Australian waters (open daily 9.30am–10pm, last admission 8pm; tel: 9262 2300; entrance fee). Although there are no salt-water crocodiles in NSW waters, visitors to the state who aren't travelling further north can see these man-eaters at the aquarium. Sydney's waters certainly are home to sharks, and nose-to-nose confrontations with these and other inhabitants of the shoreline are possible from the safety of the aquarium's transparent tunnel. ❑

RESTAURANTS, BARS & CAFÉS

Restaurants

Asian Food Halls
Dixon Street, Haymarket
Open: daily, continuous. **$**
A vast and very econom-
ical choice: Chinese,
Vietnamese, Japanese
and Malaysian menus on
offer, ready-made or
cooked while you wait.
Some places are
licensed.

BBQ King
18–20 Goulburn Street,
Haymarket
Tel: 9267 2586
Open: L & D daily. **$$**
Authentic Chinese menu
(notably Peking duck and
Chinese barbeque pork)
in an atmosphere redo-
lent of Imperial Canton.

Casa Asturiana
77 Liverpool Street
Tel: 9264 1010
Open: L Tues–Fri & Sun,
D daily. **$$**
One of Sydney's oldest
Spanish eateries. Wide
range of tapas, or special-
ities including fine paella
and Asturian bean stew.

CMC
The Promenade, Cockle Bay
Wharf, Darling Harbour
Tel: 9283 3393
Open: all day daily, to 2am
Fri, Sat. **$$**
Indoor and outdoor
tables with views across
Darling Harbour. Food is
Modern Australian with
Lebanese-Mediterranean
influences.

Eastern August Moon
54 Dixon Street, Chinatown
Tel: 9212 1899
Open: L & D daily. **$$**
Simple, good-quality Chi-
nese. Try the shang tong
chicken or three special
sauce chicken.

Emperor's Garden
213–215 Thomas Street
Tel: 9281 9899
Open: 9.30am–11pm daily. **$**
Good food, good prices
and average decor. BYO.
Also serves breakfast.

Fish Markets Sushi Bar
Blackwattle Bay, Pyrmont
Tel: 9552 2872
Open: L daily. **$**
Japanese seafood fresh
from the market. Friendly
service. BYO.

Golden Harbour
31 Dixon Street, Chinatown
Tel: 9212 5987
Open: L & D daily. **$$**
Popular Chinese with
daily yum cha. Best crispy
skin chicken in Sydney.

Jetty Enoteca
42–48 The Promenade,
King Street Wharf
Tel: 9279 4115
Open: L & D daily. **$$**
Contemporary Tuscan-
influenced cuisine with
good service and water-
side views.

Kam Fook
Level 3, Market City, 9–13
Hay Street, Haymarket
Tel: 9211 8988
Open: L daily, D Thur–Sun. **$$**

Sydney's biggest yum
cha venue. Go for brunch
on Sunday and watch the
waiter-and-trolley specta-
cle – traditional Chinese
breakfast for 800 people.

The Malaya
39 Lime Street, King Street
Wharf, Darling Harbour
Tel: 9279 1170
Open: L & D daily. **$$$**
Authentic Malaysian cui-
sine – reputedly the best
laksa in town. Dine out-
doors, or inside in the
open-plan setting.

Nine Dragons
39 Dixon Street, Chinatown
Tel: 9211 3549
Open: L & D daily. **$**
A good all-purpose Can-
tonese restaurant with
daily yum cha. Outdoor
seating area.

Vieri Cucina Bar
Shop 433, 435 Harbourside,
Darling Harbour
Tel: 9212 4441
Open: L & D daily. **$$**
Popular Italian eatery:
seafood and interna-
tional cuisine comple-
mented by a wide
selection of wines.

Zaaffran
Shop 345, Level 2, Harbour-
side, Darling Harbour
Tel: 9211 8900
Open: L & D daily. **$$$$**
Australia's only 5-star
Indian restaurant. Tradi-
tional, home-style Indian
cooking, presented with
a contemporary flair.

Bars

Docks Hotel
Northern promenade,
Darling Harbour
Australian-themed pub
situated by the water-
front. Lively after dark,
with great views back
towards the city skyline.

Star City Casino
80 Pyrmont Street
Sydney's casino is open
24/7 but not all its bars
and eateries are. The
overall theme in this vast
gaming house is mock
Outback. Choose from
half a dozen bars: the
Lightning Ridge Bar looks
across the huge main
gaming room.

Watershed Hotel
Shop 198/357 Harbourside,
Darling Harbour
The spacious Watershed
is a fun nightspot and
bar with exciting city
views. Offers a menu of
snacks and main meals
during the day.

PRICE CATEGORIES

A three-course meal for
one, including half a
bottle of house wine,
coffee and service:
$ = under A$50
$$ = A$50–75
$$$ = A$75–115
$$$$ = over A$115
Abbreviations: L = lunch,
D = dinner. BYO = bring
your own alcohol.

SYDNEY ON DISPLAY

From maritime history and archaeology to computers and aviation, Sydney's museums offer both traditional and contemporary experiences

Sydney's museums and galleries are a justifiable source of pride for the city. Most of the major museums are close to the city centre, and most combine architectural innovation and imagination with challenging and fascinating collections.

Modern Australians are understandably curious about their country's unique history, and especially about the dramatic evolution in just over two centuries from an expanse sparsely populated by hunter-gatherers to a high-tech, multicultural, modern country. Nowhere is this evolution more apparent than in Sydney, and the city's museums do justice to the dramatic history of the city and the country.

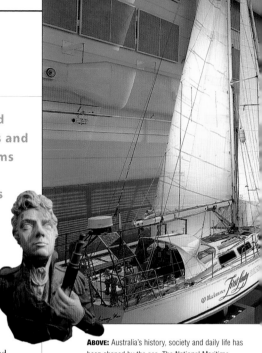

ABOVE: Australia's history, society and daily life has been shaped by the sea. The National Maritime Museum covers everything from Aboriginal seafarers to early European explorers, from submarines to surfboards. There are boats outside in Darling Harbour, including the destroyer *Vampire* and the submarine *Onslow*, and a wealth of nautical artefacts inside, including the figure head from HMAS *Nelson*.

ABOVE: The Edge of the Trees sculpture outside the Museum of Sydney, by Janet Laurence and Fiona Foley (Sydney's first public artwork to be a collaboration between a European and an Aboriginal Australian), represents human memory and experience, drawing on Eora culture and Sydney's many cultural influences. The story of Sydney's indigenous people is woven through the fabric of the museum.

BELOW: The Crazy Crooners are part of a Museum of Sydney exhibit on city sights. They are from an early sideshow in Luna Park, the Northside amusement park that opened in the 1930s, closed after a fire in the 1960s and reopened for business in 2004. The museum sits on the site of Governor Arthur Phillip's first Government House (in 1983 archaeologists unearthed the original footings of the house, which had lain preserved since it was demolished in 1846: these remains are a feature of the museum's display). The adventurous museum, which opened in 1995, offers a unique insight into the city's history. Exhibitions, films and high-tech displays tell stories of Aboriginal culture, colonial life, environment, trade, the law, and everyday dramas.

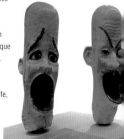

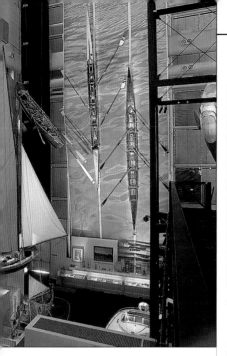

POWER TO THE PEOPLE AT AUSTRALIA'S MOST POPULAR MUSEUM

BELOW: Palaeontology can be fun. The Australian Museum has an international reputation in the fields of natural history and indigenous studies – but despite its academic credentials, it's very enjoyable to visit. Permanent displays include Indigenous Australia, artefacts that illuminate Aboriginal cultures and lifestyles; the Living Harbour and the Wildlife of Sydney; a huge collection of other birds, mammals and insects; and Australia's Lost Kingdoms, a gripping journey through evolution, featuring genuine fossils and life-size models of dinosaurs and some of Australia's extinct megafauna. Plenty for children to enjoy.

The Powerhouse Museum in Ultimo is a fine example of Sydney's dynamic late-20th-century reclamation and transformation projects. The core of the building was once the power station that serviced Sydney's tram system, and still incorporates the boiler, switch and turbine houses. The new sections, the work of architects Denton Corker Marshall, recall grand European railway stations and exhibition halls.

Within them are gathered all manner of technological marvels – transport from planes and boats and trains to bicycles and wheelbarrows; engineering achievements from crossbows to clocks, from Samurai armour to printing presses; high-tech exhibits including computers, robots and early televisions; decorative arts and design, including fashion, ceramics, furniture, musical instruments and coins; and scientific displays that cover astronomy, timekeeping, navigation, medicine and much more.

Since it opened in 1988, the Powerhouse has become Australia's most popular museum. It is a favourite with families, not least thanks to the Kids Interactive Discovery Spaces (KIDS), with a range of games and hands-on activities designed to involve children in the themes in the museum's exhibitions. They explore subjects such as music, machines, life in the home, film and television. Elsewhere, children and adults alike are encouraged to sample more than 100 interactive demonstrations on topics as diverse as the chemistry of smell, lace-making and computer animation.

Playbirds
INTERNATIONAL

PLAYBIRDS

GIRLS!
GIRLS!
GIRLS!

このショップは、
ひと続きご覧頂けます。

不断的
脱衣舞表表

CONTINUOUS
LIVE SHOW

EXOTIC
LIVE
SHOWS
AUSTRALIA'S
LARGEST
EROTIC
VENUE

LIVE
NUDE
GIRLS!

Streaks Tims

THE KINGS CROSS DISTRICT

The Bohemian side of Sydney life has existed in Kings Cross since the 1920s, and still thrives along the lively Darlinghurst Road with its collection of trendy bars and cafés

Kings Cross is more a series of images than a precise geographical locality. In 1905 the junction of William Street, Darlinghurst Road and Victoria Street – 1 km (½ mile) east of the city centre – was named Kings Cross. There has long been a Kings Cross Post Office, but never a real suburb. The name refers to an imprecise area covering the suburbs of Potts Point, Elizabeth Bay, Rushcutters Bay, the part of Darlinghurst north of Oxford Street and, at a stretch, the streets and waterfront of Woolloomooloo.

Since the 1920s, Kings Cross has been synonymous with glitz and glamour, crime and sleaze, Bohemianism and cosmopolitanism, destitution and despair. Like New York's 42nd Street, it has been the place "where the underworld meets the elite" – socialites, artists, students, homosexuals, immigrants, runaways, addicts and, more recently, young professionals have come here in search of excitement, anonymity, freedom, drugs, sex or easy money.

During the 1950s (the most conservative period in Australia's history), the area offered refuge from suburbia and strict family values. Kings Cross was then, and probably is now, one of the most ethnically, socially and culturally diverse areas in Australia.

Despite its reputation, Kings Cross is a place of extraordinary architecture, from Georgian colonial mansions to art deco apartments, gracious tree-lined streets, some of the best cafés in Sydney, a magnificent wharf area and a few of the city's top cultural sites.

Woolloomooloo

The district of **Woolloomooloo** ❶ nestles into the undercliff beneath the Domain *(see page 91)*. This small suburb of old and new terrace

Map on page 112

Map on page 112

LEFT: the less salubrious side of Kings Cross. **BELOW:** wharves converted into waterside apartments in Woolloomooloo.

houses (many of them council houses) was the scene of a bitter dispute in 1969, when it was proposed that the suburb should be destroyed to make way for high-rise redevelopment. The "Loo" was saved, and the victory marked a turnaround on issues of urban conservation in Sydney.

On Cowper Wharf Road is the Woolloomooloo Deep Sea Wharf, the largest timber wharf in Sydney and typical of the wharves of the early 20th century, many of them now destroyed. The wharf has been used as a passenger terminal, an army embarkation point and for commercial shipping. Commonly known by locals as the "finger wharf", this site lay abandoned during the 1990s, when it became a popular site for unlicensed all-night "rave" parties.

The crowds who flocked to these parties attracted police attention and the music soon stopped; the wharf now houses a stylish strip of waterfront restaurants, the avant-garde styling of "W" Hotel, and yuppified upmarket apartments upstairs.

Further along Cowper Wharf Road is **Artspace**, housing artists' studios and a gallery (open Mon–Sat; tel: 9368 1899). Opposite the studios is **Harry's Cafe de Wheels**, a mobile food van which began life as a pie cart in the 1940s serving "pie floaters" (meat pies and mashed peas). It is now a Sydney institution, and stopping by for a late-night pie is a popular pastime, even with visiting celebrities – just check the many photos of famous faces eating Harry's pies on the sides of the van. (Car parking is available, but there are no seats. Sit in your car, or nab a spot along the water's edge.)

Harry's marks the start of Garden Island, Sydney's navy base, covering most of the Potts Point foreshore. Apart from its wharves, where the navy ships dock, it has some superb historic buildings and gardens. It

Sailing is a popular pastime.

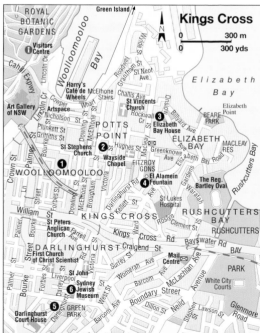

also boasts Sydney's most famous graffiti, the initials of three convicts from the First Fleet carved into a rock. The area opens to the public only once a year, but good views can be had from aboard a ferry.

Potts Point

In the 1830s, some of Sydney's wealthiest residents built mansions on what the then Surveyor General described as "the most picturesque hill about Sydney", now known as **Potts Point ❷** and Elizabeth Bay. Sadly, many of these houses have since been demolished.

Take the McElhone Stairs (113 of them) up the cliff; the steps come out at Victoria Street, an elegant tree-lined avenue that was saved from demolition in the 1970s. The two-, three- and four-storey houses that have survived, some dating from the late Georgian period, others typical of the Victorian era with wrought-iron filigree, represent the best of Sydney's terrace housing. Challis Avenue also has some interesting terraces and one of Sydney's best restaurants, the **Cicada**.

Macleay Street, at the top of Challis Avenue, is very much the preserve of the early 20th-century apartment block. The building of high-rise apartments in Sydney began just before World War I with Kingsclere, at the corner of Macleay Street and Greenknowe Avenue. The facade is one of solid simplicity but the apartments, each with four large bedrooms and servants' quarters, are on a grand scale. The completion in 1934 of Birtley Towers in Birtley Place (off Elizabeth Bay Road) with its nine storeys of red textured brick and Spanish roof tiles, ushered in the age of the art deco apartment block.

The last remaining Potts Point mansions – Rockwall and Tusculum Villa – are found in Rockwall Crescent and Manning Street respectively. They were built in the 1830s, when it was decreed that all homes in the district must be to the value of at least A$1,000 in order to maintain the right tone for the neighbourhood. Rockwall was built by colonial architect John Verge and is highly regarded for the classical

Map on page 112

Potts Point balcony ironwork. Art deco fans shouldn't miss the Macleay Regis Apartments (12 Macleay Street) and Manar House (No. 42), or the Metro Theatre in Orwell Street.

BELOW: a picnic on Woolloomooloo Bay.

simplicity of its design. Neither house is open to the public.

The Potts Point end of Macleay Street features numerous smart restaurants with slick interiors and Modern Australian menus catering to locals who are increasingly young, professional and moneyed.

Elizabeth Bay

If you head down Greenknowe Avenue and turn left into Onslow Avenue, you reach **Elizabeth Bay House ❸** (open Tues–Sun; tel: 9356 3022; entrance fee). This magnificent Georgian colonial mansion was built in 1839 to a design by John Verge for Alexander Macleay, who at that time was Colonial Secretary of NSW. The original land grant of 22 hectares (55 acres) comprised a good part of what is now Elizabeth Bay, and Macleay oversaw the development: a magnificent garden of pools, walks and plantings which stretched down to the harbour.

The house is fully furnished in the style of the period and the internal staircase, sweeping upwards from an oval saloon beneath a domed ceiling,

is regarded as one of the most beautiful in Australia. The interiors, with their generous spaces well lit by huge north-facing windows, provide a point of contrast to the formal rooms of the Victorian period that Australians are more used to.

Head along Billyard Avenue, one of Australia's most expensive streets, where the houses and apartments front onto the harbour. Boomerang, at No. 42, was the last of the great mansions in Sydney's "Hollywood Spanish" style, built in 1926. The property is private but there are views of the formal garden from Billyard Avenue, and of the front facing the harbour from Beare Park.

Kings Cross hotels

Tourist accommodation prospects in this district have picked up considerably since the 1980s. At the Kings Cross end of Victoria Street, the old terraces have filled up with backpacker accommodation. But the best innovation has been the rise of the "boutique hotel". These include **Regents Court**, with the feel of a "slightly louche apartment block",

Undercover Police now targeting kerb crawlers

Police target Kings Cross prostitution.

BELOW: the much-copied staircase in Elizabeth Bay House.

and a favourite with the arty and stylish; **L'Hotel**, a cross between Manhattan and rural France; and **Simpson's of Potts Point**, housed in Victorian surrounds and with a clientele of quiet sophisticates.

The **El Alamein Fountain** ❹ in the Fitzroy Gardens is at the heart of Kings Cross. It was built in 1961 to remember Australian efforts during World War II.

Darlinghurst Road

The strip of **Darlinghurst Road** ❺ stretching up to Bayswater Road is where the district's reputation was founded and nurtured. In the 1920s, "sly grog" shops in Kellett Street were followed by gaming clubs and cocaine outlets, while prostitution and razor gangs thrived in the slums on both sides of William Street. Big spending by American servicemen during World War II, and later during the Vietnam War, consolidated the vice trade in small clubs. Refugees from war-torn Europe found the cosmopolitan atmosphere and coffee-shop culture here more reminiscent of home than the sprawling Sydney suburbs.

Although these days they're a little too pricey for the average creative type or alternative lifestyler to live in, in the 1950s the terraces of Darlinghurst provided cheap lodgings for artists, writers and students. Art dealers and dowagers lived in the art deco apartment blocks. Clubs like the Tabou and Balalaika served drinks and risqué entertainment to the affluent; intellectuals found conversation in the coffee lounges. Since the 1970s, Darlinghurst Road has served as Sydney's "Street of Sleaze", with sex shows, gambling outfits, pinball parlours, low-life pubs, and a population of prostitutes, underworld types, drug dealers and addicts.

A more genial atmosphere can be found on Victoria Street, where a new generation of coffee bars cater to writers, artists and film-makers, with a fair smattering of lawyers, politicians and business folk thrown in. **Bar Coluzzi**, which serves the best coffee in Sydney, was first opened by a former boxing champion in William Street as a coffee bar for Italian working men. Others worth a visit are the Bombolo, Andiamo, Maxims, Parmalat and the Tropicana, which hosts an annual short film festival, TropFest, that has become a highlight on the Australian film calendar.

Also on Darlinghurst Road the themes of war and immigration, so much a part of this district, are brought together in the **Sydney Jewish Museum** ❻ (open Mon–Thur 10am–4pm, Fri 10am–2pm, Sun 11am–5pm; tel: 9360 7999; entrance fee). The museum, through a series of fascinating exhibits, tells the history of Judaism and the story of Jewish settlement in Australia. A Holocaust display and memorial, spread across several floors, reveals the horrors and survivals of the 20th century's most tragic event. ❑

Map on page 112

In 1916 the government introduced six o'clock closing to prevent late-night drinking. In response "sly grog" shops opened up to combat the prohibitive times. They thrived until the 1960s, when more liberal liquor laws were re-introduced.

BELOW: the El Alamein Fountain in Fitzroy Gardens.

RESTAURANTS, CAFÉS & BARS

Restaurants

Arun Thai
28 Macleay Street,
Potts Point
Tel: 9326 9135
Open: L & D Wed–Mon. **$$$**
Decorated in an upmarket
yet traditional Thai style.
Menu is authentic Thai
with imaginative touches
like salmon and coconut
curry. Good wine list.

Balkan Continental
209 Oxford Street,
Darlinghurst
Tel: 9360 4970
Open: L & D, Wed–Mon. **$$**
Charcoal-grilled meats
are a speciality in this
long-running Croatian
restaurant. BYO.

Balkan Seafood
215 Oxford Street,
Darlinghurst
Tel: 9331 7670
Open: D Tues–Sun. **$$**
Some of the best and
cheapest seafood in
town, cooked in the
Croatian way. BYO.

PRICE CATEGORIES

Price indications are for
a three-course meal for
one, including half a
bottle of house wine,
coffee and service.
$ = under A$50
$$ = A$50–75
$$$ = A$75–115
Abbreviations: B =
breakfast, L = lunch,
D = dinner. BYO = bring
your own alcohol.

Bayswater Brasserie
32 Bayswater Road,
Kings Cross
Tel: 9357 2177
Open: daily 7am–midnight. **$**
A long-established
eatery, serving Modern
Australian cuisine. Spe-
ciality is oysters. Large
venue with huge win-
dows for watching local
Kings Cross passers-by.

Café Sel et Poivre
263 Victoria Street,
Darlinghurst
Tel: 9361 6530
Open: B, L & D daily. **$**
Good-value French cui-
sine, served with gusto.
Opens daily at 7am for
breakfast.

Cicada
29 Challis Avenue,
Potts Point
Tel: 9358 1255
Open: L Wed–Fri, D Mon–
Sat. **$$$**
Housed in a beautiful
Victorian terrace, this
chic establishment
delivers Modern
Australian cuisine.

La Toque
91 Riley Street, East Sydney
Tel: 9356 8377
Open: L Thur–Fri, D Mon–
Sat. **$$**
Home of traditional
French cuisine, La Toque
is economical and satis-
fying. Lunch is particu-
larly good value.

Mahjong Room
312 Crown Street,

Darlinghurst
Tel: 9361 3985
Open: D daily. **$**
Chinese regional cuisine.
Private room and take-
away service available.
BYO.

Moran's
61–63 Macleay Street,
Potts Point
Tel: 9356 2223
Open: L Wed–Sun, D daily.
$$$
Named "Best New
Restaurant" by the
*Sydney Morning Herald
Good Food Guide* when it
opened, Moran's
delivers a seasonally
organised menu of Mod-
ern Australian cuisine in
leafy surroundings.

Oh, Calcutta!
251 Victoria Street,
Darlinghurst
Tel: 9360 3650
Open: L Fri, D daily. **$$**
Bistro-style restaurant
at the heart of the
tourist district, serving
subtle modern Indian
food with an Australian
twist (like stir-fried
kangaroo with sesame
seeds). BYO.

Onde
346 Liverpool Street,
Darlinghurst
Tel: 9331 8749
Open: D daily. **$**
Trattoria-style bistro with
a casual atmosphere
and some of the best-
value meals around.
Popular for its low prices

and hip inner-city loca-
tion. No reservations.

Out of India
178 Victoria Street, Kings
Cross
Tel: 9357 7055
Open: L & D daily. **$**
Large (200 seats), good-
value Indian restaurant
on three levels. Try the
special banquet meals
or the discounted Thali
meals 5–7pm.

Paramount
73 Macleay Street,
Potts Point
Tel: 9358 1652
Open: D daily. **$$$**
Excellent Modern Aus-
tralian cuisine in the
attractive Macleay
Street restaurant strip.

Shimbashi Soba on
the Sea
Shop 6, 9 Cowper Wharf
Road, Woolloomooloo
Tel: 9357 7763
Open: daily noon–10pm. **$**
One of the newest spots
for outdoor Japanese
dining on the hip, reinvig-
orated "finger wharf".

Una's
338–340 Victoria Street,
Darlinghurst
Tel: 9360 6885
Open: Mon–Sat 6.30am–
11pm, Sun 8am–11pm. **$**
An old, economical Kings
Cross favourite serving
hearty German and Aus-
trian food at low prices.
BYO. No reservations,
no credit cards.

Yamato Steakhouse
36–38 Macleay Street,
Potts Point
Tel: 9357 2446
Open: D daily. $$
A marriage of traditional
Japanese food with excel-
lent Australian produce.

Cafés

Bar Coluzzi
322 Victoria Street,
Darlinghurst
Open: daily until late,
including B
A local landmark. The
outdoor seating on the
wide Victoria Street foot-
path makes this tiny
coffee shop a lot larger.

Bill and Toni's
74 Stanley Street,
East Sydney
Open: 7am–midnight daily.
Ever-popular coffee house
in Little Italy. Economical
coffee and snacks like
focaccia. There is also a
cheap no-frills spaghetti
place upstairs.

Dean's Cafe
5 Kellett Street, Kings Cross
Open: daily until late.
A quirky place that's
been going for years.
Psychedelic and kitsch
decor attracts an array of
arty types. Good coffee,
interesting crowd, tasty,
affordable snacks.

Dov Cafe
252 Forbes Street,
Darlinghurst
A sparse, colonial feel
characterises this hip
inner-city hangout, situ-
ated in an old sandstone
building opposite the
East Sydney Art School.

Piccolo Bar
6 Roslyn Street, Kings Cross
Open: early morning to late
at night
A tiny place in the thick
of Kings Cross street
activity, and something
of an institution. Neapoli-
tan owner Vittorio
Bianchi has been brew-
ing coffee for the local
Bohemians for 40 years.

Bars

Baron's
5 Roslyn Street, Kings Cross
A long-established,
un-glitzy after-hours bar.
Has an unusual but
cosy seafaring, galleon-
like feel to its cramped,
dark decor.

Club 77
77 William Street,
East Sydney
A popular place for 18–
25-year-olds. Alternative
music until late into the
night. Has a dungeon-
like but friendly atmos-
phere. Variable hours,
depending on what's on.

Columbian Hotel
Cnr Oxford and Crown
streets, Darlinghurst
A mixed straight and gay
crowd inhabit this late-
night bar. Huge windows
open out onto Oxford
Street, great for people-
watching.

Dugout Bar
2 Oxford Street,
Darlinghurst
A tiny bar oozing atmos-
phere. Situated in a
bunker beneath the mas-
sive Burdekin Hotel, the
Dugout is quiet, intimate
and dimly lit – a hidden
gem in an otherwise loud
and glitzy district.

Kings Cross Hotel
248 William Street,
Kings Cross
Opposite the massive
Coca-Cola sign at the top
of William Street. A popu-
lar spot with backpack-
ers during the week.
Theme nights are regu-
larly held, including
"Miss Backpacker"
beauty pageants, British
tele nights (soccer or
soaps, usually) and even
the occasional drag
show. A diverse crowd on
weekends. Also hosts a
(Friday nights only) alter-
native music club.

Kinselas
383 Bourke Street,
Darlinghurst
In the heart of Taylor
Square, Kinselas
attracts a mixed straight
and gay crowd. Daily
until late. Admire the
architecture – ornate
high ceilings and art
deco embellishment
give this building a
cathedral-like feel.

RIGHT: Bar Coluzzi, a Darlinghurst institution.

THE INNER SUBURBS

After a heyday during the 19th century, most of Sydney's inner suburbs lay neglected until the 1960s, when the beauty of the domestic architecture was recognised and restored

Sydney's inner suburbs burgeoned during the Victorian era and, in keeping with that architecturally ornate period, their streets are lined with decorative terrace houses, trimmed with iron lace.

The 19th-century middle classes who built most of these houses only stayed for a generation or two before moving on to greener garden suburbs. As a result, many areas in the inner suburbs declined into slums and remained in an appalling state for the first half of the 20th century. Fortunately the artist and student communities of the early 1960s knew a bargain when they saw one. The talented but poor started to move into the Paddington, Glebe and Balmain suburbs, which soon attracted the attention of young, moneyed professionals, gradually restoring the areas and the traditional architecture (see pages 76–7).

Today they are some of the most sought-after properties in Sydney. Indeed, in a city that has generally considered its waterside suburbs as the most desirable places to live, the once run-down streets of the inner city are now inhabited by a population that ranges from alternative lifestylers and media types through to yuppies who appreciate their suburb's closeness to the CBD (Central Business District) and the fashionable reputation that helps foster their "urban elite" status.

Paddington

Oxford Street is one of the main thoroughfares of the inner eastern suburbs. About 1 km (½ mile) southeast of the city along this bitumen river, you find Paddington. It begins – and began – with the historic convict-built **Victoria Barracks ❶**, a sandstone complex still used by the Australian Army (open Thur 10am–12.30pm, Sun 10am–3pm, tours Thur 10am; tel: 9339 3330; entrance fee). The barracks were the main focus for the infant village of

Map on page 122

PRECEDING PAGES: a giant tuna at the Sydney Fish Markets, Pyrmont. **LEFT:** Balmain Market. **BELOW:** a wrought-iron balcony in Paddington.

Paddington, and they stand today as one of the finest examples of British imperial military architecture. The old jailhouse is no longer used for its original purpose, but houses a museum on the nation's military history. Across the road on Shadforth Street and on many of its nearby lanes you can see the original tiny workers' cottages, built to house the skilled artisans who worked on the construction of the attractive barracks buildings.

A block further up Oxford Street on the left is **Juniper Hall** ❷, Paddington's grandest home, built for Robert Cooper, a gin distiller, in 1824. Cooper was an ex-convict who, like so many others, ended up doing rather well from transportation, as attested to by the magnificence of this mansion. The house, probably the largest ever to be built in Paddington, fell into disrepair over many years once the rich began seeking harbourside locations and

Juniper Hall was named after the main ingredient used in Robert Cooper's successful gin factory.

the area became another grimy inner-city suburb. Juniper Hall was probably only saved from the bulldozer by the fact that it was large enough to accommodate flats and didn't have to be pulled down to make way for new accommodation space. The house is a rare surviving example of pre-1850s Victorian architecture and was restored by the National Trust in 1988. Furnished in period, the building is mainly used as office space, but also houses a National Trust shop with better-than-average souvenirs and books.

Inner suburbs shopping

Past Juniper Hall, Paddington's main shopping strip begins, with fashion for the young and trendy, excellent book, print and music shops, and corner pubs that do a roaring trade. If browsing this strip makes you hungry, there are plenty of upmarket restaurants and cafés where it's fashionable to see and be

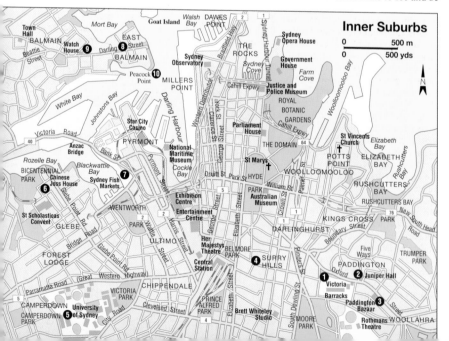

seen while dining on "Modern Australian" cuisine.

Further up on the right is the **Paddington Bazaar ❸**. This extravaganza takes place every Saturday in the grounds of the Uniting Church, and the crowds are as kaleidoscopic as the goods on sale. Always on parade are the young and fashionable, wearing the look of the moment, children and dogs scrambling in all directions at knee level, and visitors from all corners of the world speaking a babel of languages. Stallholders sell every conceivable variety of new and used clothing, plants, jewellery, pottery, leather goods, stationery and imported exotica. This is also the place to pick up a seemingly outrageous piece of clothing from a design student, who may well be a big name in five years' time: many talented students attempt to launch their careers here.

The Oxford Street shopping stretch comes to an end at the junction with Queen and Park streets. To your left, around the corner in up-market Queen Street, Woollahra, there is more excellent shopping if your tastes run to very expensive antiques. But you've hardly touched the surface of Paddington yet. From all along the length of Oxford Street, Paddington spills downhill in a maze of tree-lined streets to the tennis courts of White City and the bushland of Trumper Park. Spend half a day exploring if you can spare the time. Backtrack a block and head down Jersey Road, past the courthouse on your left and a series of Victorian houses on the right.

A few blocks on, follow your nose left into Paddington Street, one of the suburb's oldest and prettiest streets, with its shady plane trees and late-19th-century terraces. At the end, veer left into the narrow lane that is William Street. It will take you past speciality shops and the area's oldest pub, the **London Tavern**, and back to Oxford Street. But if you have a little more time, wander wherevers your fancy takes you. Paddington's back-streets abound in galleries, where you can browse through the works of local artists, photographers and sculptors, and some of the smallest lanes, such as Stafford Lane and Union, Broughton and Duxford streets, are very attractive.

Five Ways is a somewhat chaotic, but very interesting little intersection with five corners sporting shops that cover the panoply of Victorian architectural style. On one corner is the magnificent **Royal Hotel**, a three-storey Victorian pub bearing the features of the popular Classical Revival style. The balconies are a fantastic place to sit and have a drink or a meal.

Surry Hills

The street life and terrace slums of **Surry Hills ❹** are immortalised in the semi-autobiographical novels of Ruth Park, who wrote about growing up in Sydney in the 1940s.

Map on page 122

The height of the Victorian building boom lasted from 1860 to 1890. During those 30 years, 3,800 houses were built in Paddington.

BELOW: searching for bargains at the Paddington Bazaar.

Unlike nearby Paddington, Surry Hills was, for the most part, nearly always poor. There are a few substantial terraces scattered around, but many are tiny structures built on pocket-handkerchief-sized allotments.

In the pre-war period it was populated by the working class, mostly Irish Catholics such as Ruth Park's family. Post-World War II, new immigrants arrived and took over, attracted by the low rents and the proximity to the city and work opportunities.

In the 1980s, Surry Hills was the preferred address of art students and young musicians, who invented their own soundtrack in the form of urban-gothic "grunge" music. It was complemented by a dark, waif-like dress sense that later inspired a generation of Sydney fashion designers during the 1990s.

The **Brett Whiteley Studio**, a Surry Hills landmark, is an important site for art pilgrims to the city. Whiteley died in 1992 at the age of 53, at which time he was Sydney's most famous living artist. His paintings are large, sensuous and full of the light and colour of the city – one of his favourite subjects was the harbour, and probably no one has captured this icon quite so vividly. Many of his paintings are on display at what was his original studio, as well as work by friends, and Whiteley's mementoes and personal effects (open Sat–Sun; tel: 9225 1881; entrance fee).

Recently, as with so many Australian inner-city suburbs, the yuppies have arrived, and Surry Hills is being spruced up with the dollars that the young professional classes bring with them. Sydney's median house price hit A\$500,000 in 2004.

Eating out in the suburbs

Despite this recent invasion, the suburb remains one of the city's most eclectic and chaotic places. Slickly renovated terraces sit beside those bearing 30- to 40-year-old improvements in a style that now has its own term, "immigrant nostalgic", and other rickety dwellings that haven't seen a coat of paint for a century. Amid the houses there are

BELOW: verandas provide shade from the summer sun.

Greek cake shops, Asian grocers, designer-clothing outlets, chic homeware shops, stores with everything for the gay-man-about-town and pubs ranging from the old workingman style through to trendy yuppie enclaves and gay nightclubs.

The main centre of activity is Oxford Street, where there is a large range of restaurants including Asian, Spanish, Thai and Italian. The other end of Surry Hills, around Cleveland Street, is well known for its collection of Lebanese and Turkish eateries and food stores. Somewhere in the middle there is a series of excellent modern cafés and restaurants that are lifting the suburb's gourmet stakes, including **Bills 2**, **The Dolphin Hotel** and the **Clock**. The MG Garage, a large, expensive restaurant-cum-luxury-car showroom, offers some of Sydney's finest food to a celebrity clientele – quite a change from the mean streets of Ruth Park's home suburb.

Glebe – from rags to riches

In the early 1970s, Sydney author Ruth Park wrote of Glebe: "There are many senile cottages with sagging shutters and reeling gates, barely keeping afloat in a sea of unpruned greenery. The whole district is like a creaky old ship bound for oblivion, the sails rotten rags, and the timbers worm-eaten, nothing ahead but wreck and disaster."

However, the inner suburb of Glebe never sank to quite the same depths that almost destroyed Paddington. The Rev. Richard Johnson, chaplain of the First Fleet, was given the original "glebe" or grant of land for the Church. It consisted of 160 hectares (400 acres) around Blackwattle Bay. After 1826, the Church of England began selling some of its glebe land to wealthy buyers who established ornate mansions.

The Church leased its remaining glebe lands for downmarket housebuilding, most of which took place during a 20-year span after 1855. A century on, what had by then deteriorated into the slum portions of the Glebe Estate became something of a scandal. Then, in 1974, the Australian government bought the estate

Map on page 122

Ruth Park's novels detailing her early life in Surry Hills include Harp in the South *(1948) and the much later addition,* Fence around the Cuckoo *(1992).*

BELOW: taking to the water in Blackwattle Bay.

and began a process of external restoration and internal renovation of its houses for low-income families, many of whom had lived here for generations.

Today, Glebe is awash with heritage paint jobs, pruned roses in cottage gardens, polished floorboards and an air of solid prosperity – you'd have a hard time buying into the suburb for under half a million dollars. If any suburb bears the marks of the transformation of Sydney's inner city, it is this one. The quaint old cottages are well worth a look, as are the remaining 19th-century mansions and villas of Glebe Point.

Just across Parramatta Road is the **University of Sydney ❺**, Australia's oldest, established in 1850. The area has long had an academic reputation and a thriving student population. The elegant "Oxbridge" quadrangles date from the 1850s, and the Great Hall gives a good insight into the grand dreams of the university's founders.

Glebe's main thoroughfare, Glebe Point Road, runs the length of the suburb from Parramatta Road to Blackwattle Bay, and is one of the more interesting affordable restaurant areas in Sydney, offering international cuisines. Perhaps because of its student connection (although Glebe is fast pricing itself out of the student league), there are also "tat" shops, selling recycled tongue-in-chic clothes, and second-hand book shops.

The **Valhalla Cinema** screens up-to-the-minute movies with cheap ticket prices, as well as festivals of classics (tel: 9660 8050 for programme times and details). To see something of the restored Glebe Estate, turn off Glebe Point Road to the left at Mitchell Street and wander up side streets such as Derwent and Westmoreland streets.

For a more historic look at Glebe, turn left much further down Glebe Point Road at Toxteth Road and do a circuit. At the corner of Toxteth and Avenue roads is the delightful Victorian Gothic sandstone house, The Lodge, probably the former gatehouse of the grand estate, Toxteth Park. Continue down Toxteth, turn

A fisherman at Pyrmont.

BELOW:
Sydney University.
RIGHT: Glebe's
Chinese Joss House.

right into Maxwell and right again into Arcadia to see some of the area's prettiest houses.

At the intersection of Arcadia and Avenue roads, turn left into Avenue and on your left is what was once the Toxteth Park Estate, now transformed into the impressive **St Scholastica's Convent**.

At the end of Avenue Road, turn right into Victoria Street and left into Edward Street for the surprise of the day. A **Chinese Joss House** ❻, a relic of Chinese immigration during the 19th-century gold rushes *(see page 104)*, has been restored by Sydney's large Chinese community with authentic Asian features.

Pyrmont

Take Pendrill Street, just down from the Joss House gate, back to Glebe Point Road and over into Leichhardt Street, where it winds to the right past some particularly picturesque houses. These give way to bland new blocks of home units, but persevere to the end where you will find a very pretty park overlooking **Blackwattle Bay**, in which the shell

of one of the old harbourside mansions has been restored.

On the Pyrmont side of Blackwattle Bay are the **Sydney Fish Markets** ❼. These bustling daily markets offer a vast range of fish, either live or prepared for cooking, all fresh each day from the nearby ocean, and are popular with both restaurateurs and housewives. There are also seafood restaurants, sushi bars and even a cookery school above the market, offering lessons on the preparation of fresh seafood (tel: 9660 1611).

Balmain: memento of the Victorian era

The Balmain peninsula juts into Sydney Harbour just across Darling Harbour from Millers Point. It is named after William Balmain, who arrived on the First Fleet as Second Assistant Surgeon. Within a decade he had become Principal Surgeon of the colony, a magistrate and collector of customs. His services were rewarded by several land grants including the 220 hectares (550 acres) of headland that bear his

Map on page 122

The Saturday market at Balmain.

BELOW: the dramatic Anzac Bridge links Pyrmont to Balmain.

Map on page 122

Blooms at Balmain.

BELOW: a cosy Balmain café.

name. But it wasn't until the 1830s that blocks were first released for sale, when the good surgeon sold it for five shillings as part of the settlement of a gambling debt. A handful of Georgian colonial buildings and many early Victorian houses are still standing.

Most of the building in Balmain took place between about 1855 and 1890. Because the suburb soon developed harbourside light industries, the area today is a mix of Victorian working-class cottages, expensive mansions and substantial bourgeois terraces and villas set along a confusing network of tiny crooked streets, which every so often open out to reveal a glittering sliver of the harbour.

Darling Street ❽ is the peninsula's spine, strewn with restaurants and with some grand civic architecture. Clustered together near the centre of the peninsula are the High Victorian-style post office and courthouse, fire station and town hall – not to mention a charming Victorian glasshouse which remains only because of a bitter conservation

battle fought by residents. And next to the fire station is the Manor House, now a restaurant but originally built around 1869 by the colonial architect Edmund Blacket.

Like Paddington, Balmain has its Saturday market, in the grounds of St Andrew's Congregational Church, a pretty building further down Darling Street built of locally quarried stone. This market has a different flavour from its rival in Paddington. Somehow in Balmain, 1960s Flower Power lingered on to become New Age, retaining a bohemian rather than a fashionable feel.

A block or so past the church and on the same side of the road is the restored **Watch House** ❾. This old police station and lock-up was also designed by Edmund Blacket and built in 1854. The oldest lock-up in Australia, it has been variously used over the years as a doss-house, police headquarters and a home for a family with 12 children. It is now used to house temporary art exhibitions (tel: 9818 4954 for details).

The suburban streets most worth a wander are mainly north of Darling Street, but two areas stand out for their beautiful parks and water views. One is the area behind Darling Street ferry wharf and the park on **Peacock Point** ❿. Do a circuit from the wharf, left past the old sandstone Waterman's Cottage opposite, through the park with its stunning harbour views and through the little maze of streets behind, bounded by Darling and Johnston streets.

The other pleasant walk is rather longer, in a section of Balmain called Birchgrove. Begin your exploration in Wharf Road with its waterfront houses, turning left into Grove Street then right into Cove Street and right again into Louisa Road, which has many interesting houses and winds down to the beautiful reserve on Long Nose Point. ❏

RESTAURANTS & BARS

Restaurants

Al Mustafa
276 Cleveland Street,
Surry Hills
Tel: 9319 5632
Open: D Tues–Sat, 11am–
11pm Sun. **$**
Traditional Lebanese cuisine. Cushion room with belly-dancing during the dinner show. Complimentary coffee and sweets.

Becasse
48 Albion Street, Surry Hills
Tel: 9280 3202
Open: D Wed–Sun. **$$**
Upmarket French restaurant with an attractive, chic, low-key styling.

Bills 2
359 Crown Street, Surry Hills
Tel: 9360 4762
Open: all day. **$$**
Offers great food with minimum fuss and possibly the best breakfast menu in Sydney. BYO.

Boathouse on Blackwattle Bay
End of Ferry Road, Glebe
Tel: 9518 9011
Open: L & D, Tues–Sun. **$$$**
Some of Sydney's best seafood in a converted boathouse on the edge of the harbour (floor-to-ceiling glass windows).

Buon Ricordo
108 Boundary Street,
Paddington
Tel: 9360 6729
Open: L Fri–Sat, D Tues–Sat.
$$$

Established restaurant with fine Italian food, friendly atmosphere and good Italian wine list.

Clock Hotel Restaurant
470 Crown Street,
Surry Hills
Tel: 9331 5333
Open: L & D daily. **$$**
Beautifully prepared modern food in a lively bistro-pub setting.

The Dolphin Hotel
412 Crown Street, Surry Hills
Tel: 9331 4800
Open: L daily, D Mon–Sat. **$$**
A great modern Australian affair – seafood and wild duck are specialities – in a beautiful, traditional corner pub.

Longrain
85 Commonwealth Street,
Surry Hills
Tel: 9280 2888
Open: L Mon–Fri, D Mon–
Sat. **$**
Spacious new place with chic ambience and a trendy reputation, located in a 100-year-old warehouse and serving a fusion of Thai and Chinese cuisine.

MG Garage
490 Crown Street, Surry Hills
Tel: 9383 9383
Open: L Mon–Fri, D Mon–
Sat. **$$$**
Modern Australian cuisine and a luxury-car showroom co-exist in this unusual "concept" restaurant where you eat

fine food while eye-balling the sexy vehicles.

Mixing Pot
178 St John's Road, Glebe
Tel: 9660 7449
Open: L Mon–Fri, D Mon–
Sat. **$$**
Italian seafood cuisine and outdoor dining amidst the relaxed chic of inner-city Glebe.

Mohr Fish
202 Devonshire Street,
Surry Hills
Tel: 9318 1326
Open: 10am–10pm daily. **$**
Tiny and atmospheric seafood restaurant. There's more seating next door, at the sister restaurant Mohr and Mohr.

The Prophet
274 Cleveland Street,
Surry Hills
Tel: 9698 7025
Open: L Mon–Sat, D daily. **$**
Great flavour and friendly service at an old favourite on the Lebanese restaurant scene. BYO.

Shakespeare Hotel and Bistro
200 Devonshire Street,
Surry Hills
Tel: 9319 6883
Open: L & D daily. **$**
A cosy Surry Hills pub and eatery opposite the Mohr Fish restaurants. Popular all week.

Thai on Crown
118 Crown Street,
Surry Hills

Tel: 9332 3284
Open: L & D Mon–Fri. **$**
Satisfying Thai food in the lively Crown Street strip of restaurants.

Bars and Cafés

Ancient Briton Hotel
255 Glebe Point Road
A long-standing Glebe pub, situated on a busy intersection. The upstairs bar has a more modern feel than the cramped downstairs bar.

Badde Manors
37 Glebe Point Road
A colourful and quirky Glebe coffee house that is especially popular on weekends. Opposite the alternative Glebe weekend markets.

Kitty O'Shea's
384 Oxford Street,
Paddington
A crowded and sociable Irish-themed pub in the centre of Paddington. Expect big crowds on weekends.

PRICE CATEGORIES

Price indications are for a three-course meal for one, including half a bottle of house wine, coffee and service.
$ = under A$50
$$ = A$50–75
$$$ = over A$75
Abbreviations: L = lunch, D = dinner. BYO = bring your own alcohol.

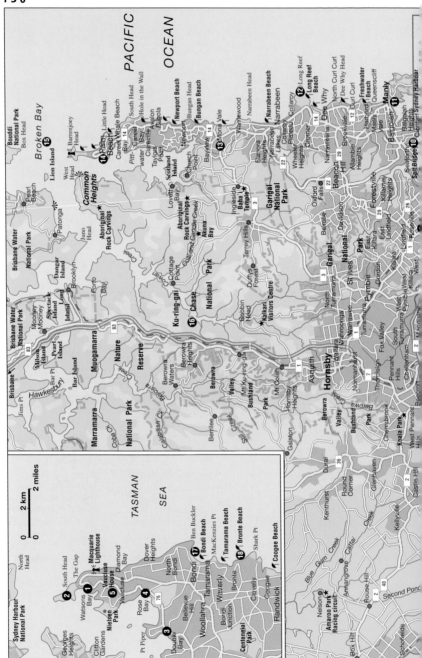

PACIFIC OCEAN

Broken Bay

Bouddi National Park
Box Head

Lion Island

Pearl Beach

Patonga

Common Heights

Juno Head

Brisbane Water National Park

Dangar Island

Mooney Mooney

Spectacle Island
Long Island
Bar Pt
Pearl Island
Bar Island

Brooklyn

Porto Bay

Hawkesbury
Jims Pt

Brisbane Water National Park

Wilson Island

Marramarra National Park

Muogamarra Nature Reserve

Calabash Ck
Coba Ck
Berowra Ck

Galston

Berrilee

Berowra Waters

Berowra Heights

Berowra

Berowra Valley Bushland Park

Mt Kuring-gai

Mt Colah

Hornsby Heights

Asquith

Hornsby

Berowra Valley Bushland Park

Bobbin Head

Ku-ring-gai Chase National Park

Duffys Forest

Terrey Hills

Cottage Point

Akuna Bay

Aboriginal Rock Carvings

Coal and Candle Creek

Cowan

Cowan Creek

Lovett Bay

Scotland Island

West Head

Barrenjoey Head

Little Head
Palm Beach
Careel Bay
Whale Beach
South Head
Hole in the Wall
Avalon
Clareville
Bilgola
Newport Beach
Bungan Head
Bungan Beach
Taylors Point
Pitt water

Church Point

Ingleside
Baha'i Temple

Garigal National Park

Bayview
Mona Vale
Warriewood
Narrabeen Head
Narrabeen Beach
Narrabeen

Elanora Heights

Oxford Falls

Belrose

Davidson

St Ives

North Turramurra

Turramurra

Warrawee

Wahroonga

West Pymble
Pymble
Gordon
West Lindfield
West Killara
Killara
East Killara
Lindfield
East Lindfield
Roseville

Wheeler Heights

Collaroy Plateau
Collaroy
Cromer
Beacon Hill
Brookvale
Dee Why
Long Reef Beach
Long Reef
North Curl Curl
Curl Curl
Harbord
Freshwater Beach
Dee Why Head

Forestville

Killarney Heights

Frenchs Forest

Seaforth
Balgowlah Heights
Clontarf
Manly
Spit Bridge
Queenscliff
Fairlight

Central Sydney Harbour

Turramurra
Fox Valley
South Turramurra
Normanhurst

Thornleigh
Pennant Hills
Cherrybrook
Cheltenham

West Pennant Hills

Beecroft

Koala Park

Belrowa Valley Bushland Park

Dural

Round Corner

Glenhaven

Kenthurst

Castle Hill

Kellyville

Blue Gum Creek

Annangrove
Cattai Creek

Rouse Hill

Second Ponds Creek

Box Hill

Schofields

Nelson

Amaroo Park Racing circuit

Garigal National Park

Garigal National Park

Sydney Harbour National Park

North Head

Georges Heights
Clifton Gardens

The Gap

South Head

TASMAN SEA

0 km 2
0 2 miles

Watsons Bay

Macquarie Lighthouse

Vaucluse
Vaucluse House

Nielsen Park

Diamond Bay

Dover Heights

North Bondi

Ben Buckler
Bondi Beach
Bondi
MacKenzies Pt
Tamarama
Tamarama Beach
Shark Pt
Bronte Beach
Bronte

Rose Bay

Point Piper

Bellevue Hill

Double Bay

Woollahra

Bondi Junction

Waverly

Clovelly

Coogee
Coogee Beach

Randwick

Centennial Park

Greater Sydney

THE EASTERN SUBURBS

Big money buys big property to the east of
the city, but even visitors on a budget can take
in the stunning cliffside views and dine on
seafood while overlooking the Pacific Ocean

The area to the east of Sydney is regarded by many residents and visitors as the best part of the city's suburban sprawl. On one frontage there is the magnificence of Sydney Harbour with its calm beaches, bays and sunny parks; on the other is the coastline where the South Pacific Ocean rolls against spectacular cliffs and beaches.

It is this superb setting that has created an enormous demand for housing, with the result that the market boasts the highest residential prices in Australia. The ideal is a north-facing water view so that the house is sunny in winter and shaded by the eaves from the fierce summer sun. When one of these houses comes on the market, the sky's the limit: waterfront homes at Point Piper can sell in excess of A$20 million. The eastern suburbs are populated by people who are openly and ostentatiously proud of the fact that they can afford the most expensive real estate in the country.

If you cannot own a water view, the advantage of the eastern suburbs is that a 10-minute drive out of the city will take you to either a harbour swimming spot or an ocean beach. Apart from these natural delights, the eastern suburbs offer a wide range of sights, from historic buildings to fine parks and shopping centres.

But the visitor and local alike tend towards the anthropological pleasures of people-watching and house-inspecting. There is a fascinating mix of cultures and religions here. The east has the highest proportion of Jewish residents of anywhere in Sydney, which has led to a wealth of synagogues and kosher food outlets. On the housing side, the amateur observer has a field day: because many residents are now coming to terms with riches beyond their imaginations, they feel com-

Map
on pages
130–1

LEFT: a grand house on the Vaucluse waterfront. **BELOW:** the Macquarie Lighthouse.

pelled to let everyone know they are rolling in it. The result is ludicrously expensive clothes, jewellery, cars, hairstyles and houses that scream of excess cash but unfortunately very little style.

The South Head peninsula

Eastsiders are proud of their natural environment, and all Sydneysiders enjoy the harbour and coastal walks, beaches and parks of this area. Begin your exploration with a stroll along **Watsons Bay ❶** and soak up the atmosphere of the village, which is steeped in history. Old fishermen's cottages can still be found along the narrow streets, although today from their humble beginnings they have been turned into the homes of some of Sydney's most prosperous individuals. Camp Cove and Green Point both played important historical roles as settlement sites during the first European arrival.

The tip of the peninsula is **South Head ❷**, where you can delight in the heart-stopping scenery on the coastal cliff walk to the **Macquarie**

Lighthouse and the Signal Station, which has been continually manned from 1790 to the present day. There is a rock shelf down near sea level which is used by fishermen but it can be very dangerous, so good advice or experienced company is advisable.

The sheer drops of **The Gap** are famous for their mesmeric effect on suicide victims, but most visitors can stand back and admire the awesome natural sculpture of the sandstone cliffs. It's also a great place to watch the Sydney to Hobart racing yachts as they clear the heads and harbour and get down to the serious business of sailing to Tasmania on 26 December each year.

Below South Head, on the harbourside, is the universally misnamed Lady Bay. Ask for directions to it and the response will be a blank stare. However, ask for Lady Jane Beach and most will respond with a knowing look. For this is Sydney's best-known nudist beach – tour boats cruise past throughout the weekend. It's the perfect symbiotic balance: voyeurs watching exhibi-

It has been suggested that the glow that shimmers over the eastern waterfront suburbs is the reflection from the gold which bedecks both male and female hands and necks.

BELOW: yachts at anchor in Watsons Bay.

tionists. If private bathing is your scene, stay away, but it's quite a sideshow for those who love to people-watch.

The interior harbour

From Rose Bay, past Point Piper and around to Double Bay and Darling Point, expensive residences hug the hilly foreshore, many of them great modern piles of glass and painted concrete stucco. There are a few spectacular old homes on the foreshore, most noticeably Carthona just to the east side of Darling Point, which was built in 1841 for the NSW Surveyor Thomas Mitchell. A ferry ride from the Quay around to Rose Bay and on to Watsons Bay is the best way of getting a look at how the other half lives.

Nielsen Park (once part of the Wentworth Estate) is one of the most beautiful spots in Sydney, a perfect little harbour cove, fronted by a sandy beach and flanked by bush-clad cliffs on either side. Stretching out beyond and to the side of the beach are stretches of national park, administered by staff housed in Greycliffe House, a superb Gothic Victorian dwelling built by the Wentworths. The Hermitage Foreshore Walk is a popular cliff-edge stroll, winding in and out of patches of native bush, and leading around to Rose Bay. The views are heartstopping. Look out for Strickland House on the way, a magnificent old harbour home, now a nursing home.

In **Double Bay** ❸ you can shop till you drop at some of the most exclusive establishments in Sydney. Long regarded as the place to see and be seen, the wealth of the surrounding residential areas has created the demand for this expensive centre. Indeed, local critics have wryly nicknamed the suburb "Double Pay" as a result of the many retailers who have set up shop to cater to locals with expensive taste. There are boutiques crammed with imported designer labels as well as fine jewellery stores. You can then rest weary feet and cool the overheated credit cards at a number of sidewalk cafés. Meanwhile, watch the people who actually dress up in

Map on pages 130–1

BELOW: The Gap, with North Head in the distance.

Map on pages 130–1

furs and diamonds to do the supermarket shopping.

Further into the harbour, **Shark Island** requires advance booking to visit and use the picnic facilities (tel: 9337 5511 for details). Named after a First Fleet marine, **Clark Island** near Darling Point was the site of Ralph Clark's vegetable garden. Clark's other claim to fame was that he kept a detailed diary setting out events in the first days of the colony. The island can be visited without notice as long as your group doesn't exceed 15 people.

Away from the water, **Cooper Park** in Double Bay is wild and wonderful, with 1930s structures, creeks and modern tennis courts. If it's time for a picnic lunch, you have the perfect place in **Centennial Park**, with over 200 rolling hectares (500 acres) of lawns, trees, bridle paths and duck ponds. Created in celebration of Australia's centenary in 1888, and dedicated to "the enjoyment of the people of New South Wales for ever", Centennial Park runs between Woollahra and Randwick, and is the jewel of the eastern suburbs' open space. Feed the ducks and eels in the ponds, hire a horse or bike, or eat in style at the park's restaurant, which serves breakfast, lunch, morning and afternoon teas.

At Lyne Park in **Rose Bay** ❹ there are tennis courts, a seaplane airport with flights to Palm Beach, Berowra or Newcastle, and a place to hire sailboards or catamarans. There is also safe swimming at Redleaf harbour pool, while at Darling Point's **McKell Park** there is the most magnificent view of Sydney at your feet. **Rushcutters Bay** and Yarranabbe Park boast combinations of mega-buck cruisers and yachts, interesting homes and views. If visiting the area in December, take a look at the yachts of the Sydney to Hobart race, which berth at Rushcutters Bay before the big race begins on Boxing Day.

Finally, the gem of the eastern suburbs is the finest example of the area's historical wealth in the beautiful **Vaucluse House** ❺ in Olola Avenue, Vaucluse (open daily; tel: 9388 7922; entrance fee). ❏

BELOW RIGHT:
Vaucluse House.

Vaucluse House

The grand home and the 7.5-hectare (19-acre) grounds of Vaucluse House constitute one of Australia's most significant historic estates. It was the residence of William Charles Wentworth (born 1790, the son of a convict), who took part in the first successful inland exploration across the Blue Mountains and co-founded the colony's first independent newspaper, the *Australian*, in 1824. He was also a founding member of the first Legislative Council, and played a major role in gaining independent government for New South Wales and in the writing of its state constitution.

Vaucluse House itself is a chaos of idiosyncratic innovations and styles. Wentworth lived here between 1828 and 1862, and continued to alter the structure whenever he found the time. One of the most unusual features is that there is no front door or formal entranceway. One was planned, but just like the "corridor to nowhere" (an upstairs hallway that comes to an abrupt end), the owner never got round to completing it. A constantly changing population of between 24 and 37 servants were required to look after the whole complex, not to mention the Wentworths' 10 children.

RESTAURANTS & BARS

Restaurants

Art e Cucina Cafe
2 Short Street, Double Bay
Tel: 9328 0880
Open: L & D Mon–Sat. **$$**
Much more than a café,
despite its name, serving
fine Modern Australian
and Italian cuisine.

Bistro Moncur
Woollahra Hotel, 116 Queen
Street, Woollahra
Tel: 9363 2519
Open: L & D Tues–Sun. **$$$**
Classic French bistro cui-
sine in a stylish Eastern
Suburbs restaurant. No
reservations.

Claude's
10 Oxford Street, Woollahra
Tel: 9331 2325
Open: D Tues–Sat. **$$$$**
An upmarket but low-key
restaurant with discreet
celebrity-friendly atmos-
phere, serving possibly
the best French food in
Sydney. BYO.

PRICE CATEGORIES
A three-course meal for
one, including half a
bottle of house wine,
coffee and service:
$ = under A$50
$$ = A$50–75
$$$ = A$75–115
$$$$ = over A$115
Abbreviations: L = lunch,
D = dinner. BYO = bring
your own alcohol.

Doyles on the Beach
11 Marine Parade,
Watson's Bay
Tel: 9337 2007
Open: L & D daily. **$$**
Australia's first seafood
restaurant (1885) and
still one of the best,
Doyles combines great
seafood and lovely views
across the harbour.

Pier
594 New South Head Road,
Rose Bay
Tel: 9327 6561
Open: L & D daily. **$$$**
Consistently voted Syd-
ney's best seafood
restaurant, this beauti-
fully sleek outfit hovers
over the harbour waters.

Prunier's
65 Ocean Street, Woollahra
Tel: 9363 1974
Open: L Mon–Fri, D Mon–
Sat. **$$$**
With a loyal clientele,
Prunier's serves old Ital-
ian favourites and some
excellent specialities.

Rose Bay Afloat
New South Head Road,
Rose Bay
Tel: 9371 7955
Open: L & D Tues–Sun. **$$**
One of Sydney's less
expensive waterside
dining experiences, this
floating restaurant has
superb views, an above
average Modern Aus-
tralian menu and a com-
prehensive wine list.

Spice Market
340 New South Head Road,
Double Bay
Tel: 9328 7499
Open: D daily. **$**
Tasty Thai fare in an
exclusive neighbour-
hood. BYO. No bookings.

Cafés and Bars

Luigi Brothers
372 New South Head Road,
Double Bay
A café-cum-grocer, this
outlet is a food-lover's
delight, with shelves
crammed full of imported
goods and the strong
smell of real coffee.

Royal Hotel
Five Ways, Paddington
Situated in the pleasant,
villagey Five Ways.
Ornate Victorian archi-
tecture and affordable
pub food.

Spring Chicken Cafe
129 Manning Road,
Woollahra
Open: daily, all day until late
Lively coffee shop in the
attractive tree-lined
streets of Woollahra.

Watsons Bay Hotel
1 Military Road,
Watsons Bay
Beer garden and fore-
shore setting, next door
to Doyles restaurant.
Especially popular on
Sunday afternoons.

Woollahra Hotel
116 Queen Street, Woollahra
Two bars (one refined,
one hip), live jazz on Sundays, pool tables, 2-for-1
cocktails on Thursdays.

RIGHT: 120-year-old Doyles seafood restaurant.

EVENTS AND FESTIVALS

No festival organiser could ask for more: a balmy climate, a beautiful waterfront setting, glorious city parks and enthusiastic inhabitants

The people of Sydney respond to the city's serene climate and natural beauty with a seemingly limitless desire for outdoor celebrations. Throughout the calendar of any year, scarcely a week goes by without some major cultural or sporting event taking place. The height of summer coincides with Christmas and the New Year, and involves carol-singing in the Domain, Christmas parties on Bondi Beach (with Santa Claus arriving by boat), the start of the Sydney to Hobart yacht race *(above)* on Boxing Day and impressive New Year fireworks in the harbour *(above right)*. Then there's the Sydney Festival in January…Mardi Gras and Chinese New Year in February…the St Patrick's Day Parade and the Kings Cross Bed Race in March… The festivities just go on and on. Whenever you visit, you'll find something to celebrate in Sydney.

ABOVE: New Year's Eve is one of Sydney's most spectacular occasions. Street parties stretch from The Rocks through Circular Quay to Bennelong Point, with impromptu gatherings celebrating at virtually any available place with a clear view of Sydney Harbour Bridge. As darkness falls, the first firework displays are set off from two barges on the harbour. This is followed by a parade of tall ships, decked out in rope light and accompanied by all manner of tugs, ferries and other vessels. Then, just before midnight, all heads turn towards the bridge for a lavish display of pyrotechnics that turn the "coathanger" into a blaze of light. An estimated one million people turn up for the annual spectacular.

RIGHT: Since 1971, the City to Surf fun run has been held on the second Sunday in August. Tens of thousands of entrants, most of them amateurs and many in fancy dress, race the 14 km (8½ miles) from Hyde Park to Bondi Beach.

TAKING TO THE WATER TO CELEBRATE THE NATIONAL DAY

Australia Day (26 January) sees a series of aquatic contests in the harbour, starting with the unique Surfboard Challenge. In the absence of surf, around 1,000 surfers have to paddle their boards over a 3.5 km (2-mile) course from the Opera House, under the Harbour Bridge to Blues Point Reserve. By mid-morning over a million people have gathered on the foreshore to cheer on the Ferrython *(above)*: four workhorses of Sydney's water transport system race from Circular Quay, around Shark Island and back to the Harbour Bridge. The afternoon is taken up with the Royal Sydney Yacht Squadron's Regatta, the world's oldest continuous regatta, featuring hundreds of sailing vessels. Finally, majestic Tall Ships race from Bradleys Head to the finish under the Harbour Bridge.

BELOW: Chinese New Year is celebrated over three weeks in February, mainly in Chinatown and around Darling Harbour. Yum cha is served all day, with exotic food stalls in the street, and parades, firecrackers, sword dancing, lions and dragons in procession, and dragon-boat races in Darling Harbour.

ABOVE: Sydney's first Gay and Lesbian Mardi Gras was held in 1978 to mark the ninth anniversary of the Stonewall riots in the USA. Police blockades were set up and 53 marchers were taken into custody. Their names and addresses were published by the *Sydney Morning Herald*, which these days prints guides to the Mardi Gras festivities. But the parade sparked off a gay revolution in Sydney, and the 1979 parade went ahead without incident. Today's Mardi Gras is the largest gay party on earth. Every February, gay and lesbian arts, cultural and sporting activities reach an outrageous climax in the Mardi Gras Parade through the streets, followed by an all-night party.

NORTHSIDE

Sydney's northern suburbs are exclusive residential areas, and it's easy to see why: spectacular ocean views, unspoilt beaches and fashionable shopping districts are all within easy reach

There's an invisible filter across the Harbour Bridge which restricts the glitz of the eastern suburbs and the mundanity of the west from laying siege to the leafy glades of the northern suburbs. At least, that's the view of many who live "on the other side of the bridge". Like all stereotypes, the myth of the north shore doesn't bear close investigation. The concrete canyons of North Sydney's advertising land display levels of crassness and ostentation to which the rest of Sydney probably doesn't aspire. Then there are the streets of northside red-roofed bungalows that exhibit the lack of individuality their owners would characterise as typical of the western suburbs.

But the northside does contain certain distinctive enclaves: the film-makers at the tip of the Barrenjoey peninsula, the Armenians of Willoughby, the Japanese expatriates of Northbridge and Ku-ring-gai, the yuppies of Neutral Bay clustered around their icon, the Oaks Hotel, and the surfers of the insular Northern Beaches. Like most visitors, they came to see the most beautiful part of Sydney but, like their forebears, they ended up staying and making it their way of life. Four communities can be discerned among the generic tag of "Northern Suburbs": the Lower North Shore, Northern Beaches, Northern Suburbs and Northern Districts.

Nowhere else in Sydney has experienced the rapid shift in character that has marked North Sydney's development since the 1960s. It has changed from a local municipality to a service satellite for the Central Business District (CBD) across the bridge. It is the centre for much of the Australian computer and advertising industries: many smaller agencies operate out of the largely

Map on pages 130–1

LEFT: Manly Beach Surf Carnival.
BELOW: the exotic Baha'i Temple near Mona Vale.

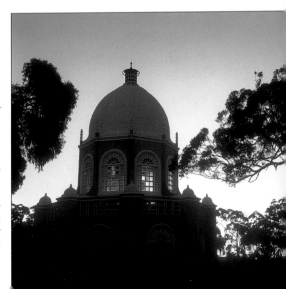

residential harbourside suburbs of McMahon's Point and Kirribilli near by. Naturally, the shopping area has developed apace and caters for that market: the Tower Square off Miller Street, Northpoint (opposite) and Shopping World (behind Mount Street which is a shopping mall itself) are the main centres.

The northside harbour

The northern side of Sydney Harbour was widely explored within weeks of the establishment of the first European colony at Sydney Cove. Indeed, the popular beachside suburb of Manly has the distinction of being visited and named before Sydney Cove itself. But for much of the first century, the inroads on the forests of the north were made by timber-cutters collecting for the buildings of Sydney town and the farmers and orchard-growers who followed in their wake.

Mosman ❻ bears the indignity of being developed as a service centre for whaling vessels – the stink of whale flesh (often up to two years deceased by the time it arrived in port) was too pungent to allow it any closer to the main settlement. Even so, there were illegal camps of "bohemians" and artists near by making the most of the wonderful interplay of bush and glowing sandstone and the effect of sparkling sunlight on water. The only remnants of the old whaling station is the "barn" used by the boy scouts at Mosman Cove. But a surprisingly large part of the bush and harbourside remain untouched, as any trip on the Manly ferry will attest.

Today Mosman is an upmarket suburb, its bay lined with luxury yachts. The impressive **Mosman Gardens** were started by two local residents in 1959, who planted and nurtured a range of native species, including dense ferns, on view via a labyrinth of paths and bridges.

Taronga Zoo

One of the most popular tourist attractions in the region is **Taronga Zoo** ❼ (open daily; tel: 9969 2777; entrance fee). Until the early 1980s, the zoo was a travesty: a ghetto of decaying grandiose buildings, cement rendered to look like rock, and concrete enclosures where the animals looked out unhappily through bars. However, all this has changed. Today, it is a fitting adornment to the harbourside peninsula it graces (*taronga* is Aboriginal for "water view"), surrounded by native bush, with intelligent use of space and water to minimise the visual effect of animal enclosures.

There are animals from every continent, as well as an extensive range of Australian wildlife including parrots and kangaroos, wombats and echidnas, fish, the country's seven most poisonous snakes and unbearably cute penguins. The Koala House is surrounded by a circular pedestrian ramp that offers a full vantage point for every sleepy "bear" dozing on the eucalyptus

Don't mistakenly refer to the north as the North Shore: the Northern Herald *once conducted a spirited debate within its letters page as to what was properly "shore", leaving the remainder with the less salubrious tag of mere "suburbs".*

BELOW: feeding the Middle Harbour gulls from the Manly Ferry.

branches. It's also the only place in Sydney to see the platypus, the egg-laying, leather-billed mammal which was regarded as a fake when the first specimens from the new colony arrived in England.

Although it can be reached by car or bus, the best way to see the zoo is by ferry from Circular Quay. Then catch the cable car to the top from the kitsch old entrance near the wharf, and look out over the animal enclosures. In summer, stay until the evening for the classical music concerts held in Taronga Park.

Northside shopping

Chatswood ❽, a close contender for the Australian suburb with the largest shopping centre, is to be found further along the North Shore railway line, just to the right off the Pacific Highway. When the city department store of Grace Bros. (recently renamed Myer) made the conspicuously successful decision to decentralise to Chatswood (and elsewhere) in the early 1970s, it started a shift to the suburbs which for ever changed the face of Australian retail-

ing. Today, **Victoria Street** leading east from the railway station is "The Strip", and several large shopping complexes lead off it: Westfield, Lemon Grove, Chatswood Chase and the Myer arcade. The extensive range of shops ensures that people of the area rarely need to travel into the city centre to shop.

Ku-ring-gai municipality

North of Chatswood you enter the heartland of northern suburbia. This is the Ku-ring-gai municipality, which has one of the lowest population densities of any suburban area on earth. From the air it is predominantly green, interspersed with large red-tile roofs, yellow tennis courts and blue swimming pools. There has been some discussion about whether Sydney's burgeoning 4 million population can afford the luxury of a Ku-ring-gai, where the average home is on 900 square metres (10,000 sq ft) of land and, outside peak hours, still only half an hour from the city. At present the bankers, doctors and lawyers who live there continue to

Map on pages 130–1

A wallaby at the zoo with a joey peering out of her pouch.

BELOW LEFT: Australia's cuddliest marsupial. **BELOW:** Taronga Zoo's Sky Safari cable car.

savour the luxury of living in the bush in the city.

A wonderful piece of 1950s domestic architecture is to be found in Clissold Road, Wahroonga. The **Rose Seidler House**, designed by eminent architect Harry Seidler, is a slender dwelling on stilts that created a furore when it was built because it didn't look like the squat suburban villas so favoured at the time. It is remarkable for its open design and for the easy flow between its interior spaces and the superb bushland beyond. Aficionados of the period will love the authentic furnishings (open Sun; tel: 9989 8020; entrance fee).

However, this isn't the part of the northside that the visitor to Sydney is most interested in. That lies along the bays and nooks and crannies of the Lower North Shore, offering superb views across Sydney Harbour to the high-rise landscape of the city centre, and the northern beaches. Discovering the north by road is a drive (or bus trip) that every visitor to Sydney should make, since it goes through much that makes

Sydney special. It can be accomplished easily on one sunny day (or less if it's cloudy and raining).

The coastal road

Starting from the city, the stepping-off point is the Sydney Harbour Bridge. Stay in the left-hand lanes, but ignore the signs tempting you off the expressway into the shopping malls of North Sydney. Take the turn-off to Mosman and Manly, and immediately enter the shopping areas of Neutral Bay and Cremorne strung along the ribbon of Military Road. (This takes its name from its initial role in 1861 as a route for taking large guns to Middle Head to fortify the colony against possible attack by Russia during the Crimean War.) On the left at the start of Neutral Bay is the Oaks Hotel: the bars are popular in the evening when office workers shrug off business clothes and slip into something more suitable to meet those who arrive in the Porsches, Saabs and BMWs double-parked outside. The beer garden at the rear is a great place to experience a traditional

BELOW: Balmoral Beach, complete with shark net.

Australian pub "cook it yourself" summer barbecue.

Balmoral Beach ⑨ is one of the best inner-harbour beaches. It may not have surf, but at the southern end masses of windsurfers take to the water. At the northern end Balmoral, like several other beaches, has a netted swimming area to keep sharks at bay. The boatshed past the baths hires out "trailer sailers" and windsurfers. This southern end of Balmoral was among the first beach areas on which topless bathing was the norm. The "island" linked to the main path by a bridge is packed with picnickers on summer weekends and over summer the tiny rotunda in the park is the venue for band recitals or jazz concerts, even Shakespearian plays on occasions.

The houses on the hillside (particularly those on Manadalong Road) are among some of the most expensive in Sydney. The Bathers Pavilion is one of those Sydney places, with its excellent food, glittering harbour reflections and temperate weather ambience, that makes you really start to think that this is the world's luckiest city.

After crossing the narrow isthmus of sand linked to the northern beaches by the **Spit Bridge ⑩**, you have a choice of either heading into Manly and North Head or straight up the highway to the numerous other beaches which line the peninsula. You may catch Spit Bridge raised to let numerous tall-masted yachts out of Middle Harbour, and you can certainly consider lunch at one of the nearby waterfront restaurants while the traffic clears. The **Manly Scenic Walkway**, beginning on the northeast side of the Spit Bridge, is an 8-km (5-mile) walking track to Manly, winding through native bushland and across the top of sandstone cliffs with heartstopping views across to the Heads. For those with the enthusiasm and energy, it is one of the finest Sydney experiences.

North Head was an island until the sea built up the sand spit which is now Manly shopping centre. For many arrivals to Sydney, this area was all they saw of the colony for the first month and a half – North Head houses the now defunct **Quarantine Station** which first opened in 1833 to protect Sydney from any imported diseases, such as smallpox. Many of the passengers and crew of detained vessels are responsible for the 2,000 rock carvings here. The last ship was impounded in 1972, and in 1984 the Quarantine Station closed. It is now administered by the National Parks and Wildlife Service as a tourist attraction, and tours of the hospital, morgue and other historic buildings are available (tel: 9977 6522 to book a guided tour). In addition, the views from here are quite simply the best in Sydney.

The popularity of Manly

"Seven miles from Sydney and a thousand miles from care", as the old sign proudly proclaimed, **Manly ⑪**

Map
on pages
130–1

TIP

The best toilets and showers on Balmoral Beach can be located at the rear of the bathers' Pavilion.

BELOW: music for jogging on Manly Beach.

is Sydney's main resort suburb.

From the wharf on the sheltered harbourside, Manly's main shopping thoroughfare **The Corso** runs for 200 metres (220 yds) to the famous surf beaches fringed by Norfolk Island pine trees. Most of The Corso is now a pedestrian mall. It was called after the Corso in Rome by developer Henry Gordon Smith who, in the 1850s, saw the potential for Manly to become the equivalent of England's Brighton Beach. It was a brave dream – in the mid-19th century ocean bathing was considered immoral, an attitude that prevailed until the turn of the 20th century.

Today, Smith's vision has come into being. Permanently bustling with tourists and buskers, The Corso is lined with souvenir shops with 1930s facades and cheap snack bars. Try the local fish and chips, sold in takeaway packages to eat on the beach. It was also Smith who started ferry services to Manly in 1854, some 60 years before Bondi became popular. His house was near the stone kangaroo which still stands in Manly.

Swim in the harbour, surf the ocean beaches, walk the sands of either, just browse along the shops of The Corso and have a pie on a bench in the mall, eat in one of the cafés or restaurants along the Esplanade, or down a beer in one of Manly's many pubs. There's no shortage of things to do here, and the bustle of the city seems distant indeed.

A major tourist attraction in Manly Cove is **Oceanworld** on West Esplanade (open daily; tel: 9949 2644; entrance fee), which is almost as popular as the Sydney Aquarium *(see page 106)*. A moving walkway takes you through a transparent underwater tunnel with sharks, stingrays and other fish swimming around you. If you are brave enough, there are often opportunities to feed the sharks.

Near by, at the wharf, is a pierside funfair, complete with rollercoasters, big wheels and sideshows.

The northern beaches

Freshwater, Curl Curl, Dee Why, Long Reef, Collaroy, Narrabeen, Warriewood, Mona Vale, Bungan, Newport, Bilgola, Avalon, Whale and Palm: the litany of northern beaches is invoked most summer mornings on radio surf reports.

Two of the most picturesque are **Freshwater** in the suburb of Harbord (which also has a restaurant in a wonderful location in the park overlooking the beach), and **Bilgola** right up on the peninsula, where a small community is snuggled into a diminutive cove far below the main Barrenjoey Road.

Long Reef ⓬ has a golf course which covers the whole headland and a wide rock shelf at water level where every tiny pond provides a journey of discovery. Much of the drive along Pittwater Road, then Barrenjoey Road, is a flickering, repeating image of beach and headland – standing on any point, you can glimpse a serried rank of head-

Legend has it that Governor Phillip named the coastal town of Manly after the physiques of the local Aboriginal men.

BELOW: a sedate picnic on Palm Beach.

**Map
on pages
130–1**

lands stretching back to Manly.

Heading towards **Mona Vale** ⑬, the best route to take is Mona Vale Road, which runs along the coastal highlands. Set high in the bushland and commanding a spectacular view 4 km (2½ miles) in from the coast is the imposingly exotic **Baha'i Temple** at Ingleside. The Baha'i faith was founded in Persia in the mid-19th century and this temple was built in 1961. The drive along the Pacific Highway now passes Ku-ring-gai Chase National Park.

Short detours into the suburban streets on either side anywhere north of Chatswood give an insight into the lifestyle of Sydney's north. These northern suburbs embody the lifestyle that many around the world consider synonymous with Australia: middle-class, complacent and smug. A cruise through the area shows why: there is little room for angst in settings as beautiful as these. It's not a place of conspicuous consumption but more a refuge from the city which is the financial powerhouse that fuels the comfort levels.

En route to the northern tip, the road passes the very exclusive suburb of **Palm Beach** ⑭. This is the favoured address of media types, film-industry folk and those who don't have to drive into the city every day. Chic restaurants and cafés line the waterfront, and windsurfing and surfing are particularly popular here.

At the very tip of the peninsula stands **Barrenjoey Lighthouse**, reached via a one-hour walk from Palm Beach. The views at the end make the effort worthwhile. The Palm Beach Ferry Service offers tours of Pittwater and **Broken Bay** ⑮, the glittering waterways on the inland side of the peninsula (tel: 9974 5235 for details).

Ku-ring-gai Chase National Park

Thirty km (19 miles) north of the city is **Ku-ring-gai Chase National Park** ⑯, which takes its name from the local Aboriginal tribe of the area, Guringai. (The first of the two hyphens in the unusual name may be an accident – preserving a line break in the original gazetting.) It

Inside the Baha'i Temple, Broken Bay.

BELOW: Palm Beach stretches almost to Barrenjoey Head.

Map
on pages
130–1

*An old poster
recalls the East
Coast's surfing
heritage.*

BELOW: yachts
anchored in Smith
Creek, part of
Ku-ring-gai Chase
National Park.

was Australia's second national park, dedicated in 1894. Unlike the first, the Royal National Park *(see page 159)*, which was to become a pleasure ground, this park's 147 sq km (57 sq miles) were set aside to preserve a sample of Sydney's original landscape, formed during the last ice age. It has some of the prettiest scenery in Sydney: from the spectacle of Lion Island crouched protectively in the middle of Broken Bay (as seen from West Head lookout) to the flooded river valleys of Cowan Creek and the picturesque Coal and Candle Creek.

Road access into the park is from the Pacific Highway to Bobbin Head or from Mona Vale Road. Towards the coast, there is another turn-off from Mona Vale Road at Terrey Hills into Cottage Point, Akuna Bay and West Head or along the shoreline from Church Point. The **Kalkari Visitors' Centre**, off Ku-ring-gai Chase Road, has maps and advice for those wanting to head out along one of the many walking tracks in the area (tel: 9457 9853). For a while, Sydney saw a rash of bumper

stickers asking "Where the hell is Akuna Bay?" Once found, its *raison d'être* is clear: it's in the middle of foreshore wilderness, where one can hire boats to explore the 120 km (74 miles) of the park's shoreline. Oddly, the main feature of Akuna Bay is that there is so little there.

Other boat-hire outlets are at Bobbin Head, Brooklyn and Church Point. There is a range of craft available, including fully equipped houseboats which can be hired for extended cruising holidays; those interested should contact the **Hawkesbury River Tourist Information Centre** in Brooklyn, at 2/5 Bridge Street (tel: 9985 7064). Travellers with less time can hop aboard a ferry for a couple of hours of gentle river cruising. The Palm Beach Ferry Service leaves from Pittwater Park, Palm Beach (tel: 9918 2747), and is a great option for visitors who want to combine a tour of the northern beaches with a peek at Ku-ring-gai, but don't want to spend the whole day in the car.

Since Australia has become more aware of its indigenous roots, one of the most popular tourist attractions in Ku-ring-gai over recent years have been the **Aboriginal rock carvings** left by the Guringai people. The soft sandstone rocks are literally covered with ancient engravings, some thought to be more than 2,000 years old. In some instances, their size is as impressive as their age: a whale image in the park is 20 metres (65 ft) long, and some sites of engravings cover more than one hectare (2½ acres). Aboriginal ancestral spirits are also depicted. Aboriginal art can be seen on the Red Hand Trail, the Ekidna Track and the Basin Track. The last of these, located on West Head, is the best known. Access is via the West Head Road and walking trail, or visitors can hop aboard a Palm Beach Ferry and arrive by water. ❏

RESTAURANTS & BARS

Restaurants

Absolutely Flabuless
2 Elizabeth Plaza,
North Sydney
Tel: 8904 9993
Open: B & L daily. $
A spacious and upbeat restaurant-cum-coffee shop with an emphasis on healthy sandwiches and salads. Tables outdoors, and large upstairs dining room open all day.

Bathers Pavilion
4 The Esplanade,
Balmoral Beach
Tel: 9969 5050
Open: B Sun, L & D daily. $$$
Understated elegance in decor and carefully selected produce characterise this upmarket beachside eatery. Good ocean views, occasionally indifferent service.

Bhaji on the Beach
315a Barrenjoey Road,
Newport
Tel: 9979 6680
Open: D Tues–Sun. $
An economical Indian diner in an attractive beach setting. Popular after a day on the beach.

Brazil Cafe
46 North Steyne, Manly
Tel: 9977 3825
Open: B, L & D Mon–Sat,
B and L Sun. $
Despite its name, serves Modern Australian and seafood cuisine in a spacious, open-plan restaurant. Water views

and outdoor dining make the most of the location. Open long hours. BYO.

Chequers
Mandarin Centre, 65 Albert
Avenue, Chatswood
Tel: 9904 8388
Open: L & D daily. $$
A popular Chinese yum cha and seafood eatery with a core of devoted regulars. Above average decor and service for a Chinese restaurant. BYO.

Fresh Ketch
77a Parriwi Road, Mosman
Tel: 9969 5665
Open: L & D daily. $$
Large seafood restaurant with water views. Spectacular put pricey entrées, regular menu changes. Gets busy, with lots of repeat visitors.

Goe Mon
161 Middle Head Road,
Mosman
Tel: 9968 4983
Open: D daily. $
Affordable, traditional Japanese cuisine in the heart of upmarket Mosman. Excellent, friendly service. BYO.

L'Incontro
196 Miller Street,
North Sydney
Tel: 9957 2274
Open: L Mon–Fri, D Mon–Sat. $
This upmarket but affordable restaurant serves an Italian and seafood menu. A tasteful

decor matches the filling Italian treats. Open late.

Jonah's
69 Bynya Road, Palm Beach
Tel: 9974 5599
Open: B Sat–Sun, L & D daily. $$$
Popular, long-established restaurant in a romantic setting with outdoor dining and water views. Modern Australian and seafood cuisine. Not cheap, but good value.

Manly Bay Seafood
39 East Esplanade, Manly
Tel: 9977 3400
Open: L & D daily. $$
A seafood restaurant in a colourful part of Manly. The decor and friendly service reflects the attractive surroundings and water views. BYO.

Minato
47 East Esplanade, Manly
Tel: 9977 0580
Open: D daily. $
A very economical Japan-

PRICE CATEGORIES

Price indications are for a three-course meal for one, including half a bottle of house wine, coffee and service.
$ = under A$50
$$ = A$50–75
$$$ = over A$75
Abbreviations: B = breakfast, L = lunch, D = dinner. BYO = bring your own alcohol.

ese dining experience in beachy surroundings. Attentive service and above average decor for a low-cost eatery. BYO.

Thai Noodle Hut
339 Penshurst Street,
Chatswood
Tel: 9417 0555
Open: L & D daily. $
Economical treats are offered in this affordable kitchen. Average decor and no-fuss service, but tasty, affordable food at nice prices. BYO.

Bars

Newport Arms Hotel
2 Kalinya Street, Newport
A long-time favourite pub with the northern suburbs' surf culture, young and old. The beer garden ($) also serves up basic, standard pub fare. Deck shoes and a suntan are de rigueur.

Oaks Hotel
118 Military Road,
Neutral Bay
A popular landmark and watering hole for the North Shore's urban elite. The spacious beer garden is something the city pubs can't offer.

Greenwood Hotel
36 Blue Street, North Sydney
A busy pub that attracts a lunchtime corporate clientele and a fashionable young after-hours crowd.

Sydney Harbour National Park

The Sydney Harbour National Park consists of a series of scattered reserves and islands, many of them preserving sections of the extraordinary natural environment of Sydney – a feast of soaring sandstone cliffs, rocky coves and crescent-shaped beaches, open woodland and pockets of rainforest. There is also an uncaged menagerie of native animals that have adapted their ways in order to survive life on the fringes of surburbia.

That such an abundance of nature can exist on the doorstep of a city that is home to more than 4 million people is nearly as remarkable as the scenery itself. Its survival is due mostly to the fact that the military traditionally held large areas of the foreshore; when the time came for the army to abandon the area, it was found that Sydneysiders had grown used to their bush-clad harbour, and showed no inclination of relinquishing even a small part of it to modern development.

The Sydney Harbour National Park Information Centre is located at Cadman's Cottage in The Rocks *(see page 84)*, where staff can provide brochures, maps and details of tours (tel: 9247 5033). In the eastern suburbs the park covers sections of Vaucluse and Watsons Bay, including the wonderful picnic/beach area of Nielsen Park, and the rocky foreshore of South Head *(see page 134)*. Five harbour islands – Fort Denison, Goat, Shark, Clark and Rodd – are also part of the park. Goat Island and Fort Denison can only be visited on a tour from Cadman's Cottage Information Centre. To visit Shark, Clark or Rodd islands, you'll need to book and pay landing fees beforehand.

If you're planning to drive into the park, you will need to purchase a vehicle day pass from the Information Centre. This costs A$3, and covers parking at Bradley's Head and North Head. Aside from any parking fees, you can get into all foreshore areas of Sydney Harbour National Park for free.

On the north side of the harbour misshapen "fingers" stretch out into the bay, making it a nightmare for taxi drivers but certainly increasing the available harbour foreshores. Heading leisurely around the harbour clockwise by boat from the bridge (at Milsons Point), one goes past Kurraba and Cremorne points, before arriving at Taronga Zoo *(see page 142)*. Here, the land

kicks south to Bradley's Head, which is vaguely reminiscent of Italy's "boot". In fact, Bradley's Head is the turning point in the harbour, from which the famous Manly ferry turns north to head towards the northern suburb of Manly.

Ashton Park, which covers the headland, does have some vestigial rainforest in its valleys. Reaching the headland, one is rewarded by views of a lighthouse and some gun emplacements built to repel the feared Russian Pacific fleet who never actually arrived in the 1850s. Those interested in fishing can try their luck here and may even catch their supper. The path continues past Taylors Bay and around to Chowder Head and Chowder Bay, both named after the thick soup dish made by early ships' crews from the abundant shellfish covering the sandstone rocks.

Suburbia breaks the rustic path at Chowder Bay but it resumes soon after, and the park at Middle Head extends right around the head to tiny Cobblers Beach. However, considerable parts of this area are still under military control. Obelisk Beach on the main harbourside and Cobblers on the middle harbourside are both recognised nudist beaches. If you'd rather observe nature than naturists, there are wonderful views from here across towards the horizon.

The tip of Middle Head is a maze of gun emplacements and tunnels dug to service them. During school holidays, the National Parks and Wildlife Service conducts historical tours of the fortifications (which again date back to the Russian scare), but there is limited access at other times. The views, however, suggest that this would have been a very pleasant spot from which to defend the nation and await invaders.

On the other side of the Spit Bridge, there is an 8-km (5-mile) walk that extends right from the wharf, much of it through national parkland. This goes past Grotto Point, home to the wonderfully evocative lighthouse which swimmers at Balmoral Beach *(see page 145)* invariably think looks like a tiny Greek Orthodox chapel on an Aegean island. The lighthouse is now abandoned, as are the nearby Aboriginal carvings made by a tribe that was wiped out by smallpox in the first days of the colony. Anyone arriving at Reef Beach by boat should beware of the swell – each year, regulars keep score of the boats that come ashore capsized.

North Head is the jewel in the crown of the Sydney Harbour National Park. Fairfax Lookout at the point provides a view of the greater portion of this widely scattered park. This headland was an island until the sea built up the spit which is now Manly shopping centre. Its isolated position made it the perfect location for a Quarantine Station in which to house immigrants suspected of carrying infectious diseases. Remarkably, the station remained operative until 1984, but is now a tourist attraction: "Ghost Tours" are led by park rangers every Wed, Fri, Sat and Sun evening; advance booking essential (at the Cadman's Cottage Information Centre).

Shelley Beach is an enclave of homes and beachfront restaurants. At this point, anyone without mountaineering aspirations would be well advised to catch the Manly Hospital bus, rather than climb the hill to reach the start of the park on the harbourside.   ❏

LEFT: an aerial view of North Head.
RIGHT: Fort Denison is part of the National Park.

SOUTHSIDE

The coastal area south of Sydney marks
the historic spot where Captain Cook
first claimed Australia for Britain, but
the region is perhaps best known
today for the pleasures of Bondi Beach

Sydney's southern suburbs residents are a coterie all to themselves. They have money, the latest in domestic gadgetry and a power boat, preferably on a private mooring. They pride themselves on being better than the west and claim to disdain the beautiful but sterile and prudish north. They have the bleak and windswept Botany Bay and the beautiful, natural (most of it) Georges River recreation area. They also have large tracts of industrialised areas.

This is the region where "Modern Australia" began, on the shores of Botany Bay when Captain James Cook stepped ashore in 1770 to survey the land for Britain and plant the seeds of European settlement. It was the plants of this southern land that gave the bay its final name. Originally called Stingray Bay, it was renamed Botany Bay by Cook after the "great quantity of new plants" (more than 3,000 species) collected by the expedition's naturalist, Joseph Banks.

The bay became the inspiration of ballads – "Farewell to old England for ever… We're bound for Botany Bay" was the plaint of one – despite the fact that 18 years after Cook landed, the First Fleet stayed only a few days here and finally moved on to Sydney Cove, a far more amenable site. Six days later, a French fleet commanded by explorer Comte de La Perouse arrived at Botany Bay, where they spent six weeks resting and refitting before continuing on their round-the-world journey of exploration. La Perouse's precautionary request that the English deliver his charts, journals and letters to France proved to be a wise move: after sailing from Botany Bay, his fleet was never seen again.

Today these historic landing sites are surrounded by oil refineries,

Map
on pages
130–1

LEFT: life-saver mural on Bondi Pavilion.
BELOW: taking it easy on Bondi Beach.

Looking for action at Bondi Beach.

BELOW RIGHT: Bondi has seen surfing for nearly a century.

power stations and container terminals. The locals generally have a healthy disregard for history. They lean more towards pleasure, flocking to the surf beaches of Maroubra and Cronulla and the largely unspoilt Georges River recreation area.

It's into this region of Sydney that most overseas tourists first alight, at Kingsford Smith Airport. The airport and its related industries take up a large chunk of the region – the runway even extends into Botany Bay to accommodate larger jet planes and the ever-increasing flow of tourists.

Bondi Beach

With 1 km (½ mile) of white sand and great waves, **Bondi Beach** ⓱ is Australia's most famous beach. The area is a hive of activity from morning to night. Body-builders and joggers warm up along the promenade before undertaking a day's work in the office, then, after about 9am, the tourists begin to arrive, along with truanting or holidaying Sydneysiders. Bondi has always been popular but, following in the wake of Miami and Venice Beach in Los Angeles, the beach has witnessed a renaissance in the last few years, and has rediscovered its hip atmosphere. Not only are there the in-line skaters along the strip, narrowly avoiding mere walkers, but swimming and surfing have returned as the sports of favour, following water-contamination scares in the 1980s and an ensuing cleaning up of the area.

The beach is well set up for visitors and families. Life-savers patrol the coastal strip, ensuring revellers swim "within the flags", lock-ups are available in which to leave valuables and changing rooms are free in the charmingly run-down **Bondi Pavilion**, built in 1928, which now regularly plays host to film and drama festivals, as well as serving its original purpose. Generally speaking, the northern stretch of the beach is best for those with young children – there is a toddlers' pool here for youngsters afraid of the waves – while the southern end is more lively with teenage and twenty-something sun-worshippers.

The demographics change again

The Ultimate Beach

Bondi Beach can claim to be the birthplace of Australia's famous love of sea and surf. Before the 1880s, swimming in the sea during daylight hours was considered the preserve only of convicts and other low-life characters. At the end of the 19th century, a few bathers braved the ocean and the disdain of society by taking to the water, but it wasn't until 1903 that a clergyman and a banker risked their reputations and started a trend that was to grip the very heart of all Australian culture. By the late 1920s hordes of Sydneysiders flocked to Bondi's golden shore every summer, and a tramline was swiftly built to link the beach with the city. The sea off Bondi, however, is occasionally violent, and in 1906 the world's first life-saving society was set up here to protect the naive swimmers. Turning the high waves into an advantage, it wasn't long before the Hawaiian surf legend, Duke Kahanamoku, brought the sport to Australian shores. Ironically, this most macho of sports was first attempted at Bondi by a woman. Although Australians today are keen to render themselves more sophisticated in international eyes, the image of Aussie beach culture lingers on, and nowhere is this more prevalent than at Bondi.

at the Bondi Baths (far south), the preserve of the Bondi Icebergs, a group of older men who swim all winter, and open the season by throwing huge blocks of ice into the water to get the temperature right. Just past the baths is the starting point for a magnificent scenic walk heading south to Clovelly, a two-hour trek exploring the clifftops, rock platforms and seaside communities of this celebrated coastline.

When you're tired of swimming, or simply want to quench your thirst out of the sun, head to Bondi's main street, **Campbell Parade**. The facades may date from the 1930s, but the bars, cafés and restaurants are innovative and largely new, although there is still a good range of eating establishments that are old favourites. There is also a range of fish-and-chip shops that are beginning to move away from the deep-fried variety and serve a range of grilled fresh fish, caught that day. Bondi's heart continues to beat well into the early hours, in bars such as the traditional Bondi Pub. From the top of the hill at the south end of Bondi there are a series of cafés offering good food, drinks, strong coffees and enviable views of the glorious sweep of famous beach.

Unlike many institutions that continue to thrive on a reputation long gone, Bondi Beach remains a highly entertaining and enjoyable experience that no visitor to Sydney should miss.

The southern surf

The way south from the city to the windswept surf beach of Maroubra is along **Anzac Parade**, a long avenue named in honour of the Australian and New Zealand Army Corps. It passes the Sydney Cricket Ground, Moore Park Golf Course, Fox Studios (Rupert Murdoch's plastic gift to Sydney), Randwick Racecourse (where the first Australian race meeting was held in 1833) and the University of NSW (established in 1949).

Tamarama Beach is another beautiful stretch of warm waters and white sand, and a popular spot for Sydney's beautiful people. Although it looks safe and protected, the surf

Map on pages 130–1

Guidelines for enjoyment-seekers.

BELOW: hanging out on Campbell Parade.

at Tamarama is notoriously dangerous – definitely not a great choice for families with young children.

After Tamarama, the road leads south to **Bronte Beach** ⑱, which is more of a family-outing destination, helped along by a natural rock pool and a beachside swimming pool that are both fun and safe for young children. Behind the beach is the attractive 19th-century mansion, **Bronte House** (closed to the public), fronted by lush landscaped gardens. Picnics can be enjoyed in the gardens, or you may prefer to try out the inexpensive cafés and fish-and-chip restaurants that line Bronte Beach.

Past Bronte is the **Waverley Cemetery**, which spreads across a large clifftop area, and which must have some of the best views of any cemetery in the world. Of interest are the grand Victorian and Edwardian graves, with their ornate statuary and elaborate epitaphs. Look out for the Irish Memorial commemorating the Irish Rebellion of 1798.

Further along the coast is **Coogee Beach**, with some of the best bronzed Aussie life-savers around.

Coogee is also home to a couple of fantastic sea baths: Wiley's Baths, a 1900s institution sporting a modern award-winning renovation, and the Women's Baths, a female-only affair, popular with Muslim and lesbian communities. Inland is the Randwick Racecourse, home to the Australian Jockey Club and site of the Sydney Cup race held every Easter.

The historic coast

Continuing south, the highway skirts Long Bay Jail, Sydney's largest prison, before terminating at **La Perouse**, lying across the northern head of one of Australia's most famous areas, Botany Bay.

La Perouse provides a reminder that Australia was very nearly a French colony. The French explorer arrived six days after Captain Phillip, but bad weather prevented his ship from entering Botany Bay. He eventually landed there the same day that Phillip raised the flag at Sydney Cove. The French stayed for six weeks, dining on flathead caught and prepared in the best French culinary traditions, before sailing off never to be seen again. Years later their ships were found wrecked on a Pacific reef.

The **La Perouse Museum**, part of Botany Bay National Park, has relics from this expedition and provides a fascinating glimpse of the early history of the area (open daily; tel: 9311 3379; entrance fee). The La Perouse monument dates from 1828 and was the concept of Baron de Bougainville, who visited the site in 1825. The National Parks and Wildlife Service of NSW looks after it, with financial contributions from the French government (tel: 1300 361 967 for the main NPWS switchboard, or 9311 3379 for Botany Bay National Park.)

The nearby **Macquarie Watchtower**, built in the early 1820s, is the oldest existing building on the Bay's

BELOW: Tamarama Beach is for posing, not swimming.

shores. Governor Lachlan Macquarie instructed that the tower be erected to house the soldiers attempting to control smuggling and other activities of ships entering the Bay. The 1882 **Old Cable Station**, built to house staff operating the 1876 telegraph line from La Perouse to New Zealand, now contains a museum honouring La Perouse's exploits and a tomb marks the grave of Père Receveur, a Franciscan monk attached to La Perouse's expedition.

Offshore, and linked by a bridge, is **Bare Island**, observed as being such by Captain Cook. After the removal of British troops in 1870, the colony's increased self-reliance led to the strengthening of Botany Bay's defences in anticipation of French or Russian attacks. The island's fort was constructed in 1881, and its barracks added in 1889, with the bridge being built early in the 20th century. Fortunately, the fort's guns have never been required to fire a shot in anger or retaliation. Tours of the island are available through the National Parks and Wildlife Service (tel: 9311 3379).

Continue from La Perouse along the Foreshore Road, which passes Port Botany and underneath Kingsford Smith Airport's 4-km (2½-mile) north–south runway reaching into the bay. Established in 1920, the airport's name commemorates legendary aviator Sir Charles Kingsford Smith. In the 1920s, huge crowds gathered at the simple airstrip to cheer the aviator and his plane, the *Southern Cross*, on his epic transPacific and trans-Tasman flights.

Botany Bay

Botany Bay ❶ was the site chosen by Cook's botanist, Joseph Banks, for Australia's first penal settlement in 1788. However, after an eightmonth voyage from England, the First Fleet soon discovered that water supplies further north in Sydney Cove were more advantageous and the Bay was deserted, but its place in Australian history remains legendary.

The 324-hectare (800-acre) area is now protected as a registered national park. This is where Cook landed, and the place which, based on his reports, was to be the site of the new Antipodean colony. Governor Phillip of the First Fleet arrived 18 years later to find a windswept landscape, unsuitable for occupation, and promptly moved his infant colony north to the shores of Sydney Harbour, showing an impressive property acumen in the process.

Pass through Brighton-le-Sands (with its warning signs of sharks in Botany Bay), and continue south to the Georges River, which winds its way through the bushland and pleasant suburbs of southern Sydney. Before reaching the town of Cronulla, a turn-off leads to the **Kurnell Peninsula** ⓴. Today the home of industry and oil refineries, the headland is of historic importance as **Captain Cook's Landing Place** and is also part of the Botany

Map on pages 130–1

BELOW: ice creams at Coogee Beach.

Bay National Park. Several monuments commemorate the eight days Cook spent at this spot in 1770 – the Captain Cook Obelisk, erected in 1870; the Sir Joseph Banks Memorial, raised in 1947; and a tablet to the memory of Seaman Forby Sutherland, who died three days after the expedition's arrival.

The park's **Discovery Centre**, on Captain Cook Drive at Kurnell, commemorates the life and achievements of James Cook (open Mon–Fri 11am–3pm, Sat–Sun 10am–5pm; tel: 9668 9111; entrance fee weekends only). Shops and picnic facilities are nearby. The National Parks and Wildlife Service have pamphlets on recommended walking trails in the area and notes on the history of the site.

Cronulla and beyond

Crossing the Captain Cook Bridge brings you to **Cronulla ㉑**, home of the city's southernmost and longest beach with its 10 km (6 miles) of sand and billowing surf. The area's Aboriginal name of Gunnamatta – "beach and sandhills" – aptly describes what has become a surfers' haven. Catch a ferry from the Tonkin Street Wharf (tel: 9523 2990) near the Cronulla Station for a tour of Port Hacking at the mouth of the Hacking River, or for a ride across to the Royal National Park.

Further south along the Princes Highway at Loftus, on the edge of the Royal National Park, is the Sydney Tramway Museum. It contains about 30 tramcars dating back to the late 19th century, some of which operate along a 2.5 km (1½-mile) track to the Royal National Park Railway Station (open Sun 10am–5pm, Wed 10am–3pm; tel: 9542 3646; entrance fee). The highway then leads to the beautiful Royal National Park.

To return to Sydney, take the Princes Highway through Sutherland and the attractive garden suburb of **Sylvania**, crossing the Georges River at Tom Ugly's Point – believed to be the result of Aboriginal attempts at the pronunciation of an early settler's name, Tom Huxley. Sylvania is the site of Paul's Famous Hamburgers, an outlet that many

BELOW:
Winifred Falls in the
Royal National Park.

Sydneysiders claim serves the best burgers in Sydney, if not the world.

Carss Bush Park, on the shores of Kogarah Bay, is a pleasant reserve with a historic cottage. This otherwise unremarkable area was made notorious in the 1980s by expatriate Clive James's hilarious reminiscences in *Unreliable Memoirs*, the first volume of his autobiographical series.

You can return to the city via the re-gentrified suburb of Newtown with its period working-class architecture, and Sydney University.

The Royal National Park

The **Royal National Park** ㉒ at Sutherland is the second-oldest national park in the world after Yellowstone in the United States. While national parks today are generally regarded as areas where the environment is preserved in perpetuity, when this park south of Sydney was declared in 1879 it was intended as a pleasure ground for city-dwellers, to be modelled after London's Hampstead Heath. In an act of great environmental brutality, some of the native Australian bush was even cleared to be replaced by more "attractive" imported plants and manicured lawns. Indeed, conservation hardly seemed to have entered the equation over the first 75 years of the park's existence. Until 1922, the trust for this 16,000-hectare (37,000-acre) region earned its income from logging, until it was found to have no power to license logging within the park. Even the army used the park as a training ground during World War II.

Access to the park is by train, ferry or road. The ferry service runs between Cronulla Wharf, directly behind Cronulla railway station, and Bundeena, a small coastal village completely surrounded by the park, as well as offering tours of Port Hacking, the beautiful waterway

that forms the northern border of the park (tel: 9523 2990 for information on the ferry services).

You can also enter the park by train straight along a spur line to **Royal National Park Station**, near the Park Headquarters on Farnell Avenue at Audley (tel: 9542 0648 for information). There are also walking trails from Engadine, Heathcote, Otford, Loftus and Waterfall stations. Rowing boats and canoes are available for hire at the picnic area at Audley.

In keeping with the early lack of concern for conservation, the roads through the Royal are not just day-access routes – several are through-roads between the south coast and Sydney (although most traffic now skirts the park boundary on the Princes Highway), and one provides the only road access to Bundeena. Lady Carrington Drive, a one-way path that follows the Hacking River Valley, may be travelled only on foot and gives an excellent idea of what the park's valley scenery is like.

The "Royal" has been part of Sydney's life for more than a cen-

Map on pages 130–1

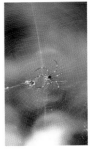

A spider gets ready for lunch.

BELOW: red kangaroos sparring.

Map
on pages
130–1

tury. It cannot truly be called a wilderness area, and you rarely have the feeling of being miles away from civilisation, but it has the decided advantage of being one of the city's most readily accessible bushlands, less than an hour's drive from the heart of the metropolis.

The park consists predominantly of heath-covered sandstone plateaux. However, despite the early attempts at destruction, the park's valleys are still full of forests with thousands of native plant species, including rainforests, woodlands, luminous green luxuriances of buttress roots, liana vines and innumerable ferns. There is also a range of tranquil lakes, waterfalls and lagoons.

The Royal also attracts birdwatchers. It is within these dense grottoes that you stand the best chance of hearing a whip bird (its call sounds like the crack of a stock whip) or seeing the exquisite lyre bird, named for its lyre-shaped tail. You may also see the satin bower bird, which derives its name from the spectacular bowers it builds out of sticks. It looks like a crow or

raven at first glance, until a closer look reveals that the bird's plumage isn't black, but a very deep iridescent mauve. In tall trees throughout the park you may also see the rainbow flash of a rosella (a type of parrot) or watch the antics of the shrieking sulphur-crested cockatoos. The coastal caves on the edge of the park are nesting sites for the resident terns and sea eagles.

The native animals are timid and most are nocturnal, so visitors aren't likely to see them with the same frequency as the 200 bird types in the park. Still, there is the chance of spotting an echidna (spiny anteater) – normally as a spiky mound disappearing vertically into the soil – or a swamp wallaby hopping into the distance. The Javanese rusa deer and fallow deer released into the park around the end of the 19th century are also still here. The park's picnic areas are closed between sunset and 7am, so unfortunately few see the ringtail and brushtail possums that frequent the park after dark.

The Royal's coastline

Along the shores of the Royal National Park there are 21 km (13 miles) of beautiful coastline: surfing beaches interspersed by rugged sandstone headlands, eroded by years of wave activity.

Era Beach and Garie Beach are the most popular surfing spots and the small town of Bundeena, within the sheltered waters of Port Hacking, is a renowned windsurfing area. The well-appointed camping area of Bonnie Vale near by is adjacent to a sandy spot with good swimming. Wattamolla, although on the ocean side, has a good swimming lagoon, and attracts snorkellers and divers exploring the inlet. Just below the southern border of the park, the foreshore road leading down to Wollongong has some of the best coastal views in Australia. ❑

BELOW: you may see a rainbow lorikeet in the Royal National Park.

RESTAURANTS & BARS

Restaurants

The Beach Pit
211 Coogee Bay Road,
Coogee
Tel: 9665 0068
Open: B Sat–Sun, L & D
Thur–Mon. **$$**
Modern Australian cuisine, including seafood,
close to the promenade.
Gets busy weekends.

Botany Bay Seafood
128 The Grand Parade,
Brighton-Le-Sands
Tel: 9599 2755
Open: L Sun–Fri, D daily. **$$$**
An upmarket seafood
eatery, with live music
Saturday evenings.

Danny's Seafood
1605 Anzac Parade,
La Perouse
Tel: 9311 4116
Open: L & D daily. **$$**
Outdoor seating overlooking Botany Bay. Menu
includes economical
seafood platters for two
and children's menu.
Live music.

Eurobay Cafe and Bar
86 The Grand Parade,
Brighton-Le-Sands
Tel: 9597 3300
Open: B Sat–Sun, L & D
daily. **$$**
A southern European
eatery and pizza place
that doubles as a coffee
house. Open long hours.

Mint Restaurant
43 Gerrale Street, Cronulla
Tel: 9523 9381

Open: L Thur–Sun, D Tues–
Sun. **$$**
A Mediterranean and
seafood restaurant with
water views. Relaxed
and intimate, with attentive service.

The Pool Caffe
94 Marine Parade, Maroubra
Tel: 9314 0364
Open: B Sun, L & D daily. **$**
A large restaurant with
outdoor seating and an
economical modern Australian and seafood menu.

Sean's Panorama
270 Campbell Parade,
Bondi Beach
Tel: 9365 4924
Open: L Sat–Sun, D Mon–
Sat. **$$**
An eccentric little place at
the north end of Bondi
Beach. The Modern Australian menu is very good
and the weekend breakfasts are legendary. BYO.

Thai Terrific
170 Maroubra Road,
Maroubra
Tel: 9349 8288
Open: D daily. **$**
A welcoming place with
trendy decor. Economical
prices and large servings.
Free delivery to hotels in
the surrounding area.

Treehorn
19 Havelock Avenue, Coogee
Tel: 9664 4005
Open: L & D daily. **$**
Vegetarian eatery offering lots of healthy, fresh
food and tasty desserts.

Laid-back but efficient
staff. Live music at
weekends.

Cafés and Bars

Bar One
Departures Lounge,
Kingsford Smith Airport
A terrific new rooftop bar
with elevated views
across the airport's runway. Relaxed and comfortable, despite all the
airport frenzy.

The Bogey Hole
473 Bronte Road, Bronte
Named after a rugged
natural pool on the
southern end of Bronte
Beach, a local favourite
for a morning cuppa or
quick lunchtime snack.

Bondi Icebergs
1 Knotts Avenue,
South Bondi
Enjoy a beer while soaking up one of the best
views in Sydney. Live
music at weekends.

Catch Seafood Cafe
Cnr Alfred and Ramsgate
roads, Ramsgate Beach
A licensed Modern Australian and seafood café
with affordable snacks
and an economical set
menu. A free bottle of
wine for bookings of four
or more.

Coogee Bay Hotel
Cnr Arden Street and
Coogee Bay Road
A large old pub that

packs them in over the
weekends. Has water
views and a bistro serving Modern Australian
and African menus.

Cozzi Cafe
233 Coogee Bay Road,
Coogee
A bright and breezy
beachside coffee shop.
Attentive staff and a convenient central Coogee
location.

Grind Espresso Bar
Rydges Hotel, Kings Way,
Cronulla
A popular coffee shop
in an otherwise café-deprived area. Serves
breakfast and a selection of budget-priced
meals. Outdoor tables.
Open long hours.

Hotel Bondi
178 Campbell Parade,
Bondi Beach
This is the real Bondi –
loud, friendly, sun-and-sea-soaked, despite its
yuppification.

PRICE CATEGORIES

Price indications are
for a three-course meal
for one, including half a
bottle of house wine,
coffee and service.
$ = under A$50
$$ = A$50–75
$$$ = over A$75
Abbreviations: B =
breakfast, L = lunch,
D = dinner. BYO = bring
your own alcohol.

THE WESTERN SUBURBS

The site of the 18th-century European arrivals' second settlement, the suburbs west of Sydney have remained an open door for new immigrants and are the basis for the city's multicultural reputation

The western suburbs of Sydney are the city's heartland, and have long been misunderstood. Home to the majority of the city's population, they also contain much of Sydney's light and heavy industry, and some of the other less scenic aspects of modern civilisation. But while the visual terrain may appear a little bleak in parts, the cultural (and gastronomic) terrain and the history are well worth a look, as are the large range of wildlife and children's attractions. There is also the phenomenal redevelopment that transformed the once humble area of Homebush Bay into the site for the 2000 Summer Olympic Games.

When those aboard the First Fleet arrived in Sydney Cove in 1788, they discovered that the area around Port Jackson (Sydney Harbour), although scenic, offered precious little in terms of fertile land and fresh water. A search for new land was promptly executed, leading to the discovery of the Parramatta River and the surrounding swathes of rich arable land (made so by millennia of Aboriginal "fire-stick" farming). Australia's second-oldest settlement, Parramatta, was established as a centre for agricultural activity. Thus the life of the infant colony was secured, and the history of the district moved into its second phase.

The main feature of today's great west is, without doubt, the mix and character of its people. Successive waves of migration brought new settlers to this less desirable and thus much more affordable area of Sydney, and it is now one of the most cosmopolitan congregations of humanity in the world.

There are three main routes etched through the west from the city centre, one on each side of the Parramatta River, and the third through the heart of the southwest.

Map on pages 130–1

LEFT: Polish Australians at a festival in Parramatta Park.
BELOW: a pelican observes life on the Parramatta River.

On the south side of the river, the Great Western Highway (Parramatta Road) incorporates the Western Motorway. On the north side is Victoria Road. Heading out to the southwest is New Canterbury Road. The metropolitan west is bordered to the north by the Hawkesbury River, to the far west by the Blue Mountains, and to the south by the foothills of the Southern Highlands.

The multicultural west

From "Little Italy" to "Vietnamatta", it's not for nothing that Australia's premier city is described as one of the most sophisticated cultural and racial melting pots in the world. Sydney is home to people from more than 200 nations and no one knows how many linguistic backgrounds. Nowhere is the concentration of different cultures greater than in the western suburbs which, by virtue of their relative affordability, have acted as a magnet for generations of new arrivals.

Leichhardt has been home to Sydney's large Italian community since the fishmongers and fruiterers,

Angelo Pomabello and the Bongiorno brothers, settled here in 1885. Norton Street, off Parramatta Road, is the main strip and provides an attractive and chic atmosphere of cafés and outdoor eating.

In nearby **Petersham** the regional theme continues, with part of New Canterbury Road forming the core of "Little Portugal". Delicious aromas emanate from bakeries, restaurants and cafés between Audley and Hunter streets, attempts to bewitch the visitor into partaking of the local community's spicy cuisine.

Further afield, in **Campsie**, lies "Korea Town". Apart from the great Korean food available along Beamish Street, further west down New Canterbury Road look out for the blue-aproned "Granny Squad", armed with baseball caps and rubbish bags, who at two o'clock every Thursday afternoon ensure Campsie stays one of the cleanest districts in the area. A little further to the southwest is **Lakemba**. Home of some infamous scrapes between local youths and the constabulary, the suburb, which is home to people of

BELOW: Arrival in Parramatta on the RiverCat Ferry.

some 120 nationalities, is also the place known as "Little Lebanon", particularly on Haldon Street, near the railway line north of Canterbury Road. Lebanese Australians have been part of Sydney life since the 1890s, and here you can benefit from the culture with some terrific and inexpensive meals, including baklava and delicious Lebanese coffee.

The suburbs of **Auburn** (near Parramatta Road and Homebush) and **Cabramatta** (off the Cumberland Highway) are the prime locations for Sydney's Turkish and Southeast Asian communities respectively. The arc of restaurants, cafés and Middle Eastern produce stores from Beatrice Street, along Auburn Road and down South Parade in Auburn mark out "Little Turkey". Sydney's finest Turkish pizza is on offer here and you can follow it with some Turkish delight *(lokum)* from the Real Turkish Delight shop, the owners of which baked their way into the *Guinness Book of Records* in 1997 with the largest single Turkish sweet ever made.

Cabramatta, known affection-ately as "Vietnamatta", is home to nearly 25,000 Australian Vietnamese. The centre of action is clustered around Hughes, Hill and Johns streets and Park Road, where you can gorge yourself on a wide range of choice "Vietnamattan" dishes and soak up the vibe of this robust and colourful community.

Parramatta

The most pleasant way to get to Parramatta is by the RiverCat Ferry from Circular Quay. The trip takes about an hour. Take an Explorer bus from the wharf (Wed–Sun), which stops at the major sites, or simply wander around on foot.

Parramatta is Aboriginal for either "head of the river" or "a place where eels lie down" – no one is quite sure which. The suburb is the demographic heart of Sydney, as well as the important commercial, industrial and residential centre of the west. It was secured from the Aboriginal Dharug, Dharawal and Gandangara people by force of arms, and was at one stage intended to be the capital of the new colony. From

Map on pages 130–1

An oars sculpture at Parramatta.

BELOW: Church Street, the heart of Parramatta.

The oldest surviving gravestone in Australia is that of Governor Phillip's butler, H.E. Dodd, who died in 1791. It can be found in St John's Cemetery on O'Connell Street.

a historical perspective, Parramatta's heyday was the time of European settlement, when it was a centre for social and cultural activity that far outshone Sydney Cove.

There is still much of interest in the area today. Start at the Parramatta Visitor's Centre at 346a Church Street (tel: 8839 3311), where you can pick up a locally produced map showing the historic sites and a brochure detailing a self-guided historic walk.

Parramatta Park ㉓ (entrance off O'Connell Street) is the site of many early Sydney constructions. The National Trust-run **Old Government House** is undoubtedly one of the most important historical buildings in Australia (open Tues–Fri 10am–4pm, Sat–Sun 11am–4pm; tel: 9635 8149; entrance fee). Designed in London by an accomplished practitioner of the neo-Gothic style, Edward Blore, Old Government House began as a relatively simple two-storey brick building in 1799, then was remodelled and extended by Lieutenant John Watts in 1815. The much admired ex-

BELOW: Old Government House, dating from 1799.

convict architect, Francis Greenway, is thought to have designed the front porch. Probably the oldest public building still standing in Australia, the house was used as a residence for governors and a meeting place for the social elite of the day. Its lime-washed walls are reminiscent of a time when Australia was viewed simply as a penal colony for the British Empire. Also located in Parramatta Park is the shell of the river-fed **Governor's Bath House**, erected by Governor Brisbane in 1823, and the ruined **Observatory**, Australia's first when it was completed in 1822.

Governor Macquarie's **Lancer Barracks** in Smith Street were completed in 1820, and are the oldest military establishment in Australia. They are still used by the army, and there is a small military museum open to the public in Linden House (open Sun; tel: 9365 7822; entrance fee). **St John's Church** in Church Street was built in 1799 and then rebuilt to its current form under the guidance of Lieutenant Watts and Mrs Elizabeth Macquarie around 1815.

Other sites of significance within

easy reach are **Hambledon Cottage**, dating from 1822, at 63 Hassell Street, and **Elizabeth Farm** at 70 Alice Street, Rosehill, which was built in 1793, just five years after the arrival of the First Fleet. Both belonged to the wool pioneers John and Elizabeth Macarthur, and each established an architectural precedent, for the single-storey city homestead and for the country farmhouse respectively. Elizabeth Farm was the original abode of the Macarthurs and is arguably the oldest standing private European building in Australia (open daily 10am–5pm; tel: 9635 9488; entrance fee).

Hambledon Cottage was the home of the Macarthurs' governess (open Wed–Thur, Sat–Sun and public holidays 11am–4pm; tel: 9635 6924; entrance fee).

Experiment Farm Cottage at 9 Ruse Street marks the site of the first grant of land in the colony. It was given to convicts James and Elizabeth Ruse, who were pardoned in 1789 as a reward for producing the first wheat crop in the colony, and registered in 1791. The land was eventually bought by a surgeon, John Harris, who built the cottage in 1834 (open Tues–Thur 10am–4pm, Sun 11am–4pm; tel: 9635 5655; entrance fee).

Homebush Bay

Homebush Bay ㉔, spreading out on the south side of the Parramatta River, is a major recreation, sports and leisure precinct for the city, as well as the site that hosted the Sydney 2000 Olympics.

Access is via the Great Western Highway and the M4 (Western Motorway), but car travel is not the best option. The massive new infrastructure that ensured a good ride to the Games means the suburb probably has a better public transport service than any other district in Australia. Pick up a RiverCat Ferry from Circular Quay, or catch a train from Central or Town Hall to the award-winning Olympic Park Station, a modern glass-and-steel structure recalling the grand old railway stations of 19th-century Europe. Once there, you can obtain a map and brochures from the **Sydney Olympic Park Visitor Centre** (tel: 9714 7545) at the corner of Showground Road and Murray Rose Avenue.

The history of Homebush Bay is that of a suburb that has suffered more than its fair share from the indignities of urbanisation. Deforested early on, it was used, at various stages, as the site for a brickworks, a racecourse, an armaments depot and an abattoir, before becoming contaminated in the 1960s and 1970s from the uncontrolled dumping of toxic waste. The changes in recent times have been vast, fast and phenomenal.

After the 2000 Olympic Games were won for Sydney in 1993, some A$3 million a day were spent in transforming the suburb and surrounding areas. Apart from the sporting venues (see page 51), there are a number of sites worth noting.

Map on pages 130–1

Woodchopping contest at the Easter Fair, held at the Telstra Stadium.

BELOW: the Telstra Stadium, built for the 2000 Olympics at Homebush Bay.

Map on pages 130–1

A koala to cuddle in Featherdale Wildlife Park.

BELOW: making friends with a wallaby at Featherdale.

The **Olympic Games Village**, which was located just across the river from Sydney Olympic Park, comprised temporary and permanent residences, being built initially to house 15,000 visiting athletes and officials, but afterwards the houses were sold off to private residents. The owners now benefit from having some of the world's best and most modern sporting facilities in their own back yard.

Olympic Boulevard, the main access between the sporting venues of Olympic Park and the Athletes' Village, was designed as a sweeping tree-lined thoroughfare.

Fronting the waters of Homebush Bay is the magnificent **Bicentennial Park**, part of which is the Millennium Parklands, a massive project designed to reclaim the area around the Parramatta River from the ravages of urban abuse and turn it into one of Sydney's main leisure areas. There are 60 hectares (150 acres) of parkland built across hills with walking and cycling tracks, playgrounds and picnic areas, and 40 hectares (100 acres) of conservation wetlands

replicating the complex ecology of one Australia's most sensitive natural environments. Tours of the area can be arranged through the Visitor Centre (tel: 9714 7545).

At the eastern end of the park, on Underwood Road at the corner of Homebush Bay Drive, is the vast Direct Factory Outlets (DFO) shopping complex (open daily 10am–6pm; tel: 9748 9800), a favourite with brand-name junkies. The site acts as the Sydney clearance centre for over 100 upmarket retailers and fashion labels. With prices below those that even the most hardened duty-free shopper would expect, DFO is a 15-minute walk from Olympic Park train station along Australia Avenue.

Wildlife parks

Koala Park, located on Castle Hill Road, West Pennant Hills, is a long-established koala research centre and sanctuary. The park also contains emus, kangaroos, wallabies, wombats and native Australian birds (open daily 9am–5pm; tel: 9484 3141; entrance fee). In Kildare Road, Doonside, is the **Featherdale Wildlife Park**, famous for having the largest private collection of Australian animals and birds. It's possible to cuddle a koala, those ambassadors for Australian tourism, or just watch one go about its business in a natural setting (open daily 9am–5pm; tel: 9622 1644; entrance fee).

More furry fauna is to be found at the **Australian Wildlife Park**, part of the Wonderland complex. You can pat the kangaroos, cuddle the koala bears, or just watch the extremely dangerous estuarine crocodiles – the "salties" as they are called by the folk from the remote north where the creatures are found (open daily; tel: 9830 9100, or 9830 9106 for 24-hour recorded information; entrance fee). ❏

RESTAURANTS & BARS

Restaurants

Costa do Sol
77 New Canterbury Road, Petersham
Tel: 9569 2319
Open: Wed–Mon 11.30am–10.30pm. **$$**
European and seafood menu with a Portuguese and Spanish influence. Caters to large groups. Gets noisy.

DFO
Cnr Underwood Road and Homebush Bay
Tel: 9748 9800
Open: 10am–6pm daily. **$**
The vast DFO shopping centre has several inexpensive unlicensed eateries. This is the best place for a snack, coffee or a quick meal when exploring the Olympic Park.

El-Manara
143 Haldon Street, Lakemba
Tel: 9740 6762
Open: B, L & D daily, 9am–10pm. **$**

PRICE CATEGORIES

Price indications are for a three-course meal for one, including half a bottle of house wine, coffee and service.
$ = under A$50
$$ = A$50–75
$$$ = over A$75
Abbreviations: B = breakfast, L = lunch, D = dinner. BYO = bring your own alcohol.

Basic Lebanese eatery. No alcohol. The good prices and tasty authentic Lebanese fare make up for the average decor and service.

Frattini
122 Marion Street, Leichhardt
Tel: 9569 2997
Open: L Mon–Fri, D Mon–Sat. **$$**
Wholesome Italian food and a genuine Italian atmosphere pervades this family-run, service-oriented BYO restaurant noted for its dumplings.

La Perla
255 Victoria Street, Gladesville
Tel: 9816 1161
Open: L Tues–Fri, D Fri–Sun. **$$**
A terrific bustling French and seafood restaurant that gets busy on weekends. BYO.

Pho Minh
42 Arthur Street, Cabramatta
Tel: 9726 5195
Open: L & D daily. **$**
One of the many Vietnamese noodle eateries in Cabramatta, basic but spacious, with very economical prices. Also has a seafood menu, and simple, no-fuss service.

River Canyon
96 Philip Street, Parramatta
Tel: 9689 2288
Open: L & D daily. **$$$**
Modern Australian cuisine and steakhouse in historic, colonial Parramatta. Has live music, outdoor dining and bar.

La Roche
Shop 5, 61 Haldon Street, Lakemba
Tel: 9759 9527
Open: B, L & D daily. **$**
Traditional Lebanese food in a no-frills, economical environment. Open all day.

Se Joung
68–72 Evaline Street, Campsie
Tel: 9718 4039
Open: L & D daily 11am–11pm. **$**
Traditional Korean food (try the raw beef dish). Has an authentic Korean feel – seating is on pillows, with small tables low to the ground. BYO.

Sofra
35–39 Auburn Road, Auburn
Tel: 9649 9299
Open: B, L & D daily, 8am to late. **$**
Turkish eatery with courtyard tables and free home delivery. An economical, no-frills affair. BYO.

Cafés and Bars

Alexander's
238 Church Street, Parramatta
A busy coffee house on Parramatta's main street that also serves up pizza and a seafood selection.

Bar Italia
169–171 Norton Street, Leichhardt
A long-established Italian coffee shop, noted for its delicious *gelati*. Open long hours – from breakfast to midnight – and also serves basic Italian fare like pasta.

Inside Out Cafe
99 Phillip Street, Parramatta
A coffee shop-cum-restaurant with a wide menu ranging from Modern Australian to seafood and Italian.

Leichhardt Hotel
95 Norton Street, Leichhardt
One of Norton Street's better pubs. Has been spruced up to give it a modern, funky edge; popular with the young crowd.

Mado Cafe
63 Auburn Road, Auburn
A Turkish coffee house open daily from breakfast until late. Pavement eating in the heart of Sydney's Turkish community. Also serves up interesting Turkish ice cream and baklava.

Oneworld Sports Bar
259 Church Street, Parramatta
This Aussie-style drinking barn on Parramatta's main road has a busy atmosphere and plenty of coverage of sporting events on the big screen.

TRIPS OUT OF SYDNEY

After just a short drive out of the city, you can be
in the lush New South Wales countryside, with
its peaceful atmosphere and hiking trails

With unspoilt natural beauty on their doorstep, most Sydneysiders take
regular trips out of the city, and visitors should try to do the same if
time allows. Within a 100-km (60-mile) radius of the city there are
12 national parks and six state recreation areas, vast stretches of coastline
and many other peaceful rural areas. An there's no shortage of things to do:
boating, swimming, board- and wind-surfing, scuba diving and snorkelling,
birdwatching, bush-walking, camping, horse-riding, cycling, hot-air bal-
looning, rock-climbing, hang-gliding, fishing and golf are all on offer, and
there's even wine-tasting and country-pub-crawling for the less active.

Getting out of town is simple. Sydney's excellent public transport system can get you to most locations with ease. Guided tours are also on offer
in many locations, as long as group activities don't cramp your style. The
Transport Infoline (tel: 13 15 00) offers public-transport timetables, trip
planners and a What's On round-up, free of charge, daily from 6am to
10pm. Or you can rent a car or camper-van from one of the many outlets
listed in the Yellow Pages telephone directory *(see page 215).*

Close to the city is the Hawkesbury River, which provides spectacular,
uncrowded and mostly unspoilt boating and sailboarding. Whatever the
craft, the scenery and atmosphere remain the same: forest-cloaked slopes
and tranquillity with a touch of civilisation if you choose to seek it out.

Out west, the stunning Blue Mountains and Wollemi national parks
offer excellent possibilities for many outdoor activities, including bush-
walking (gentle excursions or the serious type), rock-climbing, abseiling,
camping, canoeing, trout-fishing, golfing and horse-riding.

The more gentle Southern Highlands area abounds with pubs, guesthouses and farm accommodation, many of which provide day or weekend
horse-riding trips. The region is popular with golfers, too. The Central
Coast region is an array of inlets, bays and cliffs. Although much of the
coastline is fairly well populated, it's still possible to find quiet, undevel-
oped areas. If you're just searching for a patch of beach and some sun,
you'll find plenty of both.   ❑

PRECEDING PAGES: Hanging Rock, Grose Valley, in the Blue Mountains; fishing off
a jetty in Gosford on the Central Coast. **LEFT:** the Zig Zag Railway near Lithgow.

THE UPPER HAWKESBURY

To the west of Sydney, bounded by the impressive Hawkesbury River, is a treasure trove of early 19th-century colonial architecture, set amid a striking backdrop of national parks

Map on page 186

The fertile region of the Upper Hawkesbury River, 50 km (30 miles) northwest of Sydney, was discovered by Governor Phillip in 1789, who observed that the country was "as fine as I ever saw". Much of the land had been "fire-stick" cultivated and owned by the Dharug, Dharawal and Gandangara Aboriginal people for hundreds of years. Phillip named the area Green Hills and quickly colonised it on behalf of the near-starving colony of Sydney Cove. By 1794, 22 settlers were ensconced in the Upper Hawkesbury area and by 1799 they and others on the river flats were producing between half and three-quarters of the colony's food requirements.

In 1810, Governor Lachlan Macquarie arrived in the wake of Governor William Bligh (of *Bounty* fame), who had just suffered his career-damaging rebellion. Macquarie and his wife Elizabeth were both dreamers, and full of plans and optimism for the potential they saw in the new colony: in a series of breathless initiatives in their first year, bridges, roads and wharves were built and many new public buildings and other civil engineering projects embarked upon.

In response to the Hawkesbury River's propensity to swell into calamitous floods, Macquarie laid out plans for a series of township developments on higher ground in the region, leading to the foundation of what became known as "Macquarie's Five Towns". Windsor, Richmond, Pitt Town, Wilberforce and (the now defunct) Castlereagh were established and planned with carefully designed public spaces and institutions. The design of many of the buildings for which Macquarie was responsible and the layout of the towns them-

LEFT: St Matthew's Church in Windsor.
BELOW: fishing in the Hawkesbury River.

TIP

To explore the area by river, Windsor Cruises (tel: 9217 7095) offer gourmet winery cruises, and Wiseman's Ferry Cruises (tel: 4575 5387) will take you up and down the Hawkesbury, MacDonald or Colo rivers. Houseboats are available for self-charter. Operators include Able Hawkesbury River Houseboats (tel: 1800 024 979), Ripples House Boat Holidays (tel: 9985 5555) and Holidays Afloat (tel: 9985 7368).

BELOW: the Hawkesbury Museum of Local History, in Windsor.

selves reflected the governor's beliefs in the Enlightenment values of Reason and Law.

The Hawkesbury River

The **Hawkesbury River** ❶, combined with the Nepean River, is 1,000 km (620 miles) in length and forms Australia's longest eastward-flowing river. It flows into the sea at Broken Bay, 30 km (20 miles) north of Sydney *(see page 147)*. Although the city has crept ever nearer, to this day the Hawkesbury region, set in a landscape of rolling hills and calm flowing waters and surrounded by national parks, provides probably the most authentic experience of rural colonial life in Australia. While agriculture is still pivotal in the region, the Hawkesbury has long been a pleasure ground for weary city workers and day-tripping tourists, both drawn to the area's wealth of cultural, scenic and environmental attractions.

The region is and has always been defined by its beautiful river, and there's really no better way to explore its reaches than on the water.

Options range from a day tour to a week spent on a houseboat.

Windsor

The town of **Windsor** ❷, approximately 30 km (20 miles) from Sydney, is named after the royal town on England's River Thames, and is the third-oldest site of European settlement in Australia. The area was settled by farmers in 1794 and joined by road to Sydney in the same year. The town of Windsor was named and established by Macquarie in 1810, and he also personally designed the town square. Of the five Macquarie towns, Windsor is considered the prime monument to the governor's planning achievements. It is the central of the five towns, and its layout and historic buildings make it a delightful place to explore.

Some of Windsor's attractions include several Georgian sandstone buildings built by Macquarie. Two of these, **St Matthew's Church** and the Rectory on George Street, were designed by the outstanding ex-convict architect Francis Greenway and date from 1817 to 1823. The church, known by locals as the "Cathedral of Hawkesbury", is the least altered of all Greenway's existing works and thus of national significance; the Rectory is considered the best of his domestic designs.

The church's graveyard has some interesting early graves, among them the burial site of Andrew Thompson, a man held in high esteem by Macquarie as an example of the powers of reason over evil and unlucky circumstance. Thompson had been sent to Australia as a 17-year-old convict and, in Macquarie's words, "distinguished himself by persevering industry and diligent attention to the commands of his Superiors." After hard work and heroic acts of selflessness in the Hawkesbury floods of 1806 and

1809, Thompson was made a chief magistrate of the district by Macquarie, the first ex-convict to gain such a position.

The **Macquarie Arms Hotel**, also on George Street, dates from 1815 and has been used continuously as a hotel for all but 34 years of its history (it was a private residence between 1840 and 1874). Sadly, generations of alterations have left the original structure barely discernible. The 1822 **Windsor Court House** at the corner of Pitt and Court streets is the oldest courthouse in Australia and another Greenway design. It was seriously altered for a period but was restored to its original glory in the 1960s, and displays the sandstock bricks and stone lintels so typical of the early 19th century.

John Tebbutt's House and **Observatory** on Palmer Street was once the home and recreation ground of the astronomer and gentleman farmer John Tebutt, whose portrait appeared on Australia's first $100 bill (in 1996 he gave way to Dame Nellie Melba). The house was built in 1845 by Tebbutt's father and inherited by John in 1870. His descendants own it to this day. Tebutt built two observatories, one in wood in 1863, and another in brick in 1879, to accommodate his passion for observation of the stars and endless calculation of the heavens.

Operating daily from the observatory is the **Clydesdales Restaurant** (tel: 4577 4544), a mobile, horse-drawn diner that deploys the gentle plod-power of mighty Clydesdale horses to take you sightseeing while you tuck in to a good feed.

The **Hawkesbury Museum of Local History** and Tourist Information Centre (open daily 10am–4pm; tel: 4577 2310; entrance fee) is a good place to stock up on local maps and information about both Windsor and Richmond, and has some excellent displays. These include Aboriginal artefacts, chronicles from the early settlers, and other details concerning the towns' development.

Thompson Square stands as a landscape tribute to 19th-century Reason, combining rational civic orderliness and a punishment the-

Map on page 186

Fishing on the Hawkesbury.

BELOW: the rodeo comes to Windsor.

atre, replete with a whipping post for convicts, which was once its central feature.

Richmond and Wilberforce

Richmond ❸, 7 km (4½ miles) from Windsor, was settled in 1794, along with Windsor, and formally established in 1810. The historic interest of Richmond lies predominantly in the 19th-century architecture, built when the town became a prosperous centre for market activity. **St Peter's Uniting Church** was constructed between 1837 and 1845, and its graveyard contains memorials to significant early pioneers, such as the convict chronicler Margaret Catchpole.

Wilberforce ❹, a small town on the edge of the river flats on Highway 69, was named after the British philanthropist and anti-slavery campaigner William Wilberforce. The main attraction, **Hawkesbury Heritage Farm** (open Thur–Sun; tel: 4575 1457; entrance fee), is situated just outside of town, and is a repository for numerous historic buildings and "edutainments" concerning

colonial life. Many of the historic buildings have been moved to the site from elsewhere, but **Rose Cottage** (1811) was built here, and remains as the oldest surviving timber dwelling in Australia. This lath-and-mud-plaster building was also the home of the colony's first free-settler family, headed by Thomas Rose, and his descendants occupied Rose Cottage right up until 1961.

Other buildings of interest include a church built from Huon pine in 1860, and a slab cottage from the 1840s. The Heritage Farm also offers a range of attractions in addition to the historic architecture. These include rides on Clydesdale horses, a collection of farm animals, a baby-animal nursery, a native-animal section including dingos, emus and kangaroos that may be hand-fed, and numerous bushcraft demonstrations including sheep-shearing, blacksmithing, whip-cracking, and traditional sheep round-ups.

In Wilberforce itself the sun-dried brick **Schoolhouse**, built in 1820, is worth a look. It is one of only four of

Heading from Windsor to Richmond you will pass the Royal Australian Air Force base, the oldest in the country. In 1912, a Mr W.E. Hart located a flying school here, which became the current RAAF base after the air force purchased the land in 1925.

BELOW: a forested river bank in Wollemi National Park.

the schools that Macquarie commissioned in the area to have survived to the modern era. Also of interest is **St John's Church**, which has a memorial sundial on the northern wall.

At nearby **Ebenezer** (along King Road from Wilberforce), the **Ebenezer Church** and **Schoolhouse** combines Australia's oldest church building, established in 1809, and Australia's oldest schoolhouse. The church was built by free-settler Scottish farmers who arrived in the district in 1806.

On Tizzana Road you will find **Tizzana Winery** (open weekends and public holidays noon–6pm; tel: 4579 1150), established in 1887 by Dr Thomas Henry Fiaschi. This much-admired medical practitioner emigrated from Florence in 1875. He no doubt brought the full weight of his training and experience to bear when he advocated the benefits of *vino* to a congregation of nurses in 1906, saying he believed wine to be "a valuable support to a man in this thorny path of life".

Wollemi and Cattai national parks

Wilberforce is also a good base town from which to explore the superb wilderness of **Wollemi National Park** ❺ (tel: 4588 5247 for the Richmond information office). At 4,930 sq km (1,900 sq miles), Wollemi is one of Australia's most ecologically important, rugged and impenetrable national parks, containing giant and ancient stands of forest, rugged gorges and wild rivers.

In 1994, the plant equivalent of a living dinosaur, the Wollemi Pine, was discovered to international acclaim in a small gorge within the park (as a protective measure the exact location is now a closely guarded secret). Another of the park's attractions is the Glow Worm Tunnel, best reached via Lithgow

(see page 187), which is home to the iridescent larvae of the attractively named fungus gnat.

More accessible from Wilberforce is the Colo Valley section of the Wollemi National Park, offering a variety of places, such as Riverside Park (tel: 4575 5253), that are excellent for touring, sightseeing, bush-walking, canoeing and camping. Eco-touring is also available with outfits such as Eco-Escapes (tel: 9873 5959) who offer canoeing day-trips along the valley.

The 425-hectare (1,050-acre) **Cattai National Park** ❻ (tel: 4572 3100), split into two parts on the banks of the Cattai Creek and the Hawkesbury River respectively, preserves some important traces of early Australian history, fauna and remnant vegetation. You can trek, paddle a canoe, camp out or go for a horse ride here, or check out the small wilderness area of forest and wetlands preserved in Mitchell Park. Also worth a visit is the **Cattai Homestead** (open Sun noon–4pm, tel: 4572 3100), built in 1821 by Dr Thomas Arndell, an assistant

Map on page 186

BELOW: tackling the rapids in Wollemi National Park.

surgeon on the First Fleet. After being held for seven generations by the Arndell family, the homestead now provides limited public access and has displays outlining 160 years of the family's history.

Pitt Town: the finest of Macquarie's creations

Another interesting route from Windsor is along the Pitt Town, Cattai and Wiseman's Ferry roads. **Pitt Town ❼** was established by Lachlan Macquarie in 1811 and named after the illustrious British statesman and twice prime minister, William Pitt the Younger. The tiny town has largely escaped the ravages of time and development and has numerous 19th-century buildings, including the restored **Bird in Hand Hotel** that dates from 1825. It is thought by some to be the finest of the remaining Macquarie towns, its small-village ambience strongly evoking the Victorian era.

Pitt Town owes its preservation, at least in part, to its distance from the rich farming frontages near the river. Farmers had to travel too far from

the town to their plots of land, thus development was slow. Bathurst Street has a number of buildings of interest including the **Maid of Australia Inn**, which served its popular home brew between the 1850s and the 1890s, and the **St James Anglican** (1857) and **Scots Presbyterian** (1862) churches.

There are also a number of other impressively aged structures of weatherboard and slab worth a look. The Bona Vista mansion at 1888 Johnston Street, has a gentrified layout that includes an assembly of Norfolk Island pines and camphor laurels down the length of its long driveway.

Pitt Town Bottoms Road was the very early site of Sydney Cove's food salvation. It was here that Lieutenant-Governor Francis Grose granted the first allotments of fifteen 12-hectare (30-acre) farms to free settlers, for the purposes of growing produce for the colony. From here the produce was ferried down the river to Broken Bay, out into the open sea, and then down into Sydney Harbour.

In spring the trees are burdened with blossom.

BELOW: St James's Church, Pitt Town.

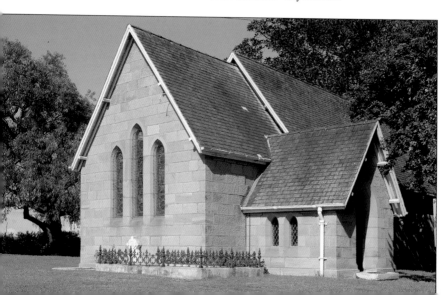

Wiseman's Ferry and Dharug National Park

Past Cattai National Park along the Wiseman's Ferry Road, you come to the picturesque old farming settlement of **Wiseman's Ferry** ❽ on the Hawkesbury River. The **Wiseman's Ferry Inn** was originally the home of Solomon Wiseman, an ex-convict who was granted land and pioneered settlement in this area. The ferry service that he started is the oldest in the country and still runs 24 hours a day. The inn provides accommodation and is rumoured to be haunted by the ghost of Solomon's wife, an unfortunate woman who is believed to have met her end here after being pushed down the front steps by her husband.

On the opposite side of the Hawkesbury is **Dharug National Park** ❾, which is famous for its examples of ancient Aboriginal rock art dating back 10,000 years (access to sites is limited; contact the park ranger for details, tel: 4320 4200). The park gets its name from the area's traditional owners, the Dharug people, and is bounded to the west by the Great North Road (which is not open to vehicle access but can be trekked).

Another pleasant tour from Wiseman's Ferry is along the MacDonald Valley up to the sleepy heritage hamlet of **St Albans**. Here you can visit the gravestones of St Albans Old Cemetery that dates back to 1837, or take a look at Price Morris Cottage built in 1833. ❑

> Map on page 186

The Great North Road was built by convict labour in 1827. The grim hangman's rock is where recalcitrant prisoners were subjected to some of the more brutal social engineering of the day.

RESTAURANTS & BARS

Bar Piazza
42 Camberwell Road, Vineyard
An Italian-style coffee shop on Camberwell Road. The place to get real coffee far from the Italian influence of Sydney's chic inner-city cafés and restaurant strips.

Clydesdales Restaurant
Palmer Street, Windsor
Tel: 4577 4544
Open: L & D daily. **$$**
Highly unusual mobile restaurant: the "dining room" is a restored 1890s bus with lace curtains, velour seats and antique fittings, pulled by three Clydesdales. It seats only eight guests for three-course lunches or five-course dinners.

Wine and dine while viewing the historic streets of Windsor rolling by. A typical dinner party lasts three to four hours. Seating is in pairs, perfect for romantic couples.

Embers
332–334 Windsor Street, Richmond
Tel: 4588 5028
Open: L & D daily. **$**
A popular and laid-back pizza eatery with pavement tables. Licensed or BYO. Friendly service and a basic but tasty menu.

Royal Cricketers Arms
385 Reservoir Road, Prospect
Tel: 9622 6498
Open: L Mon–Fri, D Sun, Tues–Fri. **$$**

Founded in 1880, The Cricketers is situated in a heritage building with large open fireplaces and a rural, vintage feel. Good Modern Australian cuisine and an extensive bar. Attracts a daytime business crowd. Plenty of room to move, and more atmosphere than many local watering holes.

The Snooty Fox
122 Windsor Street, Richmond
Tel: 4588 5808
Open: L & D daily. **$**
A large beer garden with informal bistro/ brasserie attached on a veranda with tree-shaded gardens. Often has live music to keep visitors entertained.

Trentino's on George
89 George Street, Windsor
Tel: 4587 7419
Open: B, L & D daily. **$**
Modern Australian cuisine on the site of Fitzgerald House in Windsor. Emphasis is on outdoor undercover dining, heated in winter. Also serves as a breakfast and all-day coffee stop-off.

PRICE CATEGORIES

A three-course meal for one, including half a bottle of house wine, coffee and service:
$ = under A$50
$$ = A$50–75
Abbreviations: B = breakfast, L = lunch, D = dinner. BYO = bring your own alcohol.

THE BLUE MOUNTAINS

**Less than two hours' drive from the centre of
Sydney is one of Australia's most spectacular
natural regions, where lush valleys and high
escarpments stretch as far as the eye can see**

One of Sydney's favourite recreation areas and now regarded
as part of the city's commuter
belt, the Blue Mountains once presented a frustrating barrier to the
early European settlers in their
search for more pastoral land. First
named the Carmarthen and Landsdowne Hills by Governor Phillip in
1788, the current name comes from
the effect of the refraction of light on
minute droplets of eucalyptus oil
from the millions of gum trees that
cover the mountains. Viewed from a
distance, they appear in a blue haze.

In geological terms, the Blue
Mountains form a spur in the Great
Dividing Range – a huge dissected
sandstone plateau that is the result
of long processes of sedimentary
deposits, uplifting, volcanic activity
and constant erosion. During the
past 3 million years the uplifting
process raised the tableland a further
1,200 metres (4,000 ft) and created
the cliffs, deep valleys and gorges
and accompanying rivers that make
the area so appealing today.

The mountains are just part of
one of NSW's largest national parks,
and feature a host of natural attractions. Extremely popular with bushwalkers and rock-climbers, the area
is full of history too – houses,
monuments, museums and even the
creation of the road and railway

yield a host of pioneering tales. A
visitor should set aside at least two
days to explore this area – or three
or four days if contemplating a more
in-depth look or a visit to the
Jenolan Caves.

Map
on page
186

Bell's Line of Road

To approach the mountains by the
northern road, leave Richmond *(see
page 180)*, pass over the Nepean
River and head through Kurrajong
on the **Bell's Line of Road**, which
was constructed in 1868. The route

LEFT: morning mist
shrouds the Blue
Mountains. **BELOW:**
you can tour the
mountains by
"London bus".

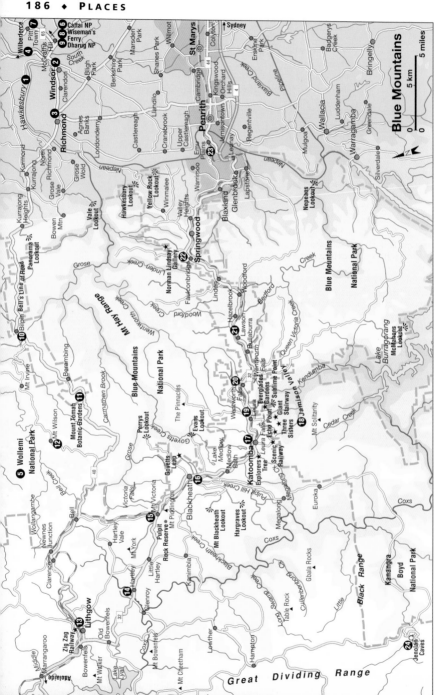

Blue Mountains

Wilberforce
Pitt Town
Cattai NP
McGraths Hill
Wiseman's Ferry
Dharug NP
Windsor
Richmond
St Marys
Sydney
Marsden Park
Wilmot
Berkshire Park
Shanes Park
Bligh Park
South Creek
Clarendon
Berkshire Park
Agnes Banks
Grose Vale
Grose Wold
Cranebrook
Llandilo
Castlereagh
Upper Castlereagh
Kingswood
Orchard Hills
Penrith
Cambridge Park
Colyton
Kingswood
Erskine Park
Badgerys Creek
Bringelly
Londonderry
Leonay
Jamisontown
Regentville
Mulgoa
Wallacia
Luddenham
Greendale
Kurmond
Norri
Richmond
Kurrajong
Grose Vale
Bowen Mtn
Emu Plains
Regentville
Warragamba
Silverdale
Kurrajong Heights
Panorama Lookout
Bell's Line of Road
Blaxland
Glenbrook
Lapstone
Nepean Lookout
Bilpin
Mt Irvine
Berambing
Bowen Mtn
Hawkesbury Lookout
Yellow Rock Lookout
Warrimoo
Valley Heights
Blaxland
Glenbrook
Lapstone
Blue Mountains National Park
Vale Lookout
Winmalee
Springwood
Norman Lindsay Gallery
Faulconbridge
Woodford
Hazelbrook
Bedford
Bullaburra
Mt Wilson
Mount Tomah Botanic Gardens
Wollemi National Park
Mt Hay Range
Grose
Wentworth Creek
Linden Creek
Woodford
Lindec
Lawson
Bullaburra
Queen Victoria Creek
The Pinnacles
Blue Mountains National Park
Perrys Lookout
Govetts Creek
Evans Lookout
Wentworth Falls
Leura
Everglades Gardens
Sublime Point
Giant Stairway
Three Sisters
Mt Solitary
Jamison Valley
Kendumba
Lake Burragorang
McMahons Lookout
Mt York
Hartley Vale
Lake Medlow
Medlow Bath
Katoomba
Explorers Tree
Leura Falls
Echo Point
Scenic Railway
Megalong Valley
Cedar Creek
Blackheath
Mt Victoria
Govetts Leap
Victoria Falls
Pulpit Rock Reserve
Mt Blackheath Lookout
Hargraves Lookout
Kanimbla
Blackheath Creek
Megalong
Euroka
Coxs
Lithgow
Zig Zag Railway
Hartley
Little Hartley
Mt York
Glenroy
Old Bowenfels
Bowenfels
Mt Walker
Lowther
Hampton
Gbala Rocks
Black Range
Kanangra Boyd National Park
Jenolan Caves
Great Dividing Range
Coxs
Little
Little Hartley
Lords Sydney
Cullenbenbong Creek
Table Rock
Clarence
Newnes Junction
Wollangambe Creek
Bell
Bell's Line of Road

Hawkesbury
Nepean
Grose
South Creek
Blaxland Creek
Wentworth Creek
Carmarthen Brook
Govets Creek
Kendumba
Pulpit Hill Creek
Megalong Creek
Blackheath Creek
Kanimbla Creek
Coxs River

0 5 km
0 5 miles

is extremely scenic and presents excellent views from its many twists and turns. Pass through the apple-growing village of **Bilpin** , which is wedged between the borders of Wollemi National Park to the north (*see page 181*) and the Blue Mountains National Park to the south. Further on, the **Mount Tomah Botanic Garden** ⓫ (open daily; tel: 4567 3000; entrance fee) are worth a visit. This Bicentennial project is an offshoot of Sydney's Royal Botanic Gardens, and displays cool-climate plants in a series of walking trails as well as a formal garden. The gardens flow across a series of terraces down the slopes of the mountain and the views are spectacular.

Between Mount Tomah and the small village of Bell, it is possible to make a side excursion to **Mount Wilson** ⓬. This area of high rainfall and rich volcanic soil has produced some of the region's best private gardens, which open to the public in spring and autumn (tel: 4739 6266 for locations and opening times). From Mount Wilson there are panoramic views of the mountain range. Many of the gardens and houses here date from the 19th century, and the village is virtually unchanged since then. One of the old houses, Withycombe, was once home to Australia's most famous author, Patrick White.

Lithgow and Hartley

Just before Bell the road divides, one route leading directly to Mount Victoria while the other goes to **Lithgow** ⓭, an industrial city set in a narrow valley on the western side of the range. Coal has been mined here since 1869, and new mines and a power station have grown up around the 19th-century buildings in the town's main street. Lithgow's novelty interest, however, is the **Zig Zag Railway**, a stretch of line built in the 1860s to descend the western

escarpment of the mountains. A steam-train ride on the line gives a sense of the difficulties encountered in opening up this inland area (tel: 6353 1795 for details).

From Lithgow return to the mountains through the village of **Hartley** ⓮. The township was established in 1838 as an outpost on the fringe of the uncharted western plains. For the pioneers continuing westwards, it was their last touch with secure settlement. Today Hartley is a historic site that reflects the spartan pioneering lifestyle of the mid-1800s. It also contains some impressive public buildings from that era, such as the 1840s post office, the oldest remaining in Australia, and the 1837 courthouse which predates the township. Built in the Greek Revival style, the courthouse was used as such for only 50 years, but in its time saw a colourful and constant flow of convicts and bushrangers confined within its lock-up. Today it houses a museum. St Bernard's Catholic Church also dates from this time.

The historic site is managed by the

Map on page 186

The site of Hartley was originally called the Vale of Clwydd, because it reminded Governor Macquarie of the Welsh valley of that name.

BELOW:
a Protea, originally from South Africa, in the Mount Tomah Botanic Garden.

NSW National Parks and Wildlife Service, and there is an information centre at Farmers Inn on the Great Western Highway (tel: 6355 2117).

Looking over the Blue Mountains.

Mount Victoria and around

Continuing east along the Great Western Highway you will reach **Mount Victoria** ⓯. At 1,110 metres (3,665 ft), it is the highest and coldest point in this part of the range. The entire Mount Victoria area is National Trust classified, and historic buildings include the post office, the 1849 **Tollkeeper's Cottage** and the 1870s **St Peter's Church**. The railway arrived here in 1868 and the old railway station now includes a museum dedicated to the region.

Several vantage points in the district give spectacular views of the Grose Valley (from Victoria Falls Lookout) and, from Pulpit Rock Reserve and Mount Piddington, the Kanimbla Valley to the south. At nearby Mount York there is a monument to the explorers of the Blue Mountains and some bush-walking trails that follow the tracks the pioneers took as they sought the route to the west.

Blackheath ⓰ is the next main town on the highway. Originally called Hounslow, the settlement was renamed by Macquarie on his return from Bathurst in 1815 because of its black and wild look. The town grew up around the railway and was a stopping place for 19th-century miners heading west to the gold fields. The local **Bacchante Gardens**, featuring more than 1,500 rhododendrons in a bush setting, are worth a visit (open daily; tel: 4787 7624; entrance by donation).

The area also has spectacular views of the tree-lined Grose Valley from Evans Lookout and **Govetts Leap**, the starting point for a variety of bush-walks, from a quick stroll to five- or six-hour hikes to the valley floor or the Grand Canyon, a chasm that has become something of a mecca for canyoning enthusiasts. The impressive **Bridal Falls** is the highest waterfall in the Blue Mountains.

The **Blue Mountains Heritage Centre**, headquarters for the Blue Mountains National Park, is on

BELOW RIGHT:
the Sceniscender cable car climbs 545 metres (790 ft).

The Blue Mountains Explorers

Lieutenant Watkin Tench reached the foothills near Penrith in 1789, and many attempts were made to cross the mountains between 1793 and 1804, when botanist George Caley eventually reached Mount Tomah and opened up the first passable route into the northern foothills. But it wasn't until 1813 that the explorers Gregory Blaxland, William Wentworth and William Lawson carefully planned their route over the Grose and Cox rivers and crossed the entire range. They eventually reached the present-day site of Hartley on the western side of the mountains. The three men founded the first viable path over this seemingly impenetrable border, and all now have towns named in their honour.

From 1815, convict labour was used to build the road along the explorers' route (the present Great Western Highway), and by 1817 a military stockade was in existence at Springwood. Caley's northern route was fully explored in 1823 by Archibald Bell, and is still called Bell's Line of Road. By 1869 a railway across the range led to permanent settlement in the area. In the 1870s the region came to be regarded primarily as a holiday centre.

Govetts Leap Road, and it is worth dropping in for its useful information on the Aboriginal history of the area and on local walks that are available (tel: 4787 8877).

From here, a trip can be made down over the escarpment into the Megalong Valley, a tranquil farming area that offers horse-riding and a different perspective of the region. Return to the main road via the Shipley Plateau, famous for its apple orchards. En route to Katoomba, stop at the **Hydro Majestic Hotel** at Medlow Bath. Built between 1880 and 1903, this Edwardian folly with art deco touches offers stunning views over the Megalong Valley (tel: 4788 1002).

Katoomba

Before Katoomba, the road passes the **Explorers Tree**, commemorating Blaxland, Lawson and Wentworth's successful 1813 journey. This is also the starting point for an ambitious bush-walk, the Six Foot Track, which leads to Jenolan Caves and takes two to three days to complete.

Katoomba ⓱, built on a series of hills that drop steeply into the Jamison Valley, is now a major tourist centre and the undisputed capital of the Blue Mountains. The town's early development was due to the discovery of coal in 1841, but it has been a holiday resort since the late 19th century, when the first guesthouses were established in the wake of the railway.

The first stop should be **Echo Point**, where there is a large information centre run by the Blue Mountains Tourism Authority (open daily 9am–5pm; tel: 1300 653 408 for information). The point gives a magnificent view over the **Jamison Valley** ⓲, including the famous **Three Sisters** rock formation. In Aboriginal legend, these ancient rocky pinnacles are believed to be three sisters imprisoned by their father as a form of protection from bunyips (fierce creatures, half-animal, half-spirit, believed to inhabit creeks and water-holes). The nearby **Giant Stairway** has 1,000 steps to the valley floor, where there are several short walks. Leura Forest is a perfect example of Australia's

Map on page 186

 TIP

The best time of day to view the Three Sisters is late afternoon, when the bus tours have moved on and the three sandstone pillars are bathed in golden light.

BELOW: siblings of Narrabeen sandstone, the Three Sisters.

*The Sceniscender
cable car.*

temperate east-coast rainforest areas.

Further along, the more adventurous can choose between swinging out over the valley in a cable car or riding on what is reputed to be the world's steepest train line. The **Scenic Skyway** was built in the late 1950s as a tourist attraction. It suspends its brave passengers 175 metres (580 ft) in the air along its 500-metre (1,650-ft) horizontal cable, offering a wonderful view of the valley below. Alternatively, the new **Sceniscender**, Australia's steepest cable car, plunges down to the rainforest floor of the Jamison Valley below.

For equally spectacular views and an even more terrifying experience, the **Scenic Railway** gives the sensation of plunging vertically 445 metres (1,460 ft) down to the valley floor (in fact it's a 45-degree incline). It was not always a scenic railway, but constructed in the 1880s to transport miners and coal between the town and the valley floor. Both the cable cars and the railway operate daily at 10-minute intervals (tel: 4782 2699; entrance fee). A short drive can also be taken out along the Narrow Neck Plateau, a wall of rock that juts out between the Megalong and Jamison valleys, affording grand views of the eucalyptus forests and farming land below.

Back in Katoomba, visit the art deco 1930s **Paragon Café**, National Trust-classified and famous for its afternoon teas and home-made chocolates. The town also has a large variety of art and craft galleries – try the **Breewood Galleries** – and several museums. For the more active there are dozens of short or strenuous bush-walks in the area, or you can even try your hand at abseiling or rock-climbing. The **Edge Maxivision Cinema** in Katoomba, with its six-storey-high screen, features an adventure-packed film on the Blue Mountains taking the audience over cliff edges and up rock faces that most of us are never likely to see any other way (tel: 4782 8900 for details).

Leura and Leuralla

Take the cliff drive to nearby **Leura** ⓳, the prettiest village in the mountains. Its historic main street, rem-

iniscent of the 1920s, has been restored and abounds with craft, antiques and tea shops. The **Everglades Gardens**, 6 km (3½ miles) from the town centre, cover 13 hectares (32 acres), with more than half given over to formal plantings arranged over six terraces. Unlike many of the mountain gardens that feature mass plantings of flowers, Everglades has a restrained, classical quality, and was designed by landscaper Paul Sorensen to blend with the surrounding bushland (open daily; tel: 4784 1938; entrance fee).

Leuralla is a stately home built in 1914 in art deco style, and was the home of Dr H.V. Evatt, the only Australian president of the United Nations General Assembly. The house includes a collection of 19th-century Australian art and many other objects of interest, as well as a restaurant and a toy museum (open daily; tel: 4784 1169; entrance fee).

Sublime Point, just out of town, is another spectacular lookout, and the luxurious Fairmont Resort is located here.

Wentworth Falls and back to Sydney

The next stop on the way back to Sydney is **Wentworth Falls ㉑**, a village named after one of the three explorers who found the way west, and is home to the famous waterfalls that spill into the Jamison Valley. Areas of rainforest exist around the edges of the waterfall.

A visit to **Yester Grange** is also recommended. This 1880s Victorian house is perched on 4.7 hectares (11½ acres) of grounds above the valley and contains a museum, art gallery and tea-rooms (open daily; tel: 4757 1110).

Continuing east, you are now in the lower mountains on the coastal side of the range. Pass through **Lawson ㉑**, named for the explorer who, with Wentworth and Blaxland, successfully crossed these mountains.

Continue on through Woodford, once the site of a convict road-building camp, to **Faulconbridge ㉒**, where you'll find the **Norman Lindsay Gallery and Museum** (open daily; tel: 4751 1067; entrance fee). One of Australia's

Map on page 186

TIP

If you visit the Blue Mountains at the end of October, take time to stop in Leura during the town's Garden Festival, when many of the beautiful private gardens open to the public (tel: 4757 2539).

BELOW: Wentworth Falls, named after one of the Blue Mountains pioneers.

TIP

The company Auswalk (tel: 6457 2220) offers old-fashioned walking tours of the district, which feature comfortable bed-and-breakfast accommodation at the end of each day.

most accomplished writers, artists and sculptors, Lindsay lived in this stone cottage for 57 years up to his death in 1969. The house contains an important collection of his paintings, drawings, etchings (he specialised in twee scenes of voluptuous Bacchanalia), novels and ship models, and is now owned by the National Trust. A whole room in the house is devoted to *The Magic Pudding*, Lindsay's most famous children's book, known throughout Australia, and there is an authentic re-creation of his original artists' studio. The peaceful landscaped gardens, set amid the surrounding bushland, include several of Lindsay's larger statues and fountains (open Fri–Sun and public holidays).

Also of interest in Faulconbridge is the **Prime Ministers' Corridor of Oaks**, in which a tree has been planted by every Australian prime minister or his family. This is also the grave site of Sir Henry Parkes, five times NSW premier and the father of the Australian Federation.

Descending the foothills towards Sydney you pass through Springwood, Blaxland (the last town to be named after a member of the trio of explorers, who subsequently helped pioneer winemaking in Australia), Glenbrook and finally Lapstone, with its 1867 Zig Zag Railway – the less famous counterpart of the Lithgow line on the other side of the mountains. The **Blue Mountains Visitor Information Centre** on the Great Western Highway at Glenbrook has details about walks and attractions in the area (tel: 1300 653 408). There is a four-hour return walking track to Red Hand Cave, the sight of some extraordinary early Aboriginal hand stencils on rock.

At **Emu Plains** ㉓ (named after the long-gone emus which originally dwelt here) you cross the Nepean River once more and can return to Sydney via the suburbs of Penrith and Parramatta *(see page 165)*. Alternatively, if you have more time, just 130 km (80 miles) from Hartley, a turn-off from the Great Western Highway will take you to the spectacular **Jenolan Caves** ㉔ in the southwest of the park *(see below)*.

BELOW: the "Grand Column" in the Jenolan Caves.

The Jenolan Caves

Skirt the Kanangra Boyd National Park along a steep, winding road and eventually round a bend to be confronted by the spectacle of the 24-metre-high (79-ft) Grand Arch, the beginning of Australia's most famous cave system. Jenolan, derived from the Aboriginal "Geonowlan", the name of a nearby mountain, is set on a spur of the Great Dividing Range, riddled with a vast cave system which was discovered in 1838. These limestone caverns contain an amazing diversity of weird formations – stalactites, stalagmites, paper-thin "straws", cave pools and rivers, and some other strangely sculpted shapes.

The cave system forms a massive underground labyrinth in the hillside. The nine caves open to the public are just a tiny part of the entire system – there are estimated to be some 300 caves, created 300 million years ago, although no one is sure of the exact number. The caves are part of a 2,500-hectare (6,180-acre) wildlife reserve which contains kangaroos, echidnas and other native flora and fauna. Bush-camping and picnic facilities are available in the area.

Map
on page
186

Adventure sports in the Blue Mountains

If you want more than a sightseeing drive through the region, there are plenty of outdoor pursuits. If golf takes your fancy, there are excellent courses at Leura, Katoomba, Wentworth Falls, Springwood and Blackheath. Horse-riders are also well catered for within the park. Riding tours mostly set off from Megalong Valley, with overnight stays in farmstyle accommodation available as part of the package. Contact Megalong Valley Heritage Farm and Visitor Centre (tel: 4787 8688) for more information.

The Blue Mountains have also become a popular centre for adventure sports including rock-climbing, abseiling and canyoning. Local operators include the Australian School of Mountaineering (tel: 4782 2014) and Blue Mountains Adventure Company (tel: 4782 1271). Packages include tuition and range from half a day to a week-long experience. Equipment is provided. Walking remains the favourite activity in this region. ❑

RESTAURANTS & BARS

Cafe Bon Ton
192 The Mall, Leura
Tel: 4782 4377
Open: L daily, D Wed–Mon,
B Sat–Sun. **$**
A relaxed place in the heart of the Mall, with courtyard tables, an attached coffee shop and economical prices. Open long hours, including weekend breakfasts.

Faulconbridge Chinese Restaurant
460 Great Western Highway,
Faulconbridge
Tel: 4751 7088
Open: D daily. **$$**
A large but intimate licensed Chinese restaurant with a wide selection of dishes, including a pricier Chef's Suggestion menu. Service is friendlier and more attentive – and prices more competitive – than in central Sydney restaurants.

Gardner's Inn Hotel
255 Great Western Highway,
Blackheath
Open: B, L & D daily. **$**
A lively pub with a well-stocked bar. There is also a roomy outdoor deck bar with table service. Serves Modern Australian cuisine all day in the restaurant.

Hana
Top Floor, 121 The Mall,
Leura
Tel: 4784 1345
Open: L & D Tues–Sat. **$**
Hana, in the "Pins And Noodles" building, is a very affordable Japanese restaurant. Its terrace tables and set lunch menu (A$11–14.50) are always popular. Licensed and BYO.

Journey
54 Katoomba Street,
Katoomba
Tel: 4782 2335
Open: B, L & D Mon–Fri,
B & L Sat. **$**
Marketing itself as an "international café", Journey has a diverse array of snacks and meals amid spacious decor including pavement tables and a function room. BYO.

Paragon Café
65 Katoomba Street,
Katoomba
Open: all day for snacks. **$**
Famous café with 1930s art deco interior, serving home-cooked foods, great coffee and delicious chocolates.

Il Postino's
13 Station Street,
Wentworth Falls
Tel: 4757 1615
Open: D, L & D daily. **$**
Mediterranean cuisine in sunny Wentworth Falls. Has courtyard tables for savouring the open-air atmosphere far from city smog. Economical prices and long hours. BYO.

Vulcan's
33 Govett's Leap Road,
Blackheath
Tel: 4787 6899
Open: L & D Fri–Sun. **$$**
Modern Australian cuisine with courtyard tables in summer. Breezy, intimate and relaxed ambience. BYO.

PRICE CATEGORIES

Price indications are for a three-course meal for one, including half a bottle of house wine, coffee and service:
$ = under A$50
$$ = A$50–75
Abbreviations: B = breakfast, L = lunch, D = dinner. BYO = bring your own alcohol.

THE SOUTHERN HIGHLANDS

With their attractive 19th-century towns and villages, framed by cool green valleys, it's little wonder that the Southern Highlands are a popular destination away from the city for locals and visitors

The accessible Southern Highlands region exudes a rural prettiness and quaintness more generally associated with England than Australia – rolling green meadows, historic villages, gentle valleys and small farmsteads.

Discovery of the area began in the late 1790s with pioneering journeys by explorers such as John Oxley (who also first discovered the site of Brisbane and ventured into NSW's Outback area). It was driven by the colony's pressing need for additional grazing grounds, when the Blue Mountains were still an impenetrable barrier westwards. By the 1820s, settlement had begun in earnest, and a dairy industry, which still predominates in the Highlands today, was developed.

Tourism has since become one of the region's most important industries: Sydneysiders have long appreciated the picturesque charm of historic towns such as Berrima, as well as the natural beauty and cooler climate of the entire area. The Highlands also encompass the stunning Wombeyan Caves, the rugged Morton National Park and sandstone Illawarra Plateau, that slopes gently towards a dramatic coastal escarpment on one side and to a series of equally dramatic cliffs and deep gullies to the west.

The historic south

To reach the Southern Highlands, head out of Sydney along Parramatta Road, then take the Hume Highway towards Liverpool. A short detour to NSW's original sheep-farming "Macarthur Country" region is recommended. **Camden ❶** was first developed around 1803 as an important centre for merino sheep-breeding experiments, which became so vital to the country's economy in the early 19th century. The old town has many historic

Map on page 196

LEFT: Kiama's famous blowhole.
BELOW: Camelot House in Camden.

buildings, including the 1849 **St John's Church** and a museum.

Nearby **Campbelltown** ❷ was first settled between 1810 and 1815 and still has some interesting buildings dating from the mid-19th century. Also of interest is **Catherine Field**, where the 1810 Gledswood Homestead and Winery is located.

Just off the freeway between Camden and Campbelltown lie the **Mount Annan Botanic Gardens** (open daily; tel: 4648 2477; entrance fee), a 400-hectare (1,000-acre) annexe to the Royal Botanic

Gardens in Sydney, housing a remarkable collection of indigenous flora, set within magnificent landscaped areas such as the beautiful eucalypt and fig arboretums.

Further south, at **Thirlmere** ❸, 7 km (4 miles) from the historic town of Picton, is the **NSW Rail Heritage Museum**, hugely popular with train buffs. Around 40 steam locomotives are on display on part of the disused Picton-Mittagong railway line (open daily, but times vary during school holidays; tel: 4681 8399; entrance fee). Steam journeys con-

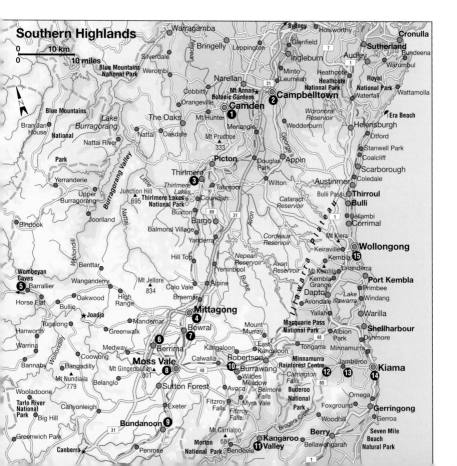

tinue to operate along a short stretch of the line, on the first and third Sundays of the month, from March through to November. The **Thirlmere Lakes National Park** is a favourite spot for canoeing or bushwalking. Heading back towards Picton, you reach the turn-off to Bargo and the **Wirrimbirra Sanctuary**, a nursery of native plants and a wildlife reserve with a number of nature trails (open daily; tel: 4684 1112).

Rejoin the Hume Highway and continue to **Mittagong ❹**, once an important coaching stop and the scene of early attempts in the 1850s to introduce an iron and steel industry to Australia. Beverley Cottee's fascinating **Victoria House** on the highway itself (open daily; tel: 4871 1682) will throw exponents of the tapestry and embroidery needle into ecstasy, and the **Sturt Craft Centre** and artists' workshops (off the highway to the left, heading from Sydney) display and sell fine Australian-made pottery, woodwork and fabric works (open daily; tel: 4860 2083).

The centre features a beautiful European-style garden. The whole area, in fact, is known as one of Australia's great gardening districts, with some of the gardens of the wealthy resort houses dating back to the 19th century. In spring and autumn, a good selection of these magnificent private gardens open for public inspection. The **Southern Highlands Visitor Information Centre** is located in Mittagong and is a good starting point with its many maps and brochures on the district (tel: 4871 2888).

Nearby is the ghost town of **Joadja**, a 19th-century mining village that still has a row of miners' cottages, a cemetery and schoolhouse dating from the 1870s (open Wed–Sun; tel: 4878 5129).

Wombeyan Caves

If you have sufficient time, another option from Mittagong is the 128-km (80-mile) round trip to the ancient limestone **Wombeyan Caves ❺** (open daily; tel: 4843 5976; entrance fee). Less crowded than the more famous Jenolan Caves in the Blue Mountains, these five caverns are remarkable for the

Map on page 196

Striking formations at the Wombeyan Caves.

LEFT: Mount Annan Botanic Gardens. **BELOW:** a restored locomotive at Thirlmere Rail Heritage Museum.

delicacy of their calcified cathedral-like formations of stalagmites and stalactites.

If you prefer books to caves, a great find between Mittagong and Berrima, on the Hume Highway, is Berkelouw Books (tel: 4877 1370), one of the state's best sources of second-hand and rare books. (Berkelouw also has stores in the city suburbs of Paddington and Leichhardt.)

The highland towns

The many small towns of the Southern Highlands have long been a summer escape for Sydney city-dwellers, who enjoy the region's cooler climate and lush, green landscape. **Berrima** ❻, founded in 1829, with its buildings constructed almost entirely of local sandstone, is the area's most picturesque and historic town. It nearly didn't survive – in later years the railway bypassed Berrima, sending the town into a decline, and it was relieved only by 1960s conservation efforts that restored many of its 1830s buildings to their former glory. These include the jail (still in use),

The historic sandstone church at Berrima.

the courthouse (the site of Australia's first trial by jury) and the Surveyor General Inn. The **Berrima Courthouse and Museum** (open daily; tel: 4877 1505; entrance fee) provides a fascinating insight into 19th-century-style justice and has some excellent brochures on the district.

Other Berrima attractions include a plethora of tea, craft and antiques shops, some decidedly expensive but still worth a look. Service here is generally at a rural pace, but it is worth taking the time to savour a traditionally English Devonshire Cream Tea of hot scones, strawberry jam and cream, served with a "cuppa". If you decide to stay in Berrima, the historic **White Horse Inn** is like stepping back in time.

Just off the Hume Highway, the 1862 resort town of **Bowral** ❼ is most famous for its flowers, and especially the Tulip Time Festival in October, as well as being a desirable retirement area for the wealthy. Bowral was also the home town of Australia's most famous cricketer, Sir Donald Bradman, and the scene of his first century (as a twelve-year-

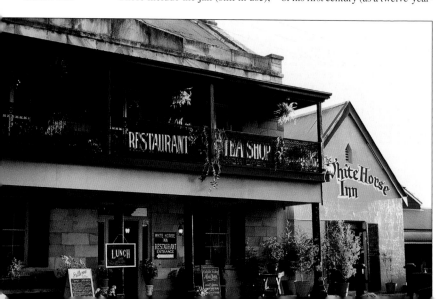

old schoolboy). The **Bradman Museum** is full of cricketing memorabilia and photographs of the sporting hero in action (open daily; tel: 4862 1247; entrance fee).

The exclusive **Milton Park Hotel**, with its overtones of an English manor set in manicured gardens, is near by. It was originally built in the 19th century as the rural seat of the Anthony Hordern family. There are some superb private gardens in the area, including Moidart and Buskers End, both open seasonally.

South from Bowral, **Moss Vale 8**, named after the farm of an early settler, is a market town that is home to the **Cecil Hoskins Nature Reserve** and the impressive **Throsby Park**, built between 1834 and 1837. This remnant of the once-substantial Throsby family estate is open to the public on selected days (tel: 4887 7270 for current details). For golfers, Dormie House, right on the 18-hole Moss Vale golf course, should prove a good stopping point.

From Moss Vale, you can make a trip south to Sutton Forest and Exeter, near the edge of rugged Morton National Park. This quiet region lies across an enormous bush-covered plateau that has been dissected into gorges and chasms by the process of erosion. It is popular with bush-walkers, cyclists, equestrians and the generally health-conscious, who flock to establishments such as Solar Springs Health Resort and Peppers Mount Broughton Country Resort.

A plentiful range of lodgings, from caravans through guesthouse, hotel, motel and farm accommodation to the luxury top-end of the market is available in the Southern Highlands. In the quaint town of **Bundanoon 9** – Aboriginal for "deep gullies" – try the 1910 Tree Tops Guesthouse, looking like something out of an Agatha Christie novel, which is perfect for

the murder mystery weekends that take place here on occasion. Heading towards the coast, there are several guesthouses and hotels in Wildes Meadow.

Map on page 196

Towards the south coast

Towards the coast, the rolling hills of the Highlands district give way to spectacular escarpment country with its rugged bush, waterfalls and dramatic views.

From Moss Vale take the Illawarra Highway to **Burrawang 10**, a tiny historic village with a general store that has been trading since the late 19th century. Next stop is the small village of **Robertson**. In town, **Ranelagh House**, built to resemble an English manor, and at one time a Franciscan seminary, is in operation again as a guesthouse and is a good place to drop in for afternoon tea.

Heading southerly from Robertson, take the turn-off to Pearsons Lane, 2 km (1 mile) west of the town. This road leads down to the northeastern edge of **Morton National Park** (tel: 4871 2888), with access to Belmore Falls and

Bowral holds an annual Tulip Festival.

Sir Donald Bradman

Australia's finest cricketer and batsman, Donald George Bradman, affectionately known as "the Don", was born in Bowral in the Southern Highlands in 1908. He attracted attention at an early age, batting golf balls against a local water tank with only a thin strip of wood. He made his Test cricket debut in 1928, at the relatively early age of 20. Two years later, he scored a record 334 not out in a Test against England and, in a match against Queensland, the highest first-class innings (452 not out) ever achieved – a record he would continue to hold until 1959.

His international career spanned 20 years, during which he played in 52 Tests and captained Australia for over a decade. His unequalled reputation stems from his unique batting average of 99.94 runs per innings – he made more than 35,000 runs throughout his career. Sadly, in his final Test, he famously needed only a further four runs to reach an average of 100, but was dismissed for a "duck" on the second ball. Bradman retired from the game in 1948 and died in 2001, aged 92. But his name continues to grace cricket halls of fame, both in Australia and the world over.

Robertson sprang to fame as the location for the smash-hit film Babe, *a quintessentially Australian story about a talking pig that thinks it is a sheepdog.*

Fitzroy Falls. The latter are the area's most dramatic waterfalls, plunging over 80 metres (270 ft) into the valley below. The Fitzroy Falls Information Visitor Centre is near by (tel: 4887 7270) and there are some excellent walking tracks in the area, including a 3-km (1¾-mile) clifftop stretch that provides views across the escarpment.

Take the Nowra Road to **Kangaroo Valley** ⑪, a lovely historic village nestling within a scenic rural landscape. Of major interest here is the **Pioneer Farm Museum** housed in a 90-year-old homestead (tel: 4465 1306). Past the township is the **Cambewarra Lookout**, with a vista across the surrounding country of escarpment rainforest interspersed with stretches of scenic dairy farmland; the views along this drive are among the best in Australia. Turn onto the Princes Highway for the township of Berry, which boasts a clutch of historic buildings including the **Bunyip Inn**, housed in a 1889 bank and operating as a small hotel.

Also from Robertson, about 3 km

(1¼ miles) along the Illawarra Highway and the turn-off on the Jamberoo Mountain Road, are Carrington Falls, with deep rock pools, walking tracks and viewing points. Further along is the **Minnamurra Rainforest Centre** ⑫ (tel: 4236 0469), which features a boardwalk through the rainforest habitat and access to the Minnamurra Falls. At the township of **Jamberoo** ⑬ is a scenic nature reserve and excellent views of the Southern Highlands landscape.

Kiama and Wollongong

Another good scenic option from the Southern Highlands is to return to Sydney via the coast road. From Jamberoo, continue east to **Kiama** ⑭. Famous for its spectacular ocean blowhole, the site was discovered by explorer George Bass in 1797 as he charted the southern coastline, and the town was founded in the 1830s. Kiama is now an attractive fishing and tourist centre, with buildings dating from the mid-1800s and pelicans nesting on its shores. The **Villa Dalmeny** is a National Trust-listed mansion on the

THE SOUTHERN HIGHLANDS ◆ 201

coast, which now serves as a fine hotel and a gourmet restaurant.

From Kiama, the road curves inland and follows the eastern shores of the fishing and boating waterways of Lake Illawarra, past the grim industrial suburb of Port Kembla and into **Wollongong** ⓖ. The state's third-largest city after Sydney and Newcastle is also the country's coal, steel and shipping industrial centre. However, Wollongong's superb location at the foot of the Illawarra Plateau makes it an appealing city. First settled in 1815, the town grew up around a small harbour and now has a population of more than 200,000. Its long coastline is dotted with historic light-houses, world-class surf beaches and restaurants overlooking the ocean. The city also has a pleasant shopping area and is, incongruously, home to the largest Buddhist temple in the southern hemisphere and the country's largest art gallery outside of a main city.

Above Wollongong, high on the coastal escarpment, there are excellent lookouts from Mount Kembla and Mount Kiera with views over the city and down the coast. Bulli Pass and Sublime Point are also recommended.

Continuing along the Princes Highway, past the Royal National Park (*see page 159*), will lead back into the centre of Sydney. ❑

Map on page 196

There are many fine golf courses here.

RESTAURANTS & BARS

Bundanoon Hotel
Erith Street, Bundanoon
A classic country-style pub. A relaxed, friendly place with a traditional Australian rural atmosphere and a regular clientele of locals.

Cafe de Railleur and Ye Olde Bicycle Shoppe
9 Church Street, Bundanoon
Tel: 4883 6043
Open: L daily, B Sat–Sun. **$**
A country-style home-made cake and pastry shop with light lunches. BYO. Eat in or hire a bike and take a picnic hamper to the park.

Fitzroy Inn
26 Ferguson Crescent, Mittagong
Tel: 4872 3457
Open: L Thur–Sun; D Wed–Sun. **$$**

A refurbished inn that serves a wide array of meals, often incorporating vegetables grown on the premises and fresh eggs from the Fitzroy's own flock of hens.

Hordern's
Milton Park Country House Hotel, Hordern's Road, Bowral
Tel: 4861 1522
Open: L & D daily. **$$**
A licensed restaurant with elegant country-style decor. Uses local produce in its delicious menu. Situated in the former mansion of the local Hordern family.

Lone Star
Cnr Flinders and Achilles streets, Wollongong
Tel: 4226 3700
Open: L & D daily. **$**

A child-friendly Texas-style steakhouse, offering a free meal for kids under 12 when dining with an adult. Lots of sweets, desserts and ice-cream treats. Phone-ahead takeaways available if you're just passing through.

The Old Schoolhouse Restaurant
Cnr Hoddle and Church streets, Burrawang
Tel: 4886 4331
Open: L Sat–Sun, D Fri–Sat. **$$**
Fine country dining with an international feel. Uses local produce, prepared under the direction of a renowned local chef in a relaxed, rustic decor.

Surveyor General Inn
Old Hume Highway, Berrima

Tel: 4877 1226
Open: L & D daily. **$$**
Situated in spacious rural grounds, the convict-built Surveyor General has traded since 1834 and is Australia's oldest continuously licensed inn. Hearty, country-style fare is on offer: cook your own steak on the barbecue or sample the à la carte menu at the Bushranger Bistro.

PRICE CATEGORIES

A three-course meal for one, including half a bottle of house wine, coffee and service:
$ = under A$50
$$ = A$50–75
Abbreviations: B = breakfast, L = lunch, D = dinner. BYO = bring your own alcohol.

SYDNEY'S FLORA AND FAUNA

You can see examples of Australia's unique wildlife in the city parks, the national parks around Sydney, and even in some suburban gardens

ABOVE: Once killed for their fur and decimated further by disease, koalas have dwindled in numbers from several million to a few hundred thousand. Koalas (not "bears" but tree-living marsupials) no longer live wild around Sydney, but can be seen at Taronga Zoo and various wildlife centres to the west of the city.

Few countries on the planet possess a more bizarre and distinctive array of native flora and fauna than Australia, where, for 40 million years, species have developed in complete isolation from the rest of the world. While modern Sydney is not exactly a wilderness, its native parks preserve large areas of natural landscape and protect the bushland borders of Greater Sydney from urban advancement. Indigenous flora and fauna of the original Sydney landscape cling tenaciously to the last vestiges of wilderness, and in some cases adapt remarkably well to the exigencies of city living.

Bicentennial Park, for example, provides wetlands for many native species as well as for migratory waders from the northern hemisphere. Many reptiles can be found resting on warm rocks around the city, and the jarring call of the kookaburra *(right)* is heard in city parks at dawn and after sunset.

ABOVE: For bird-lovers, Australia is the Land of Parrots: about one-sixth of the world's species are found here, and no other country has such a richness and diversity of forms. Among the more spectacular species you will encounter in and around Sydney are the noisy sulphur-crested cockatoo and the brilliant rainbow lorikeet *(above)*.

BELOW: Australia has a deserved reputation for dangerous creatures – spiders, scorpions, jellyfish and at least 30 lethal snakes. But you are very unlikely to encounter any of them in Sydney, with the possible exception of the Sydney funnel-web spider *(below)*, which often sets up home in rockeries and shrubberies in suburban gardens. Unusually for spiders, the male is deadlier than the female: while she spends most of her life in a burrow, he spends the summer and autumn searching for females to mate with – and often wandering into houses or garages, where he does not hesitate to attack humans. The venom can be lethal, and if you are bitten you should go straight to hospital.

BELOW: The waratah is the floral emblem of New South Wales. Found mainly on the coastal plains and tablelands, and in the Blue Mountains, there are several kinds of waratah, all with tough, dark-green leaves, often tooth-edged. The waratah's vivid flower (the genus name *Telopea* means "seen from afar") measures 7–10 cm (2–3 ins) in diameter. It is really hundreds of individual flowers crowded into a dense head, and the bright-crimson "petals" are in fact modified leaves called bracts. Waratahs flourish in rocky and sandy soil, and burst into flower in the spring (September–November).

BELOW: Australia has more than 600 species of wattle (acacias), thriving in most forms of habitat, from the arid centre to cold mountain regions. They are usually the first plants to reappear after bush-fires. The golden wattle *(below)* is the most common and widespread, and even features on Australia's national coat of arms. It is a shrub or small tree that grows 4–8 metres (13–25 ft) tall, with long, leathery, bright-green leaves. Each spring (1 September is Wattle Day in Australia) it produces large, fluffy, golden flower heads, each with up to 70 very small, sweetly scented flowers.

ABOVE: Marsupials – including kangaroos, wallabies, koalas, wombats and possums – were thick on the ground when the first Europeans landed here. As Sydney grew, most of them retreated to the surrounding countryside, where many of them survive as protected species in the national parks. An exception is the brushtail possum *(above)*, which has adapted well to city life and often comes into contact with people. Brushtails are generally nocturnal, hiding during the day in a hollow log or tree-trunk, or even inside house rafters, but are sometimes seen in daylight in the city parks. They can often be heard padding across rooftops at night, sometimes emitting piercing shrieks to establish territories.

THE CENTRAL COAST

The former rural communities that once existed independently of the city have now become commuter-belt residential areas and popular activity spots for Sydney's weekenders

For a quick respite from the city and a chance to wallow in vast tracts of natural Australiana, head north on the Pacific Highway to the NSW Central Coast. If you're travelling by car or rail you will reach the region after an hour's journey north from the city.

The Central Coast starts on the banks of the spectacular Hawkesbury River in the south and ends about 80 km (50 miles) to the north. It is bounded to the east by an impressive stretch of beaches, headlands and estuaries, and to the west by the ramparts of the Great Dividing Range. Getting there is no problem, as it is serviced by a superb expressway running through the dramatic sandstone escarpments of the Hornsby Plateau. Non-drivers can catch the air-conditioned Inter-City train from Central Railway Station, near Darling Harbour, and alight at Woy Woy, Gosford, Wyong or any one of the Central Coast's pleasant towns.

Without bordering on the ostentatious, the Central Coast is warmly receptive, being perfectly geared for the day-tripper, weekend rambler or those looking for a longer stay. In recent years it has become a retirement mecca (sometimes known as "God's waiting-room") for elderly Sydneysiders seeking a bit of water frontage without the hustle and bustle of city living. With vast stretches of enclosed waterways set against the backdrop of beautiful bushland, most of it national park reserve, it presents some of the finest scenic combinations along the NSW coast.

Gosford

Gosford ❶, with a population of 80,000, is a comfortable, compact city slung on the banks of Brisbane Water. The central visitors' information centre for the district is

Map on page 206

LEFT: angling at The Entrance.
BELOW: dinghies on the beach at Terrigal.

Gosford Regional Gallery and Arts Centre.

BELOW: pelicans waiting for fish at The Entrance.

located on Mann Street (tel: 4385 4430 or 1800 151 699). Once a purely rural area, today many of its pay packets are actually earned in Sydney by commuters who jump aboard the efficient rail service each day for the one-hour ride to the city.

On weekends their reasons for living on the coast become obvious. The place is a leisurely oasis, as anyone who sits down over a cold beer in one of the Brisbane Water's boating clubs will discover. In summer the locals can be found cooling off or carving the waves of a glittering strand of beaches and lagoons to the east. For uncluttered stretches of sand try Copacabana, McMasters or Ocean beaches. If you want to meet the locals, rock on down to Avoca, Forrester's or Bateau Bay beaches on any summer Sunday.

North of Gosford, near the small township of Ourimbah, is the **Forest of Tranquillity**, an award-winning forest "garden" featuring tracts of rainforest in which birds and animals thrive, set against a backdrop of massive sandstone cliffs. Guided walks are available on Saturdays, and there are a variety of self-guide walking tracks around the park. From November to February, the park opens late for Twilight Magic: a guided rainforest stroll, feeding of wallabies and birds, followed by a light show (Wed–Sun evenings; tel: 4362 1855; entrance fee). In November and early December, fireflies add their twinkle to the scene.

Rumbalara Reserve

For another sample of the Central Coast's natural aspects, drive back towards central Gosford where, just east of the city, you will strike **Rumbalara Reserve ②**. *Rumbalara* is Aboriginal for "rainbow", which is an appropriate name as the reserve presents the broad spectrum of the area's scenic diversity. Its rugged, bush-covered slopes are character-

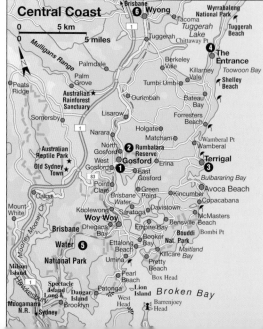

istic of the natural scenery and comprise several vegetation zones, including temperate rainforest. Rumbalara's three lookouts also command excellent views of the vast Brisbane Water, North Gosford, **Barrenjoey Lighthouse** and surrounding rural areas.

The reserve's Rock Shelter offers an inkling of what life here was like before the arrival of the colonists. The weathered recess in the Hawkesbury sandstone is believed to have accommodated migratory Aborigines of the Guringai (or Kuring-gai) tribe who visited the area every summer.

The Guringai were coast-dwellers who relied on the sea and estuaries for food. In winter, when many fish head north to warmer waters, the tribe would move inland to hunt possums, kangaroos and birds.

Linked to Rumbalara Reserve by Mouat Walk is the **Katandra Walking Trails** area, a network of bush tracks offering five scenic hikes of varying difficulty. The shortest is a 45-minute stroll while the longest is a challenging three-hour effort.

Terrigal

Just 15 minutes' drive from Gosford, **Terrigal** ❸ is a small resort town set in a beautiful arc of coast. Locals and Sydneysiders know it mostly for its lively pubs and riotous summer weekends. Popular with young children are the paddle boats for hire at weekends on the Terrigal Lagoon. Just south of the town, the **Skillion Lookout** offers views out along the spectacular coastline.

To the north along the coastal Entrance Road can be found appealing spots such as Wamberal, Shelley Beach and Towoon Bay. Keep driving and you will strike **The Entrance** ❹, a township which was once to Sydneysiders what Brighton is to Londoners: a nearby fun park on the sea. Today, however, most of the holidaymakers have moved to haunts further north, leaving The Entrance to its own devices, but the peak summer period will still find its beach choked with low-budget city escapees. The town also leads to Tuggerah Lake, another of the enclosed waterways of the Central Coast.

Map on page 206

Because of its raucous call, the kookaburra has been called the laughing jackass.

BELOW: exploring the rock pools around the Skillion, near Terrigal.

Any invitation that involves a boat should be automatically accepted. Pack or hire fishing gear and a prawn net and you might just land your own supper. Less fortunate anglers can always pick up delicious seafood platters at almost any of the area's fish restaurants.

National parks of the Central Coast

Around the foreshores of the Central Coast lie remote stretches of near-wilderness enclosed within the district's national parks, offering an escape from the bustle of the busy holiday settlements.

Brisbane Water National Park ❺ spreads out from the northern shores of Broken Bay *(see page 147)*. Access to the southeast corner of the park is via Blackwall Drive from Woy Woy through to the holiday towns of Ettalong Beach and Umina, picking up Patonga Drive to reach the sleepy village of Patonga. On the way, if you have time, pull off the road into **Pearl Beach**, the district's most upmarket town, where exclusive holiday "shacks"

provide time out for those at the wealthier end of Sydney's creative talent pool. The park itself covers some 12,000 hectares (29,500 acres) and is comprised mostly of woodland and heathland areas, although some of the gorges support thickets of subtropical rainforest vegetation. Waratah Patch, Waratah Trig and Coora Swamp are areas of the park known for their wonderful displays of wild flowers. In the northern section of the park (access via Woy Woy Road) the main attraction is the **Bulgandry Aboriginal Site**, where a special boardwalk leads past more rock engravings of the Guringai Aboriginal people.

Bouddi National Park is a relatively small reserve of just 1,200 hectares (3,000 acres), covering the northern headland of the magnificent Broken Bay. Head south from the township of Kincumber along the Scenic Drive, which, true to its name, offers wonderful views of the coastal landscape. Bouddi is an easily explored park comprised of heathlands, subtropical rainforest and some of the loveliest and least

Many Aboriginal rock engravings are well preserved.

BELOW: Pearl Beach in Brisbane Water National Park.

populated beaches in the area. There are walking trails down to the beaches, and camping is permitted in several spots.

For information about both parks contact the **NSW National Parks and Wildlife Service** in Gosford (tel: 4320 4200).

Wyong and the Australian Reptile Park

The railway town of **Wyong ⑥** is a perfect springboard for jaunts into the nearby Yarramalong and Dooralong valleys and to beaches to the northeast.

By doubling south again on the Old Pacific Highway, you can pick up signs to the late Eric Worrell's famous **New Australian Reptile Park** at North Gosford (open daily; tel: 4340 1146; entrance fee). For accessible wildlife it is well worth the visit. You can hand-feed kangaroos, see a rare platypus frolicking in the depths and acquaint yourself with exotic native birds. And, of course, there are the reptiles, which range from mighty crocodiles to goannas and lethal adders, pythons

and cobras. At prescribed times park keepers demonstrate the art of "milking" venom from some of the world's deadliest snakes, all of which are indigenous to Australia.

Map on page 206

Staying along the Central Coast

Should the prospect of seeing the attractions of the Central Coast in a day prove too daunting, you might be tempted to linger longer. This is traditional Australian summer holiday territory, which means the land of the ubiquitous caravan complete with canvas lean-to and "barbie". There are plenty of camping grounds in the towns and along the foreshores where travellers can hire a caravan or a cabin very cheaply, or pitch a tent. Camping is also available in the national parks, but camp permits and a small fee are generally required, so check in advance.

If camping outdoors is not your style, try one of the many inexpensive motels or more expensive resorts which have been springing up like mushrooms since the 1960s. Some more unusual options are

The coastlands are rich in flora.

LEFT: beach fishing at sunrise.

Fishing on the Central Coast

Fishing is one of the Central Coast's most popular activities, and year round you will spot keen anglers setting their bait and sitting back to wait. It is not hard to see why: there are virtually inexhaustible stretches of foreshore here, offering opportunities for all types of angling, including rock, boat, beach, jetty, lake and estuary fishing.

The large enclosed areas of Tuggerah Lake and Brisbane Water are two of the most popular areas with anglers, as are the many coastal rock platforms, such as the Skillion near Terrigal. However, almost any vantage point in the region will suffice. Fish species that abound in these waters include flathead, tuna, blenny, whiting, bream and luderick. Holidaymakers lucky enough to pull in a catch take advantage of the barbecues that are a standard feature of campsites to cook their own supper.

There are plenty of bait and tackle shops (buy or hire equipment), boat-hire outlets and boat ramps. Check with locals for the best fishing spots and always be aware of weather forecasts and safety issues, particularly with rock and boat angling.

Map on page 206

Salty Rose, a bed-and-breakfast with a bushland setting near Avoca, or Headlands, an environmentally friendly outfit, with individual bungalows, sitting right on the edge of Bouddi National Park. Further north, there are some more great up-market resorts, such as Kims at Toowoon Bay.

Outdoor activities

RIGHT: yachts sail all along the Central Coast.

For surfers, the Central Coast is a rich hunting ground. Try McMasters Beach, Avoca and Copacabana for a mixture of beach and point breaks. Terrigal and Norah Head are famous for their big waves in the right swell.

Canoeing and wind-surfing are other popular activities on the waterways, and further north, in the Tuggerah Lake area of the Central Coast, fishing and boating opportunities are also plentiful.

Landlubbers will enjoy bushwalking the thousands of hectares of subtropical rainforest, heathland and woodland, and the superb stretches of coastal beaches preserved within the national parks of the region. There are plenty of designated walking tracks along with camping opportunities, making for a cheap, healthy and incomparably scenic holiday. ❑

RESTAURANTS & BARS

Cafe Sicilian
131 Henry Parry Drive, Gosford
Tel: 4322 0434
Open: B, L & D Tues–Sat. **$$**
A popular Italian restaurant with an especially busy weekend trade and live band. Gets noisy. Even the owners sing when the trade is particularly healthy. Bookings recommended.

Central Coast Leagues Club
Dane Drive, Gosford
Tel: 4325 9888
Open: L & D daily. **$**
A classic Aussie leagues club, complete with poker machines galore, discounted drink prices and a choice of eating – All-You-Can-Eat Buffet, A-la-Carte Eatery and Peking Garden Chinese restaurant. All good value. Relaxed, community atmosphere, particularly lively during major sports telecasts and live entertainment nights.

Dragons Door
620 Terrigal Drive, Erina
Tel: 4367 0388
Open: L & D daily. **$**
A service-oriented Chinese restaurant with a wide array of economical meals. Caters well for group diners. Quick service and friendly staff.

Lone Star
Shop 1038, Westfield Shopping Centre, Wyong Road, Tuggerah
Tel: 4353 5552
Open: L & D daily. **$**
An American diner in the "highway steakhouse" style, complete with country music, Texan artefacts and neon beer signs. Economical set menu, children's menu, takeaway service and phone-ahead quick pick-up. Free meals for kids when dining with adults. Licensed.

Shorethyme
9 Mitchell Street, Norah Head
Tel: 4396 4507
Open: B & L Sat–Sun, D daily. **$$**
Modern Australian cuisine and an imaginative menu. Gets rave reviews and repeat customers. Prompt, friendly service amid hip decor and displays of original artworks. Plenty of local wines on the menu.

Supermex
Shop 10, Church Street, Terrigal
Tel: 4384 6289
Open: L daily, B & D Sat–Sun. **$**
A Latin American cantina serving basic, affordable Mexican-style snacks. Quick service, tasty treats in a no-frills style. BYO.

Woodport Inn
207 The Entrance Road, Erina
A large "country club" type of place, with plenty of parking and room to move inside. Has a choice of bars, lunch and dinners in the bistro, and weekend DJs until late.

TRANSPORT

GETTING THERE AND GETTING AROUND

GETTING THERE

By Air

About 50 international airlines visit Sydney. Qantas is the main Australian carrier, with the most flights to the largest number of destinations, and an extensive domestic network as well.

Other major players include British Airways, Singapore Airlines, Air Canada and United Airlines. Check with your travel agent; all of the airlines listed offer comparable levels of comfort and safety, so the choice of carrier can be made on the basis of cost and convenience.

Flights between Australia and Europe take about 22 hours, although with stopovers and delays the journey could take more like 30 hours. A stopover in an Asian capital (or on the Pacific coast or Hawaii if travelling from Canada or the US) is worth considering.

Flights to Australia can be expensive. The peak season for travel is around December, with prices tapering off from January to April. Apex fares will reduce the flat economy fare by about 30–40 percent during the less busy periods. If you are flexible and can fly at short notice, check with dis-

count flight centres for fares on unsold tickets. Note that with many of the heavily-discounted fares, refunds and changes in flight times are generally ruled out. A small departure tax, payable in Australian dollars, is levied on all travellers leaving Australia, but this is now included in the cost of an international ticket.

AIRLINES

British Airways:
Tel: 1300 767 177 (Sydney)
Tel: 08705 222 999 (UK)
Tel: 1 800 403 0882 (N. America)
www.ba.com
Qantas:
Tel: 13 13 13 (Australia)
Tel: 0845 774 7767 (UK)
Tel: 1 800 227 4500 (N. America)
www.qantas.com.au
United Airlines:
Tel: 13 17 77 (Australia)
Tel: 0845 844 4777 (UK)
Tel: 1 800 538 2929 (N. America)
www.united.com
Air Canada:
Tel: 1300 655 767 (Sydney)
Tel: 08712 201 111 (UK)
Tel: 1 888 247 2262 (N. America)
www.aircanada.com
Singapore Airlines:
Tel: 13 10 11 (Sydney)
Tel: 08706 088 886 (UK)
Tel: 1 800 742 3333 (N. America)
www.singaporeair.com

By Sea

Up until the 1960s, arriving in and departing from Australia by boat was a common and reasonably inexpensive practice, but in these days of cheap air fares, sailing Down Under has become something of a luxury activity. That said, if time and money permits, there is no better introduction to this city of the sea than arriving by boat.

Ocean liners berth at the Overseas Passenger Terminal at Circular Quay and the Darling Harbour Terminal. Passengers are required to pass through customs on arrival.

The following companies include Sydney as a destination or stopover on their intineraries:
Cunard Line tel: 0845 071 0300 (UK), 9250 6666 (Sydney); www.cunard.com
P&O tel: 0845 355 5333 (UK), 9364 8400 (Sydney); www.pocruises.com

GETTING AROUND

From the Airport

Sydney International Airport is also Australia's main international airport. Officially called Kingsford Smith International Airport, it is 10 km (6 miles) south of the city, and known to many Sydneysiders as "Mascot Airport", after the nearby suburb. The domestic airport is a further 2 km (1 mile) away: passengers in transit should use the shuttle buses provided by the appropriate airlines.

The efficient AirportLink train (built for the 2000 Olympics) is the fastest and most convenient way to reach the centre of Sydney. There are rail stations in both the domestic and the international terminals. Trains run every 10 minutes from 5.09am to 11.45pm, and the journey into the city takes only 13 minutes. A single ticket from the airport to the City costs A$11.80*

A taxi from the airport to the city centre will cost around A$25 one way, and should take around 20 minutes in light traffic. Each terminal has its own sheltered taxi rank with supervisors on hand in peak hours. All the major car hire (rental) companies have offices at the airport terminals.

Orientation

Sydney is not a planned city. It was carved out of the soft sandstone hills that rise above the harbour as space was needed for the growing population. Thus, the layout can seem (and, in fact, is) fairly chaotic. That said, it is also a surprisingly easy city in which to find your way around, perhaps because there are always the landmark foreshores of the harbour to look out for.

The city sits slightly inland from the coastline on the southern shores of the harbour. The airport is further south again. The Rocks area is within minutes of the city centre, forming its western, harbourside flank. Darling Harbour is set further west again, but is still within strolling distance of the city. The Kings Cross district is a good half-hour walk from the city.

If you follow the harbourside parkland beyond the Opera

EXPLORING THE CITY

A good way to get an overview of the city is to take a ride to the top of Sydney Tower, or visit one of the great harbour lookouts, particularly North or South Head. Pick up a good map, and always find out if it is possible to travel by ferry or foot – by far the most pleasant means of exploring this beautiful city.

House in an easterly direction and continue east in a direct line, you will reach the start of the southern beaches at Bondi, about 7 km (4 miles) from Sydney's centre. If you follow the curving shore of the harbour eastwards, you will reach South Head. Follow the harbour foreshore west and you will reach the inner western suburbs, before hitting the mouth of the Parramatta River, the water artery of the west that leads to Olympic Park at Homebush Bay and the historic suburb of Parramatta. Take the Harbour Bridge or the Harbour Tunnel to reach the leafy northern suburbs with their spectacular harbourside settings and, further along, the golden stretch of the northern beaches.

Public Transport

Buses

Buses operate from the city, ferry wharves and railway stations. The main bus termini are in Wynyard Park on George Street, at Circular Quay and at Railway Square near Broadway and Central station. Visitors can call the State Transit Authority for information on connecting routes, ticket prices and timetables. Free maps are available from outlets at the airport, Circular Quay, Wynyard Bus Station and Queen Victoria Building.

If you catch the **Sydney Explorer** (red buses), you will travel in a 28-km (17-mile) circuit around the city's major tourist

attractions. A one-day ticket (A$36) allows you any number of journeys on the circular route up to midnight the same day.

The **Bondi Explorer** travels a 30-km (18-mile) circuit around the eastern harbourside bays and coastal beaches. There are recorded commentaries on board, and passengers can get on and off as they please using the same ticket. The Bondi Explorer departs from Circular Quay every 30 minutes from early morning to late afternoon. A Bondi Explorer ticket (A$36) also allows you free travel on all regular Sydney Buses within the Bondi Explorer circular route up to midnight on the same day.

Ferries

Sydney is a harbour city, and ferries have been part of its transport scene since the arrival of the First Fleet in 1788. Today, ferries provide an efficient commuter service to many of the harbourside areas, with all services beginning and ending at Circular Quay.

Some of the city's tourist attractions, including Taronga Park Zoo, Manly and Darling Harbour, are best reached by ferry. A fleet of 27 vessels includes high-speed JetCats, the grand old Manly ferries and the RiverCats that run along Parramatta River. Plan your itinerary around at least a couple of rides. Ring the Info Line (see box) for information.

Sydney Ferries run harbour

TRAVEL INFORMATION

Bus, Train, Ferry Info Line (State Transit Authority) tel: 13 15 00, 6am–10pm daily. **TransitShop kiosks**, for tickets and timetables, are located at Circular Quay (corner of Loftus and Alfred streets), Wynyard Station (Carrington Street station entrance), Railway Square and at the Queen Victoria Building (York Street entrance). **Countrylink Rail and Coach Reservations** tel: 13 22 32.

cruises (with commentary) morning, evening and night, which take between one and two hours and are not expensive. There are also a number of private operators including Captain Cook Cruises and Matilda Cruises, leaving from Circular Quay and Darling Harbour. Trips on offer include everything from a one-hour whiz around the top sights, to a full dinner afloat. A very special trip is to be had aboard the HMAV *Bounty*, a replica of Captain Bligh's 18th-century tall sailing ship.

Captain Cook Cruises tel: 9206 1122
Matilda Cruises tel: 9264 7377
Bounty Cruises tel: 9247 1789

Trains

The safe, efficient and comprehensive railway system, **CityRail**, is a great way to get to suburban destinations, as well as providing an excellent inner-city service. The City Circle connects the city stations of St James, Museum, Circular Quay, Wynyard, Town Hall and Central. Travel out to Bondi Junction on the Eastern Suburbs line. Trains for all suburban lines can be caught at Town Hall and Central Station, which is also Sydney's main country terminal. Trains run until midnight.

It's worth noting that after peak hours in the evenings, stations and trains are sparsely staffed; passengers are advised to use the "Nightsafe" section of the platform and to travel in the train guard's carriage, marked by a blue light. Ring the Bus, Train, Ferry Info Line *(see box, page 213)* for further information.

Some of the outlying country destinations mentioned in this guide may be reached by train, including the Blue Mountains, Southern Highlands and the Central Coast. Country and interstate train travel is the domain of the government service, Countrylink. There are Countrylink Travel Centres throughout the city and suburbs, including at Central and Town Hall stations and Circular Quay. Reservations, tel: 13 22 32.

Taxis

Sydney taxis can be hired in the street if they are showing the "Vacant" sign. There are plenty of taxis waiting in front of hotels, but it is recommended that passengers phone for a taxi during busy times. There is an additional charge of A$1 on the fare for phone bookings. Taxis use meters and tipping is not necessary as a rule. A short trip will cost A$6–$7. Toll fees, of which there are now several in Sydney, are all added on to the bill. It is often possible to pay by credit card, for which there is a surcharge.

All taxi drivers are required to display an offical photo ID licence on their car's dashboard or sun visor. Complaints should be made to the individual taxi company involved (displayed on the side of the vehicle) or to the NSW Taxi Council (tel: 9332 1266).

If you are travelling with a child under 12 months of age and you don't have a suitable restraint, you must ask for one when booking a cab. It is compulsory for all passengers to wear seat belts.

ABC Taxis tel: 13 25 22
Legion Cabs tel: 13 14 51
Premier tel: 13 10 17

RSL Taxis tel: 9581 1111
Silver Service Taxis tel: 13 31 00
Taxis Combined Services tel: 8332 8888

Water Taxis

Harbour taxis operate 24 hours a day and provide a quick and convenient, if somewhat expensive, way to get to the waterfront restaurants and harbour attractions. They can also be used for daytime and sunset cruises, and will pick up and drop off anywhere, provided that there is a navigable pier.

Taxis Afloat tel: 9955 3222.
Water Taxis Combined tel: 1300 666 484.

Driving

Visiting overseas drivers are not required to obtain a NSW driver's licence or an International Driving Permit, provided they have an up-to-date driving licence from their home country. If the licence is not in English, it is a good idea to carry a translation.

Most of NSW's road rules are based upon international rules, and it is simply a matter of following the signs, sticking to specified speed limits and so on. But there are a few points that drivers should be aware of. Drivers should

MONEY-SAVING TICKETS

Travel by public transport can be expensive if you purchase individual tickets as you go. There are a range of day tickets and passes available to cut the cost.
TravelPass
This ticket allows you unlimited seven-day travel on buses, trams and ferries provided you stay within set zones, or you can buy a bus-only pass.
TravelTen
This gives you 10 bus or ferry trips for nearly half the cost of paying for each trip separately. More than one person can use this ticket; simply validate the ticket the appropriate number of times at the machines that are found on board buses and at the ferry wharves.
SydneyPass
If you intend to use public transport extensively, the best value of all has to be the SydneyPass. Available for three, five or seven days, it offers unlimited hop-on, hop-off travel on all regular Sydney Buses and Sydney Ferries services, plus the Sydney Explorer and Bondi Explorer, three Harboursights Cruises, return transfers on AirportLink trains, and free travel on all regular CityRail trains within the Red TravelPass zone.

TRANSPORT

equip themselves with a complete up-to-date road directory, available at your car hire outlet.

● Drivers must give way to the right, unless otherwise indicated, to pedestrians (keep an eye out for zebra crossings), and to all emergency vehicles.

● The speed limit in most built-up city and suburban areas is 60 kph (37 mph) unless otherwise indicated.

● Parking can be a problem in and around the city centre. Carry change for meters and read the signs carefully, keeping a lookout for the areas that change into clearways during peak periods (cars are automatically towed away if found in these spots).

● It is the responsibility of the driver to ensure restraints (including for children and babies under 12 months old) are used by passengers at all time.

● There is a 0.05 percent blood alcohol limit for drivers, which is widely enforced by the use of random breath tests carried out by the police.

Car Hire

Car rental companies have offices located throughout the Sydney area, including the airport. Car hire provides the flexibility to discover the NSW countryside, and offers many opportunities to take detours from main roads and highways in order to explore small towns. It is also possible to hire campervans. If you have not already organised car hire as part of a package, you should shop around for the best deal: the smaller independent operators tend to be cheaper.

An important point to consider is insurance. Many companies have an excess charge of A$700–1,500, which means that you pay that amount in the case of an accident. It is wise to pay a little bit extra per day to reduce the figure. When you are getting a quote from the company, ask for the full amount including insurance and charges for items such as baby restraints. Many

Yellow Water Taxis

car hire companies do not insure normal vehicles for off-road travel, which means that the driver is liable.

For disabled drivers, all the major hire companies have a small number of cars with hand controls. To be sure of availability, you should contact them well in advance.

Breakdown Services

The NRMA (National Roads and Motorists Association) provides roadside service to members, and has reciprocal arrangements with motoring organisations overseas. Most car hire outlets arrange their own roadside service, but the NRMA is a good point of contact for all sorts of motoring advice.

The Road and Traffic Authority can provide information about road rules and conditions.
NRMA tel: 13 11 11 for roadside

CAR HIRE COMPANIES

Apollo Motorhome Holidays (Campervans) tel: 9556 3550 or freecall 1800 777 779
Avis tel: 13 63 33
Britz Campervan Rentals tel: 9667 0402 or freecall 1800 331 454
Budget tel: 13 27 27
Dollar Rent A Car tel: 9955 3970
Hertz tel: 13 30 39 or freecall 1800 550 067
Kings Cross Rent-A-Car tel: 9361 0637
Thrifty tel: 1300 367 227

assistance, or 13 11 22 for travel, touring and general enquiries.
Roads and Traffic Authority tel: 13 22 13.

Cycling

Sydney now has continuous cycle paths stretching from as far west as Penrith, through Windsor, Dural and Riverstone all the way to Botany Bay and the North Shore. For free maps and a complete list of Sydney's cycling tracks, contact the Roads and Traffic Authority (tel: 13 22 13).

For an excellent run, with wonderful views, take a ride along the track from Tempe to Homebush along the Cooks River; or Botany Bay waterfront to Brighton; or Glebe to Parramatta along the Parramatta River.

Visitors who prefer to cycle in the picturesque surroundings of Centennial Park may have to share the dedicated cycle lanes with horses, in-line skaters and recreational runners, but do not let this deter you. The park was used as part of the 2000 cycle road race at the 2000 Olympics as its open plan allows riders to reach impressive speeds.

For further information for cyclists, call:
Centennial Park Cycle Hire tel: 9398 5027.
Bicycle Insitute of New South Wales (commonly known as Bicycle NSW) tel: 9281 4099, or events hotline (freecall) 1800 686 854.

ACCOMMODATION

ACTIVITIES

A – Z

A CCOMMODATION

THE BEST DISTRICTS TO STAY IN AND A GUIDE TO THEIR HOTELS

Choosing a Hotel

Where to stay in Sydney is an important question. The City rates high for convenience, but the nearby Rocks area outdoes it in terms of street life. Both areas, however, are expensive. Darling Harbour is ideal if you only have a couple of days with the family, and want to see some of the major attractions.

The urbane Kings Cross area is the best location for young, childless travellers (both budget and other), while the resort suburbs of Manly and Bondi make good choices for those who want to combine a city and seaside holiday. Double Bay is an exclusive little corner of the world – a boutique-sized urban village, for those who are fussy about their street life.

Some six percent of international visitors to Sydney are backpackers. They cluster in certain areas, predominantly Kings Cross and the City, and the beachside suburbs of Bondi, Coogee and Manly. There are many establishments where financially challenged travellers can unload their packs for under A$20 a night, yet be assured of clean and comfortable facilities. The ever-reliable Youth Hostel

Association has a giant city complex with rooftop swimming pool, while the Y on the Park offers accommodation ranging from dormitories (single-sex and mixed) to apartments. Other budget options include the Lord Nelson Brewery Hotel and the Hotel Bondi, a local landmark with some fairly impressive views across one of the world's most famous beaches.

Those with a little more cash to spare should focus on the burgeoning boutique market. The majority of these hotels are former homes, often of some historic or architectural value, converted into intimate tourist accommodation. Top of the range is the Regents Court Hotel – sleekly styled apartments set in a 1920s gentlemen's boarding house. The tiny L'Otel, also in Kings Cross, is determinedly European, with its rooms designed in many different styles, a restaurant, fashionable bar, and windows overlooking the café strip of Victoria Street.

Other favourites include Simpsons of Potts Point, housed in an 1892 former family home with wonderful stained-glass windows, and The Russell, offering a tranquil 19th-century retreat and a rooftop garden at the heart of

The Rocks. Ravesi's in Bondi has the perfect holiday location: with ocean views, good food and an appealing seaside atmosphere. A disadvantage of boutique hotels is their size – many offer only a few rooms so book ahead.

There are more than 5,000 luxury hotel beds in Sydney, with standards meeting those of their international counterparts. No one with the money to spare should have trouble finding top-class accommodation, but there are a few places that stand out as exceptional.

The ornate Observatory Hotel in The Rocks has a staircase modelled on the one in Elizabeth Bay House (see page 114), as well as a star-ceilinged swimming pool and some genuinely impressive antiques. The Ritz Carlton in Double Bay has a Mediterranean theme and an impressive guest list, including the likes of Bob Hawke and Madonna.

The Park Hyatt sprawls across the northwest flank of Sydney Cove in The Rocks and is probably Sydney's most luxurious hotel. Features include harbour frontage with unbeatable views of the Harbour Bridge, large rooms and excellent 24-hour service. Sydney also has a wide range of international luxury chains – Inter-Continental,

Marriot, Sheraton and Hilton.

Whatever your room rate, it can generally be assumed that all Sydney hotels will offer a range of "basics": air-conditioning in the summer, televisions and en suite facilities (although showers are far more common than baths). For a little more cash, many of the city's hotels have on-site swimming pools for guests to cool off in after a hot summer's day of sight-seeing, and often tennis courts or a gym.

Overseas offices of the **Australian Tourist Commission** (see Tourist Information, page 237)

have listings of hotels and motels. You can reserve accommodation through your travel agent or airline. Within Australia, book through the state tourist offices, domestic airlines and hotels chains.

The **Tourist Information Service** at Eddy Avenue (corner Pitt Street), Central Railway Station (open daily 8am–10pm; tel: 9669 5111) can assist with standby accommodation at 3, 4 and 5-star hotels, and accepts bookings from overseas.

Accommodation might be harder to find when Australians

themselves go travelling, during the school holidays. These are staggered state by state, except for the year-end period (Dec–Feb), when all schools close.

The price bands in our listings are based on a standard double room without breakfast (unless otherwise indicated), for a midweek night. Many Sydney hotels offer weekend discounts of up to 30 percent: be sure to ask when making a reservation.

To call a Sydney hotel from overseas, dial the national code (61), the NSW area code (2), then the eight-figure local number.

ACCOMMODATION LISTINGS

CENTRAL SYDNEY

ACCOMMODATION · ACTIVITIES · A – Z

HOTELS

The City

Astor Martin Place
1 Hosking Place
Tel: 9292 5016
Contains 100 studio and one-bedroom apartments in the heart of the city. The complex also includes a swimming pool for cooling off after a hard day's sight-seeing. **$$$**

InterContinental Sydney
117 Macquarie Street
Tel: 9253 9000
www.sydney.intercontinental.com
Soaring out of the shell of the historic Treasury building in the business district, this 31-storey, 498-room hotel combines old-world style with modern facilities. Four restaurants. **$$$**

Merchant Court
68 Market Street, City

Tel: 9238 8888
emailus.sydney@swissotel.com
In the very centre of the city, atop the Sydney Central Plaza building. 361 rooms, furnished in Australian maple, with great views. In-house spa and sauna. **$$$**

Sydney Marriott
36 College Street
Tel: 9361 8400
www.marriott.com
Facing Hyde Park, this 241-room hotel enjoys a fine reputation for the quality of its rooms and service. Amenities include rooftop pool and spa, and modern-Australian cuisine in the Windows on the Park restaurant. **$$$**

Capital Square Hotel
Cnr of Campbell, George & Day Streets
Tel: 9211 8633
Good-value boutique hotel in the heart of Sydney's entertainment district. Korean BBQ,

Thai and Japanese restaurants. 94 rooms. **$$**

Park Regis
27 Park Street
Tel: 9267 6511
www.parkregissydney.com.au
Occupies the top 15 floors of a 45-storey building, well placed in the central business district, near the Town Hall. 120 rooms, of no great character, but light, airy, efficient and good value. **$$**

Travelodge Sydney
33 Wentworth Avenue
Tel: 8224 9400
www.travelodge.com.au
Modern, efficient, no-frills but reasonably-priced accommodation just one block south of Hyde Park. 406 rooms on 18 floors. **$$**

The Rocks

Four Seasons
199 George Street
Tel: 9238 0000

Maps, pages 68, 92 and 100

www.fourseasons.com/sydney
Formerly The Regent Sydney, this hotel has claims to be Australia's finest. In a wonderful location at Circular Quay; impressive atrium foyer, 620 rooms and suites on 34 floors and every possible facility, including a luxurious new spa. **$$$$**

PRICE CATEGORIES

Price categories are for a standard double room without breakfast:
$= under A$100
$$ = A$100–175
$$$ = A$175–250
$$$$ = over A$250

Observatory

89–113 Kent Street,
Millers Point
Tel: 9256 2222
www.observatoryhotel.com.au
Designed by prominent
Sydney architect Phillip
Cox, this beautiful
establishment offers
absolute luxury in the
heart of The Rocks
precinct. Opulent yet
intimate ambience. 20-
metre indoor pool. 77
rooms, 23 suites. Spe-
cial rates for internet
reservations. $$$$

Park Hyatt

7 Hickson Road,
Tel: 9241 1234
www.sydney.park.hyatt.com
Possibly Sydney's most
luxurious hotel, opened
in 1990 and completely
renovated in 1998.
Clinging to the best
spot on the inner city's
harbour shore, in a low
gracious building within
a few minutes' walk of
the city centre. Great
views from the har-
bourkitchen restaurant
and bar. 158 rooms.
$$$$

The Russell

143a George Street
Tel: 9241 3543
www.therussell.com.au
A charming boutique

hotel in The Rocks dis-
trict. Friendly, intimate
surrounds, and conve-
nient. 29 rooms (some
with shared bathroom
facilities). $$$$

Shangri-La

176 Cumberland Street
Tel: 9250 6000
www.shangri-la.com
Another huge Sydney
hotel (561 rooms on 36
floors), but with a lot of
style. The Horizons Bar
is one of the city's best,
and the Japanese
restaurant is excellent
too. $$$

Lord Nelson Brewery Hotel

19 Kent Street
Tel: 9251 4044
www.lordnelson.com.au
The best value for
money in Sydney, this
historic pub provides
cheap, comfortable
rooms in the city's
liveliest district. $$

Grand Mercure Apartments

50 Murray Street, Pyrmont
Tel: 9563 6666
Stylish two- and three-
bedroom apartments
with private balconies,
full kitchens and laun-
dry, plus hotel services
and facilities including
50-metre indoor
rooftop pool, spa, gym
and sauna. $$$$

Crowne Plaza Darling Harbour

150 Day Street, Darling
Harbour
Tel: 9261 1188
http://darlingharbour.
crowneplaza.com
Formerly the Park Royal
at Darling Harbour, this

12-storey hotel with
349 rooms has a bou-
tique feel, while provid-
ing all the facilities
expected of an inter-
national business hotel.
Great location near the
Darling Harbour water-
side. $$$

Four Points by Sheraton

161 Sussex Street,
Darling Harbour
Tel: 9290 4000
www.starwood.com/fourpoints
One of Sydney's largest
hotels (631 rooms on
15 floors), although its
elegant, curved design
facing Darling Harbour
belies its size. Award-
winning Corn Exchange
restaurant and pleas-
ant Dundee Arms pub.
$$$

Novotel Sydney on Darling Harbour

100 Murray Street, Pyrmont
Tel: 9934 0000
www.novotel.com
A large comfortable
hotel geared towards
business travellers,
with gym, tennis court
and sauna. 525 rooms.
$$$

Aarons Hotel

37 Ultimo Road, Haymarket
Tel: 9281 5555
www.aaronshotel.com.au
Good standard motel-
style accommodation
right in the middle of
the city. The restaurant,
Café nine, has cabaret
Thur–Sun. 94 rooms. $$

Goldspear Hotel

Cnr of Campbell & George
Streets, Haymarket
Tel: 9211 8633
www.goldspear.com.au
A newish boutique hotel
adjacent to the Capitol
Theatre and on the
fringe of Chinatown. $$

Hotel Ibis Darling Harbour

70 Murray Street, Pyrmont
Tel: 9563 0888
A modern (1995) three-
star hotel on the west
side of Darling Harbour.
Standard rooms are not
large, but comfortable
enough. Good value for
its location. Fine views
across the harbour,
especially from the Sky-
line restaurant and bar,
with outdoor terrace.
256 rooms. $$

Mercure Hotel Lawson

383 Bulwara Road, Ultimo
Tel: 9211 1499
Friendly, efficient ser-
vice in this 96-room
modern hotel located
behind Darling Harbour.
$$

The Maze Backpackers/ CB Hotel

417 Pitt Street, City
Tel: 9211 5115
www.mazebackpackers.com
A 200-room hostel in
the heart of the city,
with TV lounges, juke
box, games room etc.
Dorms, doubles, twins
and singles, no
ensuites. Cheap and
cheerful. $

Sydney Central YHA

11 Rawson Place,
Haymarket
Tel: 9281 9111
sydcentral@yhansw.org.au
Technically a youth
hostel, but it's also an
excellent centrally-
located hotel in a her-
itage building opposite
Central Station. Less
than $100 for an
ensuite double/twin,
with special rates for
YHA members. $

OUTSIDE THE CENTRE

HOTELS

Manly Pacific Parkroyal
55 North Steyne, Manly
Tel: 9977 766
Situated right on the beach, this large hotel has a lively, resort-style atmosphere. **$$$**

Radisson Kestrel Hotel
8–13 South Steyne, Manly
Tel: 9977 8866
This beachside hotel has 83 comfortable rooms and a restaurant with balcony and beach views. **$$$**

Ravesi's on Bondi Beach
Cnr of Campbell Parade & Hall Street, Bondi Beach
Tel: 9365 4422
This is a great place to combine a beachside holiday with a trip to a busy metropolis. Great beach views and an intimate atmosphere. **$$$**

Regents Court
18 Springfield Avenue, Potts Point
Tel: 9358 1533
www.regentscourt.com.au
Converted in the early 1990s to become Sydney's first true designer hotel, in a quiet cul-de-sac. Rooftop garden with barbecue. 30 studio apartments. **$$$**

Ritz Carlton
33 Cross Street, Double Bay
Tel: 9362 4455
If you want luxury away from the city, then this is one of your best bets. Designed with a Mediterranean theme, it provides a discreet retreat in one of Sydney's prettiest suburbs. **$$$**

Sebel of Sydney
23 Elizabeth Bay Road
Tel: 9358 3244
Sydney's oldest five-star hotel, tucked away in Elizabeth Bay, the best part of Kings Cross. Popular with celebrities, who love its discreet, club-like atmosphere. 143 rooms, 23 suites. **$$$**

Simpsons of Potts Point
8 Challis Avenue, Potts Point
Tel: 9356 2199
www.simpsonspottspoint.com.au
Simpsons is an elegant boutique hotel (14 rooms) in a historic 1892 family home. It is within walking distance of the city, and minutes from Macleay Street's restaurants. **$$$**

Vibe North Sydney
88 Alfred Street, Milsons Point
Tel: 9955 1111
Long a favourite with corporate travellers, this hotel (formerly the Duxton) looks across the harbour from a North Shore perspective, with views of the Harbour Bridge and Opera House. 165 rooms, including executive suites. **$$$**

All Seasons on Crown
302–308 Crown Street, Darlinghurst
Tel: 9360 1133
An elegant boutique hotel in the city's restaurant district. The hotel has its own popular Crown Café. 93 rooms, some with harbour views. **$$**

Kirketon Hotel
229 Darlinghurst Road, Darlinghurst.
Tel: 9332 2011
www.kirketon.com.au
A well-run boutique hotel in a convenient location. Stylish design – enough to get it voted one of 21 hip hotels for the 21st century. Remarkably good value. **$$**

L'Otel
114 Darlinghurst Road, Darlinghurst
Tel: 9360 6868
This luxury "European-style boutique hotel", in the heart of Kings Cross, has 16 all-white rooms, described as a fusion of French chic and hi-tech. **$$**

Periwinkle Guesthouse
19 East Esplanade, Manly
Tel: 9977 4668
Friendly family-style accommodation on the sea at Manly. Bathrooms are shared. **$**

HOSTELS

Sydney has a large number of backpacker lodges, mostly around Kings Cross, the southern beaches and the inner west. Many of these are independently run, while others are part of large youth/backpacker networks.

Lamrock Hostel
7 Lamrock Avenue, Bondi Beach
Tel: 9365 0221
A "boutique" hostel, this

Maps, pages 112, 122 and 130–131

place deserves a special mention for its great location just up from the beach and its friendly, intimate atmosphere. **$**

Nomads Backpackers
Tel: 1800 819 883
Hostel franchise with beach suburbs and city centre accommodation available. **$**

Glebe Point YHA
262 Glebe Point Road
Tel: 9692 8418
A bright comfortable hostel with friendly staff who organise BBQs and backpackers activities. Great city views from roof recreation area. **$**

Y on the Park
5–11 Wentworth Avenue, Darlinghurst
Tel: 9264 2451
This terrific value-for-money hostel offers everything from dorm-style accommodation to en-suite rooms. All rooms are clean and comfortable. **$**

PRICE CATEGORIES

Price categories are for a standard double room without breakfast:
$= under A$100
$$ = A$100–175
$$$ = A$175–250
$$$$ = over A$250

OUTSIDE SYDNEY

HOTELS

The accommodation options in Sydney's surrounding countryside range from gourmet retreats to health spas, luxury B&Bs and bush cottages. Prices vary according to season, so you should telephone for details. Check out our recommendations, or contact the tourist information authorities for the different areas *(see page 237)*.

Northside

Barrenjoey House
1108 Barrenjoey Road, Palm Beach
Tel: 9974 4001
A traditional-style guesthouse.
Jonah's
69 Bynya Road, Palm Beach
Tel: 9974 5599
A gourmet retreat in exclusive Palm Beach.

Blue Mountains

Cleopatra
118 Cleopatra Street, Blackheath
Tel: 4787 8456
One of Australia's best gourmet retreats, set in beautiful bushland.
Echos
3 Lilianfels Avenue, Katoomba
Tel: 4782 1966
Modern luxury and old-fashioned atmosphere.
Fairmont Resort
Sublime Point Road, Leura
Tel: 4782 5222
One of the luxury resorts built in the

1980s when the area was revived as a holiday escape.
Jemby Rinjah Lodge
336 Evan's Lookout Road, Blackheath
Tel: 4787 7622
A private bush retreat just outside one of the main mountain towns.
Lilianfels
Lilianfels Avenue, Echo Point, Katoomba
Tel: 4780 1200
A five-star resort with a renowned restaurant.
Little Company Retreat
2 Eastview Road, Leura
Tel: 4782 4023
Elegant guesthouse-style accommodation in this pretty town.
Withycombe
Withycombe Church Road, Mount Wilson
Tel: 4756 2106
A gracious B&B in the beautiful village of Mount Wilson.

Southern Highlands

Bunyip Inn
122 Queen Street, Berry
Tel: 4464 2064
Cosy, historic accommodation in this pretty, out-of-the-way town.
Links House
7 Links Road, Bowral
Tel: 4861 1977
A pretty, boutique-style hotel.
Peppers Mount Broughton
Kater Road, Sutton Forest
Tel: 4868 2355
A luxurious retreat with a gourmet restaurant attached.
Ranelagh House
Illawarra Highway,

Robertson
Tel: 4885 1111
An imposing old mansion in a historic Southern Highlands town.
Solar Springs Health Retreat
Osborne Avenue, Bundanoon
Tel: 4883 6027
The area's luxury health resort.
Tree Tops Guesthouse
1011 Railway Avenue, Bundanoon
Tel: 4883 6372
An early 20th-century retreat.
Twin Falls Cottages
Throsby Road, Fitzroy Falls
Tel: 4887 7333
A modest bush retreat in the region's escarpment country.
Villa Dalmeny
72 Shoalhaven Street, Kiama
Tel: 4233 1991
A National Trust classified home, offering famous gourmet cooking.

Central Coast

Headlands
83 Highview Road, Pretty Beach
Tel: 4360 1933
An "eco" retreat on the edge of national parkland.
Kims
16 Charlton Street, Toowoon Bay
Tel: 4332 1566
Resort-style accommodation.
Salty Rose Boutique B&B
31 Surf Rider Avenue, North Avoca
Tel: 4384 6098
An intimate retreat on this beautiful coastline.

Maps, pages 130–131, 186, 196 and 206

BED AND BREAKFAST

B&Bs are big in Sydney and the surrounding areas, and many family homes are geared up to cater for one or two couples. This is an inexpensive way to stay in the city, with the added benefit of local knowledge to draw on. Some of these places welcome family groups, while others are child-free zones.

There are two online directories of B&B accommodation in the area:
www.sydneybandb.com.au
www.bedandbreakfastnsw.com.
Or contact the following organisations:
Bed and Breakfast Sydneyside, PO Box 555, Turramurra, NSW 2074; tel: 9449 4430.
Homestay Network, 5 Locksley Street, Killara, NSW 2071; tel: 9498 4400.

Call Wendy Robinson (tel: 03 9534 2683) to obtain a copy of her excellent publication, *Robinson's Guide to Bed and Breakfast and Rural Retreats in NSW*.

TRANSPORT

ACTIVITIES

THE ARTS, NIGHTLIFE, FESTIVALS, SHOPPING AND SPORTS

ACCOMMODATION

THE ARTS

Art Galleries

Sydney has a lively gallery scene. The best way to get in touch with what's on is to buy a copy of *Art Almanac*, a monthly pocket-sized booklet that lists galleries and their current exhibitions. The publication costs A$2 and is available at good bookshops and galleries. Some of the best public and commercial galleries are listed below:

Annandale Galleries
110 Trafalgar Street, Annandale
Tel: 9552 1699
Wide range of works by local painters and sculptors. Open Tues–Sat 11am–5pm.

Art Gallery of New South Wales
Art Gallery Road, The Domain
Tel: 9225 1744
The leading museum of art in the state, and one of Australia's foremost cultural institutions. Open daily 10am–5pm, Wed to 9pm.

Australian Galleries
15 Roylston Street, Paddington
Tel: 9360 5177
Features established contemporary Australian artists including Jeffrey Smart. Open Mon–Sat 10am–6pm.

Coo-ee Aboriginal Art Gallery
98 Oxford Street, Paddington
Tel: 9332 1544
Some of Australia's best known Aboriginal artists, including the work of Emily Kngwarreye. Viewing by appointment.

Darren Knight
Top Floor, 840 Elizabeth Street, Waterloo
Tel: 9699 5353
Interesting range of contemporary artists including Noel McKenna. Open Tues–Sat 11am–6pm.

Gould Galleries
92 Queen Street, Woollahra
Tel: 9328 9222
Some of Australia's biggest names, including Arthur Boyd, Charles Blackman and Sidney Nolan. Open Tues–Fri 11am–6pm, Sat 11am–5pm, Sun 2–5pm.

Gitte Weise
Level 2, 94 Oxford St, Darlinghurst
Tel: 9360 2659
New angles on the contemporary scene. Open Tues–Sat 11am–6pm.

Hogarth Galleries
Aboriginal Art Centre, 7 Walker Lane, Paddington
Tel: 9360 6839
Australia's oldest established Aboriginal fine art gallery, presenting works by established and emerging artists. Open Tues–Sat 10am–5pm.

Manly Art Gallery and Museum
West Esplanade, Manly
Tel: 9949 1776
Paintings, photographs and ceramics by Australian artists, plus international exhibitions. Open Tues–Sun 10am–5pm.

Mori Gallery
168 Day Street, Darling Harbour
Tel: 9283 2903
Showing both established and new contemporary artists. Open Wed–Sat 11am–6pm.

Museum of Contemporary Art
Circular Quay West, The Rocks
Tel: 9252 4033
Contains several unique art collections, including work by Australia's finest contemporary artists. Open daily 10am–5pm.

New Contemporaries
Level 3 South, Queen Victoria Building, George Street
Tel: 9268 0316
A non-commercial gallery, supported by the owners of the building, presenting an ever-changing display of what its name suggests. Open Mon–Sat 10am–6pm, Sun 11am–4pm

Ray Hughes
270 Devonshire Street, Surry Hills
Tel: 9698 3200
Emphasis on vibrant Australian works and more unusual overseas works. Open Tues–Sat 10am–6pm.

ACTIVITIES

A – Z

Roslyn Oxley 9 Gallery
Soudan Lane, 27 Hampden Street, Paddington
Tel: 9331 1919
Features new work in a range of media, from painting and sculpture to photography, performance, installation, video and other electronic media. Open Tues–Fri 10am–6pm, Sat 11am–6pm.

Sherman Galleries Goodhope
16–18 Goodhope Street, Paddington
Tel: 9331 1112
Exhibits contemporary Australian painters and sculptors, and occasional exhibitions of international artists. Open Tues–Sat 11am–6pm, Sun noon–5pm.

Utopia Art Sydney
2 Danks Street, Waterloo
Tel: 9699 2900
Specialises in Aboriginal work. Open Wed–Fri 10am–5pm, Sat noon–5pm.

Theatre

The Sydney Theatre Company (STC) is the town's most prominent drama company. Established in late 1978, it is housed in Australia's second best theatrical venue (after the Opera House), the magnificent Wharf complex in Walsh Bay. The company stages new and innovative works, which are dutifully attended by Sydney's theatre-goers. But in truth, what the conservative patrons want (and most often get) are the shows that have already been tried and tested overseas, or anything written by chief chronicler of modern life in Australia, playwright David Williamson. To be fair, though, the company runs an excellent research and development programme, which has launched many a brilliant career. And, old or new, its main productions are always highly professional and eminently watchable.

Belvoir Street is home to Company B, under the direction of Neil Armfield, the "actors' director". Staging works drawn from a surprisingly broad field, this is Australia's most critically acclaimed company. The Stables, which is literally that – an old horse stable in the back blocks of Kings Cross – premieres many of the plays newly written in Australia. The work is often innovative, as are the myriad ways that the designers utilise a space scarcely bigger than most people's living room – this is what they call an intimate experience.

The Bell Theatre Company does a roaring trade in Shakespeare under the direction of actor/manager John Bell. The company has a fairly high output so there is every chance that the visitor can catch an antipodean rendering of a play by the Bard.

The blockbuster musicals imported from Broadway and London's West End can usually be seen at the Theatre Royal, the Capitol or Her Majesty's Theatre.

Sydney's theatrical troupes also make use of the climate to stage open-air performances. Two of the most popular are Shakespeare by the Sea, which takes place at Balmoral Beach, and the Sydney Fringe Festival each summer, which features the work of new playwrights at various venues around the city.

Bell Shakespeare Company
88 George Street, The Rocks
Tel: 9241 2722
A touring company that stages unusual productions of Shakespeare. In Sydney, the company appears at the Playhouse Theatre in the Opera House.

Belvoir Street Theatre
25 Belvoir Street, Surry Hills
Tel: 9699 3444
An old tomato sauce factory is now home to the innovative Company B. This is the place to see alternative, well-crafted work.

Capitol
13 Campbell Street, Haymarket
Tel: 9320 5000
Built in the 1920s to a design inspired by the grand palaces of Italy, this 2,000-seat theatre hosts major musicals and large concerts.

Her Majesty's
107 Quay Street, Haymarket
Tel: 9266 4800
A large venue for blockbuster musicals and popular international performances.

Stables Theatre
10 Nimrod Street, Kings Cross
Tel: 9361-3817
Home to the Griffin Theatre Company, which performs new Australian works in this very challenging small venue.

BUYING TICKETS

Performance venues often sell tickets through ticket agencies such as Ticketek and Ticketmaster. Names and numbers of venues are published in all listings of what's on.

HalfTix is an agency that takes unsold tickets from the various companies and sells them cheaply (often half price) on the day of performance. You won't necessarily score tickets to the latest blockbuster musical, but you'll often get in to see a fairly popular local show. Obviously, you will do better in this respect on quieter nights (usually earlier in the week).

Some companies also sell unsold tickets cheaply a half-hour before the performance starts, direct from the venue.

Ticketek 195 Elizabeth St, inside Myer Sydney department store (Cnr of George and Market streets), Theatre Royal, MLC Centre, 106 King Street, and other outlets
Tel: 9266 4800
http://premier1.ticketek.com.au

Ticketmaster 1st floor, 66 Hunter Street
Tel: 13 61 00
www.ticketmaster.com.au

HalfTix 91 York Street and Ticket Central booth in Darling Park Monorail Station, Sussex Street
Tel: 9261 2990
www.halftix.com.au

OPERA

Opera Australia *(right)* has the third busiest programme in the world after Covent Garden and the Vienna Staatsopera. Its seasons run in the Opera Theatre from January to March, and June to November, but its most spectacular performance is its free and hugely popular Opera in the Park held in the Domain in January.

State Theatre
49 Market Street, City
Tel: 9373 6861 (box office); 9373 6660 (tours)
A 2,000-seat theatre built in 1929 in Cinema Baroque style. It now hosts the Sydney Film Festival and a variety of musical performances and special events.
Sydney Theatre Company
The Wharf Theatre, Pier 4, Hickson Road, Millers Point
Tel: 9250 1777
Sydney's main company performs Australian, foreign and classic works at the Wharf and in the Drama Theatre at the Opera House.
Theatre Royal
MLC Centre, King Street, City
Tel: 9224 8444
Host to large-scale musicals.

Concerts

The responsibility for providing Sydney with its classics falls to the Sydney Symphony Orchestra (SSO) and the Australian Chamber Orchestra (ACO). The SSO, established in 1932, performs around 150 concerts a year. Its home ground is the Concert Hall in the Opera House, but its biggest gig is definitely Symphony under the Stars, when thousands turn up for a free summer evening concert in the Domain. The ACO, also a Concert Hall team, is better known for the youth of its performing members and the eclecticism of its programmes.
Australian Chamber Orchestra
Sydney Opera House, Bennelong Point
Tel: 9250 7777 (box office)

This young orchestra plays about 24 concerts at the Concert Hall each year.
Musica Viva
Tel: 8394 6666
This large chamber music association organises tours of national and international music groups. Concerts are held Mar–Nov in the Opera House Concert Hall and the Seymour Centre in Chippendale.
Sydney Symphony Orchestra
Sydney Opera House, Bennelong Point
Tel: 9250 7777 (box office)
The largest orchestra in the southern hemisphere, the SSO plays about 100 concerts a year at the most famous opera venue, the Opera House Concert Hall.

Dance

The Australian Ballet, the main classical dance company, is based in Melbourne, but has two seasons each year in the Opera Theatre. The world-renowned company performs all the old classical favourites as well as new works by Australian composers and choreographers.

The Sydney Dance Company, which is based at The Wharf, did the seemingly impossible when it first started in the 1970s; it created a contemporary dance company in a city that was then vaguely suspicious of such things, and made it viable, enduring and most of all, wildly popular. The mover and shaker of the company is choreographer Graeme Murphy, who has been at the artistic helm since the beginning. The work is devastatingly skilled, funny, sensual and highly intelligent.

The Bangarra Dance Theatre, under the direction of Stephen Page, is a mostly Aboriginal company performing works that draw both on traditional indigenous forms and contemporary styles. Their work is highly regarded both at home and abroad.
Australian Ballet
The Sydney Opera House, Bennelong Point
Tel: 9250 7777 (box office)

This Melbourne-based national ballet company has two seasons at the Opera House: Mar–Apr and Nov–Dec.
Bangarra Dance Theatre
The Wharf Theatre, Pier 4, Hickson Road, Millers Point
Tel: 9251 5333
Combines Aboriginal, Western and other dance traditions.
Sydney Dance Company
The Wharf Theatre *(as above)*
Tel: 9211 4811
Sydney's main contemporary dance company performs at The Wharf and the Opera Theatre.

NIGHTLIFE

Bars

Fashionable bars
Banc
53 Martin Place, City
Tel: 9233 5300
An elegant bar in this upmarket restaurant, frequented by city professionals.
Bondi Icebergs
1 Knotts Avenue, South Bondi
Tel: 9130 3120
Enjoy a beer while soaking up one of the best views in Sydney. Live music Fri–Sun nights.
East Village
234 Palmer Street, Darlinghurst
Tel: 9331 5457
A young, groovy bar in the heart

of the city's hippest district.

Grand Pacific Blue Room
Oxford Street, Paddington
Tel: 9331 7108
A cool and hip bar for the young and trendy of Sydney.

Horizons Bar
Shangri-La Hotel, 176 Cumberland Street, The Rocks
Tel: 9250 6013
The classy atmosphere and sensational harbour views here lend themselves to enjoying a glass or two of native Australian wine.

Krug Room
Restaurant Forty One, Level 42, Chifley Tower, 2 Chifley Square, City
Tel: 9221 2500
An up-market drinking spot, with a view and prices to match.

Slip Inn
111 Sussex Street, City
Tel: 8295 9999
This complex of five bars, a restaurant and a nightclub is continually popular with Sydney's young city types.

The Soho Lounge
171 Victoria Street, Kings Cross
Tel: 9358 6511.
The young and fashionable of Kings Cross cram into this lounge bar in the Piccadilly Hotel.

Traditional Pubs

Customs House Bar
Sydney Renaissance Hotel, Macquarie Place, City
Tel: 9259 7316
Drinking spot for office workers.

Hero of Waterloo
81 Lower Fort, Millers Point
Tel: 9252 4553
Historic ambience in Sydney's reputedly oldest pub.

Hotel Bondi
178 Campbell Parade, Bondi Beach
Tel: 9130 3271
This is the real Bondi – loud, friendly, sun-and-sea soaked.

London Tavern
85 Underwood Street, Paddington
Tel: 9331 3200
Serves lunch and dinner, and a great place for a cosy drink.

Lord Nelson Brewery Hotel
19 Kent Street, The Rocks
Tel: 9251 4044
Charming historic atmosphere.

WHAT'S ON IN SYDNEY

For the most comprehensive guide to what's on in Sydney, buy the *Sydney Morning Herald* on Friday for its lift-out "Metro" section. CitySearch (www. sydney.citysearch.com.au), the paper's website, also has extensive culture and entertainment listings.

The *Sydney Star Observer* is a widely available free newspaper listing the best gay and lesbian events.

Newport Arms
Kalinya Street, Newport
Tel: 9997 4900
The northern beaches' most popular watering-hole.

Oaks Hotel
118 Military Road, Mosman
Tel: 9953 5515
A big boozy yuppie place on the North Shore.

Royal Hotel
Five Ways, Paddington
Tel: 9331 2604
Ornate Victorian architecture and great food.

Gay Bars

Beauchamp Hotel
267 Oxford Street, Darlinghurst
Tel: 9331 2575
For mature gays.

Gilligans
Oxford Hotel, Darlinghurst
Tel: 9331 3467
Cocktail bar that attracts a smart, fashionable straight and gay crowd.

Lizard Lounge
Exchange Hotel, 34 Oxford Street, Darlinghurst
Tel: 9331 2956
Popular lesbian bar.

Midnight Shift
85 Oxford Street, Darlinghurst
Tel: 9360 4463
Quirky and extravagant nightclub.

Newtown Hotel
174 King Street, Newtown
Tel: 9557 1329
Dim, smoky interior, noted for kitschy drag shows with camp humour.

Stonewall Hotel
175 Oxford Street, Darlinghurst
Tel: 9360 1963
Sweaty atmosphere and ultra-modern decor hidden inside an old-fashioned, colonial building.

Music Venues

Jazz

The Basement
29 Reiby Place, Circular Quay
Tel: 9251 2797
One of Sydney's best jazz venues. Mostly international acts, but also local bands.

Soup Plus
383 George Street, City
Tel: 9299 7728
Basement restaurant in the heart of the CBD presenting trad jazz, mainstream and occasional bebop groups.

Starfish Club
Bondi Surf Lifesaving Club
A Monday-evening club for jazz diehards.

Unity Hall Hotel
292 Darling Street, Balmain
Tel: 9810 1331
Traditional group the Roger James Band have had their gig here for 20 years.

Woollahra Hotel
Cnr Queen & Moncur Sts, Woollahra
Tel: 9363 2782
Presents contemporary groups on Sunday evenings.

Wynyard Hotel
Cnr Clarence & Erskine streets, City
Tel: 9299 1330
Traditional jazz styles.

Rock and Pop

Annandale Hotel
17 Parramatta Road, Annandale
Tel: 9550 1078
The place for indie and rock fans.

Hopetoun Hotel
416 Bourke Street, Surry Hills
Tel: 9361 5257
Rock, hard blues and Ska.

Selina's
Coogee Bay Hotel, cnr Coogee Bay Road & Arden Street, Coogee
Tel: 9665 0000
Well-known suburban rock venue on the Coogee beachfront.

TRANSPORT

The Metro
624 George Street, City
Tel: 9287 2000
International and local acts at the city's main rock venue.

Folk and Blues

The Cat & Fiddle Hotel
456 Darling Street, Balmain
Tel: 9810 7931
Mainly home to acoustic acts, pop, folk and blues.

Eastwood Hotel
115 Rowe Street, Eastwood
Tel: 9874 1100
Rhythm and blues music.

Excelsior Hotel
64 Foveaux Street, Surry Hills
Tel: (freecall) 1800 000 549
A venue for R&B and indie rock enthusiasts.

The Loaded Dog
Annandale Neighbourhood Centre,
79 Johnston Street, Annandale
Tel: 9660 2828
A traditional folk music venue which holds small concerts on a semi-regular basis.

Sandringham Hotel
387 King Street, Newtown
Tel: 9557 1254
Spacious venue with live music most nights of the week.

Cinema

Check the daily papers for cinema listings, and the weekend papers for the best film reviews. SBS, Australia's multicultural broadcaster, runs an excellent half-hour film review programme

GAMBLING

Sydney has only one legal venue for gambling: the Star City Casino. Located in Darling Harbour, it offers acres of gambling tables set within massive gaming rooms, the decoration of which is based upon the Australian landscape. There are also shops, cafés, bars, live shows, and a 352-room hotel.

Star City Casino
355 Bulwara Road, Ultimo; tel: 9777 9000 or 1800 700 700 (toll-free).

on Wednesday evenings, which covers most of the major releases.

Many of the city's multi-cinema complexes are located along George Street. This is where you'll find all the big blockbuster movies and latest releases.

Sydney also has plenty of small art-house and foreign-language cinemas in the city and inner-suburbs. Foreign-language films are rarely, if ever, dubbed in Australia; all carry English subtitles.

Academy Twin
3a Oxford St, Paddington
Tel: 9361 4453
Long-established non-mainstream release cinema.

Chauvel Cinema
249 Oxford Street Paddington
Tel: 9361 5398
Innovative programmes, with classics each Monday night.

Dendy Cinemas
MLC Centre, Martin Place, City
Tel: 9233 8166;
624 George Street, City
Tel: 9264 1577;
261–263 King Street, Newtown
Tel: 9550 5699
Varied cinema programmes, just to the left of mainstream.

Greater Union
525 George Street City
Tel: 9267 8666;
232 Pitt Street, City
Tel: 9264 1694
Multi-cinema mainstream.

Hoyts
505 George Street, City
Tel: 11680 (info line)
Multi-cinema mainstream.

IMAX Theatre
Southern Promenade, Darling Harbour
Tel: 9281 3300
Mega movies on a giant screen.

The Verona
17 Oxford Street, Paddington
Tel: 9360 6099
Part art-house, part-Hollywood showing "cross-over" product.

Valhalla
166 Glebe Point Road, Glebe
Tel: 9660 8050 or 0055 20 100 (info line)
Shows an eclectic mix of foreign films including animation and

documentaries.

Village
545 George Street, City
Tel: 9264 6701
Multi-cinema mainstream.

Walker Cinema
121 Walker Street, North Sydney
Tel: 9959 4222
Small venue showing smart art-house fare.

Comedy

Double Bay Comedy Club
16–18 Cross Street, Double Bay
Tel: 9327 6560
Live comics and a meal or just the show later in the evening.

Jokers
Star City Casino, 80 Pyrmont Road, Pyrmont
Tel: 9777 9000
The city's biggest and least subtle entertainment venue features local and international comedians.

The Comedy Store
Cnr of Crystal Street & Parramatta Road, Petersham
Tel: 9564 3900
This is comedy New York-style, brash and un-PC.

The Old Manly Boatshed
40 The Corso, Manly
Tel: 9977 4443
Monday night comedy and dinner.

Unicorn Hotel
106 Oxford St (cnr Hopewell St), Paddington
Tel: 9360 3554
Out-of-town acts and local talent.

SYDNEY FOR CHILDREN

The city has many activities on offer that will appeal to even the most demanding children. Conveniently, two of the leading attractions are located in Darling Harbour: the **Monorail** (kids love it) and **Tumbalong Park**, with a free playground and a stage for free concerts.

The "Search and Discover" section on the second floor of the **Australian Museum** lets children get their hands on all sorts of

ACCOMMODATION

ACTIVITIES

A – Z

exciting exhibits that most museums would keep out of bounds. The **Powerhouse Museum** has stimulating Kids Interactive Discovery Spaces (KIDS), designed to involve younger children in hands-on activities related to the themes in the museum's exhibitions. They explore subjects such as music, machines, life in the home, film and television.

The **Opera House** runs children's events such as the Babies Proms, which allows toddlers to get close to the musical instruments (tel: 9250 7111). The **Art Gallery of New South Wales** holds special family events on Sundays, such as renditions of Aboriginal Dreamtime stories (tel: 9225 1700).

Fox Studios (Lang Road, Moore Park) has two state-of-the-art playgrounds, one for under-fours, the other for 4–12-year-olds: ball pits, giant mazes, tunnels, cargo nets, climbing, jumping, sliding and exploring – multi-story funhouse for kids of all ages. The playground areas have tables and shaded seating for parents, along with a huge grassed area for the kids to run and play (tel: 9383 4333).

SHOPPING

What to Buy

Aboriginal Art

Aboriginal artists sell their work in art centres, specialist galleries and craft retailers and through agents. Each traditional artist owns the rights to his or her particular stories, motifs and tokens. Indigenous fabric designs by artists such as Jimmy Pike are eagerly sought. Bark paintings are the most common

SYDNEY EVENTS

Sydney is Australia's events capital, and visitors to the city should try to time their stay to coincide with one of the big "party" days on the calendar, such as the magnificent spectacle of the Sydney to Hobart Yacht Race which leaves from Sydney Harbour on Boxing Day each year, or the February Mardi Gras. More on Sydney's events can be found on pages 138–9.

The following is a run-down of what's on where, with some useful contact numbers provided.

Spring (Sep–Nov)

Royal Botanic Gardens Spring Festival, September. Spectacular seasonal displays, complete with brass bands, art shows and food stalls. Tel: 9231 8111

Spring Racing Carnival, September. Sydney's top racing event, culminating in the Sydney Cup. Tel: 9663 8400

Aurora New World Festival, late September. A multicultural celebration at Darling Harbour. Tel: 9286 0100

Manly Jazz Festival, early October. Tel: 9977 1088

Australian Rugby League Grand Final, late September. Tel: 9339 8500

Glebe Street Fair, late September. Tel: 9692 0051

Summer (Dec–Feb)

Carols in the Domain, December. Tel: 9596 8199

Sydney to Hobart Yacht Race, 26 December. Thousands watch the start in Sydney Harbour.

Christmas & New Year's Eve Parties, Bondi Beach. Tel: 9265 9007.

Concerts in the Domain, January. Free night-time performances by Opera Australia and the Sydney Symphony Orchestra.

The Sydney Festival, January. A three-week festival of local and imported music and theatre. Tel: 8248 6500

Opera in the Park, end January. Tel: 9318 1099

Symphony under the Stars, mid-January. Tel: 9265 0444

Ferrython, Australia Day (26 January). Tel: 9207 3170

Survival Concert, Australia Day. Tel: 9331 3777

Sydney Fringe Festival, late January–early February. Tel: 9365 0112

Gay and Lesbian Mardi Gras, February/March. A hugely popular parade and street party. Tel: 9568 8600

Chinese New Year, mid-February festival featuring food, firecrackers, lion and sword dancing and other excitements. Tel: 9368 7277

Autumn (Mar–May)

Golden Slipper Festival, March. Popular horse-racing event. Tel: 9930 4000

Royal Easter Show. The country comes to town: wood-chopping, cattle contests, sideshows. Tel: 9704 1111

Archibald, Wynne and Sulman exhibitions, March–April. Popular art event. Tel: 9225 1700

St Patrick's Day Parade, mid-March. Tel: 9211 3410

King's Cross Bed Race, mid-March. Madness on Darlinghurst Road. Tel: 9358 1144

Sydney Writers Festival, late May. Book-readings, public lectures and special literary events. Tel: 9252 7729

National Rugby League State of Origin Series, May–June. Tel: 9339 8500

Winter (Jun–Aug)

Sydney Film Festival, mid-June. About 250 screenings in two weeks, many in the grand old State Theatre. Tel: 9280 0511

Biennale of Sydney, mid-July (even-numbered years). International arts festival. Tel: 9368 1411

City to Surf Race, early August. Thousands of runners join the race from the City to Bondi. Tel: 9282 2747.

form of Koori (Aboriginal) art, but look out for contemporary works on board, boomerangs and didgeridoos.

Antiques

The Paddington and Woollahra district is full of antique shops. Worthy pieces to seek out include clocks, jewellery, porcelain, silverware, glassware, books and maps. Start your search in Queen Street, off Oxford Street.

Clothing

A distinct style of clothing has evolved in rural Australia (an area collectively known as "the Bush"). Driza-Bone oilskin coats, Akubra hats (wide-brimmed and usually made of felt) and the R. M. Williams range of bushwear (including boots and moleskin trousers) are good examples. Blundstone boots, made in Tasmania and renowned for their durability, are another.

Australian merino sheep produce fine fleece ideally suited for spinning. All sorts of knitwear, from vivid children's clothing to Jumbuk brand greasy wool sweaters (which retain the sheep's natural water resistance), is available throughout the city.

Food and Drink

Local delicacies include macadamia nuts, bush honey, royal jelly, chocolates and the inevitable Vegemite, a savoury spread. Australian wines can be bought at any pub or bottle shop, with fair quality wines starting at A$10 a bottle.

Gemstones

Australia is the source of abut 95 percent of the world's opals. "White" opals are mined from the fields of Andamooka and Coober Pedy in South Australia. "Boulder" opals – bright and vibrant – come from Quilpie in Queensland, while the precious "black" opal (actually more blue than black) is mined at Lightning Ridge

and White Cliffs in New South Wales. After opals, sapphires are Australia's most-mined gemstones, and creative Australian jewellery designers work wonders with them.

Many jewellery shops in the central shopping district, particularly in Pitt and Castlereagh streets and around The Rocks, sell Australian opals and sapphires, either set or loose.

Where to Buy

The City is Sydney's retail heartland, with all the major retail chains represented. The nearby Rocks and Darling Harbour precincts provide a good range of shops offering products with an Australian theme.

The inner-city "villages" of Paddington, Newtown, Surry Hills, Glebe, Balmain and Double Bay are great spots to do some browsing for a more eclectic, unusual range of products. On the North Shore, Mosman offers great fashion and homeware-buying opportunities.

Australiana
Aboriginal Art and Tribal Art Centre
117 George Street, The Rocks
Tel: 9241 5998
Artifacts and craftworks for sale.
Australian Wine Centre
Shop 3, 1 Alfred Street, Circular Quay

Consumer Rights

If you have a complaint or query concerning shopping, contact the NSW Department of Fair Trading (tel: 13 32 20) to find out what your rights are. If the goods purchased are defective in any way, customers are entitled to a full refund, but be prepared to accept a credit note or exchange.

Larger stores generally offer greater consumer protection. Ask to speak to a manager or customer service officer if you are unhappy with the service.

Tel: 9247 2755
A great gift can be made of Australia's excellent quality, reasonably priced wine.
Australian Geographic Shop
Shop 34 Centrepoint, Pitt Street, City
Tel: 9231 8013
Many excellent Australian products to do with the great outdoors.
Flame Opals
119 George Street, The Rocks
Tel: 9247 3446
One of Sydney's many opal jewellers.
Gavala Aboriginal Arts & Cultural Centre
Shop 32, Harbourside, Darling Harbour
Tel: 9212 7232
Aboriginal art and crafts.
Ken Done
123 George Street, City
Tel: 9251 6099 (and other stores)
This popular Australian artist makes his work up into a wide range of fashion items.
Red Earth Body Products
Sydney International Airport
Tel: 9667 1286
Terrific Australian cosmetics.
R. M. Williams
389 George Street, City
Tel: 9262 2228
Suppliers of bush gear including riding boots, Akubras *(see Clothing)* and oilskin bushman's coats.

International Brands

Sydney is getting together a respectable collection of big-name international designer stores, so if this is your thing head down to Castlereagh Street, the city's most exclusive retail colony. The luxurious Chifley Square, also in the City, comes a close second.

These are some of Sydney's finest designer outlets:

Adrienne Vittadini
Shop 7, 20 MLC Centre, 74 Castlereagh Street, City
Tel: 9231 1120

Cartier
43 Castlereagh Street, City
Tel: 9235 1322

Chanel
70 Castlereagh Street, City
Tel: 9233 4800

Giorgio Armani
175 Elizabeth Street, City
Tel: 9283 5562

Hermès
Shop C21, Skygarden, 77 Castlereagh Street, City
Tel: 9223 4007

Tiffany & Co
Chifley Plaza, 2 Chifley Square, City
Tel: 9235 1777

Books

Sydney has plenty of big bookstores with all the major releases, as well as a series of small outlets catering to the pleasures of the bookshop browser.

Abbey's
131 York Street, City
Tel: 9264 3111
Arguably Australia's biggest range of crime fiction, plus classics, text books, reference, fiction and audiobooks.

Angus & Robertson
Imperial Arcade
168–174 Pitt Street
Tel: 9253 1188

Ariel
42 Oxford Street, Paddington
Tel: 9332 4581
Excellent range of cinema, travel, food, design, architecture and current fiction.

Berkelouw Books
19 Oxford Street, Paddington
Tel: 9360 3200
New books downstairs, antiquarian and rare upstairs, secondhand further up again. First floor café.

Better Read Than Dead
265 King Street, Newtown
Tel: 9557 8700

The Bookshop
207 Oxford Street, Darlinghurst
Tel: 9331 4140
Specialises in gay and lesbian publications.

Collins Booksellers
Shop 34, Queen Victoria Building, 4554 George Street
Tel: 9267 6596

Dymocks Sydney
424–6 George Street
Tel: 9235 0155

Gleebooks
49 Glebe Point Road, Glebe
Tel: 9660 2333
Some 35,000 titles, including academic texts; strong on popular culture and sci-fi. Second shop at No. 191 sells children's and secondhand books.

Horden House
77 Victoria Street, Potts Point
Tel: 9356 4411

Rare books, manuscripts, prints, maps. Specialises in Australiana and Pacificana. Closed: Sat–Mon.

Kinokuniya Bookstore
The Galeries Victoria, Level 2, 500 George Street
Tel: 9262 7996

Lesley Mackay's
346 New South Head Road, Double Bay
Tel: 9327 1354
Queen's Court, Queen Street, Woollahra
Tel: 9328 2733
Excellent range, including new fiction and full backlist of classics. Separate children's shop connects with the Double Bay branch.

State Library of NSW Bookshop
Macquarie Street, City
Tel: 9320 1611
Great collection of Australian publications.

Shopping Centres

AMP Tower
Centrepoint, Level One, 100 Market Street, City
Tel: 9229 7444
A large retail area located at the base of Sydney Tower, featuring over 150 shops.

Argyle Department Store
12 Argyle Street, The Rocks
Tel: 9251 4800
Boutiques, gourmet restaurants and cafés, open until 8pm weekdays.

Chatswood Chase
345 Victoria Avenue, Chatswood
Tel: 9419 6255
Located on the North Shore, this popular centre, with over 100 retailers (including many local names), manages to be practical and elegant at the same time. Parking on site.

Chifley Plaza
Chifley Square Shopping Mall, Hunter Street, City
Tel: 9221 4500
Modern shopping plaza with luxury specialist shops including Tiffanys, Max Mara and Kenzo. Food court.

Harbourside Shopping Centre, Darling Harbour
Tel: 9281 3999

DEPARTMENT STORES

Sydney's main department stores are Myer (formerly Grace Bros) and David Jones. They offer an extensive range of goods from food to fashion, hardware to homeware. The David Jones Elizabeth Street Store has extraordinary flower displays in spring.

Gowings, which has been operating since 1868, is a men's store selling good quality clothes and various pieces of Australiana. It is now popular with Sydney's young and fashionable of both genders.

David Jones, Cnr of Elizabeth & Castlereagh streets, City; tel: 9266 55;
Cnr of Market & Castlereagh streets, City; tel: 9266 5544.

Gowings, Cnr George & Market streets, City; tel: 9264 6321.
Myer, 436 George Street, City; tel: 9238 9111.

200 shops which appeal to both tourists and local residents.

Market City
13 Hay Street, Haymarket
Tel: 9212 1388
A range of clothing chain stores and independent boutiques above the weekend market.

MLC Centre
King Street, City
Tel: 9224 8333
Close to Martin Place Station. You will find all the famous brands here, spread throughout the 80 or so shops; also boutiques, bars and restaurants.

Moore Park SupaCenta
2a Todman Street, Kensington
Tel: 9313 8340
Located in one of the southern suburbs, this centre has many of the big names in homewares including Ikea and Freedom.

Pitt Street Mall
A pedestrian shopping mall leading to a number of shopping arcades.

Queen Victoria Building
455 George Street, City
Tel: 9264 9209
This renovated ornate sandstone building (see page 73 for more details) offers boutiques and quality retailers.

Skygarden
77 Castlereagh Street, City
Tel: 92311 1811
Many high-quality local and international designer boutiques.

The Strand Arcade
255 Pitt Street, City
Tel: 9232 4199
Victorian arcade with 80 boutiques selling quality jewellery, leather goods and coffee shops.

Westfield Shopping Centre
Bondi Junction, 500 Oxford Street
Tel: 9387 3333
One of nine big Westfield Malls, this one is conveniently close to the city and offers parking and all the major stores under cover.

Markets

Sydney's enticing markets offer a myriad buying opportunities. Sharp-eyed bargain hunters will usually be rewarded if they browse for long enough among the huge variety of merchandise.

While some produce markets are open throughout the week, other "community" markets open only on weekends. Most stallholders handle cash only, so be prepared to bargain over the cost of your purchase.

Balmain Markets
St Andrews Church, cnr Darling & Curtis streets, Balmain
This "alternative" market offers a wide range of foodstuffs, clothing, locally made ceramics and woodwork. Open 7.30am–4pm Sat.

Flemington Markets
Parramatta Road, Flemington
A half-hour drive from the city. Wide range of goods and fresh produce. Open 10.30am–4.30pm Fri; 9am–4.30pm Sat–Sun.

Fish Markets
Blackwattle Bay, Pyrmont
An amazing choice of seafood, delis, sushi bars and fresh produce. Open 7am–4pm daily.

Glebe Markets
Glebe Public School, 193 Glebe Point Road, Glebe

Community-style market of around 200 outdoor stalls. Crafts, jewellery and secondhand clothes. Open 10am–5pm Sat.

Paddy's Markets
9 Hay Street, Haymarket
Sydney's oldest market, with 1,000 stalls. Huge range, from fresh produce to appliances and clothing. Open 9am–4.30pm Sat–Sun.

Paddington Bazaar
Uniting Church, cnr Oxford & Newcombe streets, Paddington
Trendy market, with works by local artisans. Open 10am–5pm Sat.

The Rocks Markets
George Street, The Rocks
Hundreds of stalls sell antiques, paintings, homeware. Also offers weekend street performances featuring the best of Australian buskers. Open 10am–5pm Sat–Sun.

SPORT

Spectator Sports

All you have to do to keep up with spectator sports in Sydney is open any newspaper or flick channels on the TV, where, on weekends, you can find broadcasts of everything from lawn bowls to netball.

If you are keen to see one of the big football or cricket games, you'd be well advised to ask your travel agent to find out about tickets prior to arrival. The ticket agency, **Ticketek** (tel: 9266 4800), handles ticketing for most of the big spectator games in Sydney. The main spectator sports sites are as follows:

Sydney Cricket Ground
Moore Park
Tel: 9360 6601/0055 63132 (match information).
Hosts all the major cricket matches and Australian Rules Football.

Aussie Stadium
Moore Park
Tel: 9360 6601

Hosts all major rugby league and union games (bar the finals, which are at Telstra Stadium).

Telstra Stadium
Olympic Park
Tel: 8765 2000
Sydney's largest stadium, hosting all the most important rugby league and union, Australian Rules and soccer matches.

Sydney to Hobart Yacht Race
The ultimate spectator yacht race; sets off from Sydney Harbour on Boxing Day.

Sydney Flying Yacht Squadron
McDougall Street, Milsons Point
Tel: 9955 8350
Departure point for spectators of 18-footer yacht races.

Horse Racing

Sydney's racing season comes to full flower in spring and autumn. However, other events are held throughout the year in the city's four main racing venues, often from Wednesday through to Sunday. The **Sydney Turf Club** (tel: 9930 4000) can handle most information inquiries.

Canterbury Park Racecourse
King Street, Canterbury
Tel: 9930 4000

Royal Randwick Racecourse
Alison Street, Randwick
Tel: 9663 8400

Rosehill Gardens Racecourse
76 McDougall Street, Milsons Point
Tel: 9955 8350

Warwick Farm Racecourse
Hume Highway, Warwick Farm
Tel: 9602 6199

Participant Sports

Golf

Sydney has around 100 golf courses. Most are inexpensive, well equipped and very scenic. Ask at your own golf club before leaving home about reciprocal membership arrangements with Sydney clubs. The **NSW Golf Association** (tel: 9264 8433) is a good starting point for golf players from abroad looking for a round in Sydney.

The following courses have been selected for convenience and quality. Some are private, and whether you get a round or not may depend on reciprocal membership rights.

The Australian
Bannerman Crescent, Rosebery
Tel: 9663 2273

Long Reef Golf Course
Anzac Avenue, Collaroy
Tel: 9971 8188

The Lakes
Cnr of King & Vernon Avenue, East Lakes
Tel: 9669 1311

Moore Park Golf Club
Cnr of Cleveland Street and Anzac Parade, Moore Park
Tel: 9663 1064

NSW Golf Course
Henry Head, off Anzac Parade, La Perouse
Tel: 9661 4455

Royal Sydney Golf Club
Kent Road, Rose Bay
Tel: 9371 4333

Swimming

Swimming in Sydney is the best way to deal with the heat. Most of the major hotels have their own pools, but many serious lappers find that these are a bit short for a good workout. Many of the chlorinated swimming pools have salt water, and some are heated in winter.

A good alternative to chlorine is a swim in one of the sea baths that dot the coastline.

Andrew (Boy) Charlton Pool
Mrs Macquaries Road, Domain
Tel: 9358 6686

Bondi Icebergs
Notts Avenue, Bondi
Tel: 9130 3120

Coogee Women's Baths
Beach Street, Coogee.

North Sydney Olympic Pool
Alfred Street, Milsons Point
Tel 9955 2309

Sydney International Aquatic Centre
Sydney Olympic Park, Homebush
Tel: 9752 3666

Wiley's Baths
Southern end of Coogee Beach
Tel: 9665 2838

Jogging & Walking

A jog or walk around the Botanic Gardens and Domain near the City, or along one of the many suburban coastal beaches, is worth the effort. But the ultimate jog in Sydney is the annual City to Surf Fun Run each August, when you can pit your fitness against thousands of others.

Two sensational walks are the Bondi to Clovelly cliff walk and the Spit Bridge to Manly walk through harbourside bushland. Centennial Park is a great spot for all activities.

Centennial Park and Moore Park Trust
Grand Drive, Centennial Park
Tel: 9339 6699

City to Surf Fun Run
Tel: 9282 2747 or 1 800 555 514

Tennis

Play in the early morning and/or late afternoon to avoid the sun. Ask about equipment hire when ringing to book a court. A good stop for information is **Tennis NSW** (tel: 9331 4144).

Primrose Park Tennis
Young Street, Cremorne
Tel: 9908 2366

Millers Point Tennis Courts
Kent Street, Millers Point (near The Rocks)
Tel: 9256 2222

Rushcutters Bay Tennis Centre
Waratah Avenue, Rushcutters Bay
Tel: 9357 1675

White City
30 Alma St, Paddington
Tel: 9360 4113

A - Z

TRANSPORT

ACCOMMODATION

AN ALPHABETICAL SUMMARY OF PRACTICAL INFORMATION

ACTIVITIES

Admission Charges

Several of Sydney's cultural sites are administered by the Historic Houses Trust (tel: 9692 8366), who also look after the Museum of Sydney. Admission to the museum and such buildings as Vaucluse House, Elizabeth Bay House, Hyde Park Barracks and the Justice and Police Museum costs the same – $7 for adults, $3 children/concessions and $17 for a family ticket. A few of the Trust's properties (including The Mint and Government House) are free to enter.

General admission to the National Maritime Museum, the Art Gallery of New South Wales and the Museum of Contemporary Art is also free, but they all charge for temporary exhibitions.

Entry to the Australian Museum costs $8 for adults, $3 for children.

Budgeting for your Trip

Australia has low inflation, and the basics – food, accommodation, admission charges – are still comparatively inexpensive. A plate of noodles or pasta in an average restaurant costs about A$10. A bottle of Australian wine from a liquor store starts at about $8, a 260ml glass of beer (about half a pint) costs from $2.50, and a cup of coffee or tea about the same.

Public transport in the city is very reasonable if you use the various saver tickets available *(see page 214)*. Taxis have a flagdown charge of $2.65; then it's $1.53 a kilometre. Add 20

percent to the fare between 10pm and 6am.

Hiring (renting) a small car costs from $45 per day. Petrol (gasoline) costs around 90c per litre, more expensive than in the US but cheaper than in most European countries. A half-day coach sightseeing tour is $36–150 per person.

A room at a backpacker hostel can be as little as $20 a night, and a room in a five-star hotel $250 and upwards. Sydney has a full range of accommodation in between *(see page 216)*.

Business Hours

Banks generally open 9.30am–4pm Monday to Thursday, and 9.30am–5pm on Friday. Currency exchange facilities at the airport

A – Z

are open all hours. Most shops are open 9am–5.30pm Monday to Friday and to 4pm Saturday. Many of the large city and suburban centres now open all day Sunday as well, although often with slightly shorter hours (generally 10am–4pm). Thursday night is late-night shopping, when some shops stay open until 8 or 9pm. However, visitors will find plenty of late-night shops operating all week including chemists, gift stores and bookshops, particularly around the major tourist centres. There are many 24-hour outlets for grocery items, including major supermarkets.

Climate

Sydney is usually mild and sunny with beautifully warm (though often quite humid) summer days, cooled in the evenings by southerly breezes. The average maximum temperature for January and February, Sydney's hottest months, is 26°C (78°F), and the minimum is 19°C (66°F). The average maximum for July, Sydney's coldest month, is 16°C (60°F) and the minimum, 8°C (46°F).

The wettest months are March and June. During the peak season in summer, travellers can expect rain on about 12 days a month – although this is likely to be little more than a brief shower.

Crime and Safety

Common-sense rules apply when visiting Sydney. Because of its high tourist profile, crimes against tourists have become something of an issue. Most often, these offences are in the order of petty thefts in popular visitor locations. Keep wallets out of sight, do not leave valuables visible in the car or luggage unattended.

Kings Cross has a fairly unsavoury reputation, but unless you get involved in something you shouldn't, the crime there is not likely to affect you directly. In fact, Kings Cross, with its constant urban buzz, is probably a lot safer

than the average suburban street come midnight. It's best to avoid Hyde Park after dark, particularly if you're on your own.

Many city and suburban train stations are either unstaffed or run with a skeleton staff during off-peak periods. Some stations have "night safe" areas on the platforms, with security cameras and an intercom for contacting staff, and trains have a blue light on one of the front carriages, indicating that there is a guard travelling in the carriage. Generally, travel on public transport is safe at any time in the inner-city area. Avoid longer, quieter trips after 10pm.

Sydney police are generally helpful and friendly. The emergency number is 000.

Customs

Australia has extremely strict regulations about what can and cannot be brought into the country. Before disembarking from the plane, visitors are asked to fill in an Incoming Passenger Card. Australian Customs officers check the information on the cards when passengers disembark, and may initiate a baggage search. There are heavy fines for false or inaccurate claims. It is always best to declare an item if in doubt.

Strict quarantine laws apply in Australia to protect the agricultural industries and native Australian flora and fauna from introduced diseases. Animals, plants and their derivatives must be declared on arrival. This may include items made from materials such as untreated wood, feathers or furs. The import or export of protected species, or products made from protected species, is a criminal offence. It is also illegal to export any species of native flora or fauna without a permit.

All food products, no matter how well processed and packaged, must be declared on arrival.

All weapons are prohibited, unless accompanied by an international permit. This includes

guns, ammunition, knives and replica items.

Medicinal products must be declared. These include: drugs that are illegal in Australia (narcotics, performance enhancers, amphetamines); legally prescribed drugs (carry your doctor's prescription with you); non-prescription drugs (painkillers and so on); and vitamins, diet supplements and traditional preparations.
Customs Information Centre tel: 1 300 363 263 (in Australia); 61 2 6275 6666 (outside Australia); www.customs.gov.au

Duty-free allowances

Anyone over the age of 18 is allowed to bring into Australia A\$400-worth of goods not including alcohol or tobacco; 1,125 ml (about 2 pints) of alcohol (wine, beer or spirits); 250 cigarettes, or 250 grams of cigars or tobacco products other than cigarettes.

Members of the same family who are travelling together may combine their individual duty/tax free allowances.

Disabled Travellers

Sydney caters reasonably well for people with disabilities, but you would be wise to start making enquiries and arrangements before leaving home. A good place to begin is with the **National Information Communication Awareness Network** (**NICAN**), a national organisation that keeps a database of facilities and services with disabled access including accommodation and tourist sights. They also keep track of the range of publications on the subject.

The **Australian Quadraplegic Association** (**AQA**) publishes *Accessing Sydney*, which lists a wide variety of places with disabled access, as well as various services. They will also provide over-the-phone information.

The **State Library of NSW** offers a good telephone service, where operators deal promptly with queries on topics such as

equipment hire and access to medical and other services.
AQA 1 Jennifer Street, Little Bay, NSW 2036; tel: 9661 8855
NICAN PO Box 407 Curtain, ACT 2605; tel: 1 800 806 769
State Library of NSW Disability Service, tel: 9273 1583

E lectricity

The current is 240/250v, 50Hz. Most good hotels have universal outlets for 110v shavers and small appliances. For larger appliances such as hairdryers, you will need a converter and a flat three-pin adaptor.

Embassies & Consulates

In Sydney

British Consulate General Level 16, 1 Macquarie Place; tel: 9247 7521; bcgsyd1@uk.emb.gov.au
Canadian Consulate General Level 5, 111 Harrington Street; tel: 9364 3000; recorded information: 9364 3050
Consulate General of Ireland Level 30, 400 George Street; tel: 9231 6999
US Consulate General MLC Centre, 19–29 Martin Place; tel: 9373 9200; after-hours emergencies, tel: 4422 2201

Overseas Missions

Canada Australian High Commission, Suite 710, 50 O'Connor Street, Ottawa, Ontario K1P 6L2; tel: (613) 236 0841 (plus consulates in Toronto and Vancouver)
Ireland Australian Embassy, Fitzwilton House, Wilton Terrace, Dublin 2; tel: (01) 664 5300; email: austremb.dublin@dfat.gov.au
United Kingdom Australian High Commission, Australia House, The Strand, London WC2B 4LA; tel: (020) 7379 4334; www.australia.org.uk (plus consulates in Manchester and Edinburgh)
United States Australian Embassy, 1601 Massachusetts Avenue, Washington DC NW 20036-2273; tel: (202) 797 3000; email: library.washington@dfat.gov.au (plus

EMERGENCY NUMBERS

Police, Fire, Ambulance
Tel: 000
Doctor Services (for hotels)
Tel: 9962 6000
Dental Services
Tel: 9692 0333

consulates in New York, Los Angeles, San Francisco, Miami, Detroit, Atlanta etc)

Entry Requirements

Visitors to Australia must have a passport valid for the entire period of their stay. Anyone who is not an Australian citizen also needs a visa, which must be obtained before leaving home – except for New Zealand citizens, who are issued with a visa on arrival in Australia.
ETA visas The Electronic Transfer Authority (ETA) enables visitors to obtain a visa on the spot from their travel agent or airline office. The system is in place in over 30 countries including the US and the UK. ETA visas are generally valid over a 12-month period; single stays must not exceed three months, but return visits within the 12-month period are allowed. ETAS are issued free, or you can purchase one online for A$20 from www.eta.immi.gov.au.
Tourist visas These are available for continuous stays longer than three months, but must be obtained from an Australian visa office, such as an Embassy or Consulate. A $20 fee applies. Those travelling on tourist visas and ETAs are not permitted to work while in Australia. Travellers are asked on their applications to prove they have an adequate source of funding while in Australia (around $1,000 a month).
Temporary residence Those seeking temporary residence must apply to an Australian visa office, and in many cases must be sponsored by an appropriate organisation or employer. Study visas are available for people

who want to undertake registered courses on a full-time basis. Working holiday visas are available to young people from the UK, Ireland, Japan, the Netherlands, Canada, Malta and Korea who want to work as they travel.
Department of Immigration and Multicultural Affairs tel: 13 18 81 or the nearest mission outside Australia. www.immi.gov.au

G ay and Lesbian Visitors

Sydney is awash with facilities and attractions for gay and lesbian travellers, and the old discriminatory attitudes are rarely seen these days. However, random violence towards gays is not unknown, particularly in the area around the gay heartland of Oxford Street. The best way to avoid trouble is to stick to the main streets, and walk with friends at night. The gay community has organised its own security outfit for the area, which seemed to help the problem considerably.

One of Sydney's premier events is the Sydney Gay and Lesbian Mardi Gras, which is accompanied by a major cultural and arts festival, held in February each year. The free *Sydney Star Observer* is the city's most popular gay and lesbian paper for news, gossip and what's on; overseas subscriptions can be arranged for forward planning.

The International Gay and Lesbian Travel Association is a professional body for people involved with gay tourism. Visitors can ring to be put in touch with providers of different travel services.
International Gay and Lesbian Travel Association tel: 9818 6669
Sydney Gay and Lesbian Mardi Gras tel: 9568 8600
Sydney Star Observer tel: 8263 0500

Guides and Tours

Tour companies offer a broad choice of excursions, from half-days in Sydney to long-haul journeys into the Outback. Harbour cruises range from a general sightseeing tour to specialised visits to historic Fort Denison. There are also local walking tours – around The Rocks, for instance – and tours for cyclists, wildlife-lovers and others with special interests. *(See pages 213–4.)*

Health & Medical Care

Australia has excellent medical services. For medical attention out of working hours go to the casualty department in one of the large hospitals or, if the matter is less urgent, visit one of the 24-hour medical clinics around the city and suburbs. Look under "Medical Centres" in the *Yellow Pages*, or ask at your hotel.

No vaccinations are required for entry to Australia. As in most countries, HIV and AIDS is a continuing problem despite efforts to control its spread. Heterosexual and homosexual visitors alike should wear condoms if engaging in sexual activity.
Emergency medical assistance, tel: 000

Pharmacies

"Chemist shops" are a great place to go for advice on minor ailments such as bites, scratches and stomach trouble. They also stock a wide range of useful products such as sun block, nappies (diapers) and non-prescription drugs.

If you have a prescription from your doctor, and you want to take it to a pharmacist in Australia, you will need to have it endorsed by a local medical practitioner.

Local Health Hazards

The biggest danger for travellers in Australia is the sun. Even on mild, cloudy days it has the potential to burn. Wear a broad-brimmed hat and, if you are planning on being out for a while, a long-sleeved shirt made from a light fabric. Wear SPF 15+ sun-block at all times, even under a

hat. Avoid sunbathing between 11am and 3pm.

Care should be taken while swimming in Sydney. Rip tides resulting in dangerous conditions are fairly common along Sydney's beaches, but it is not always obvious to those unfamiliar with the coastline. The best advice is to swim only at beaches that are patrolled, and to swim between the yellow and red flags. Never swim at night after a few drinks.

The shark bells do ring from time to time along the beaches, but it is usually a false alarm. Some of the harbour beaches have shark nets, so if you are nervous, swim there.

Snakes and Spiders

Sydney is home to two dangerous spiders, the funnel-web and the redback. Because you will not necessarily be able to identify these creatures, seek medical help for any spider bite. Dangerous snakes are also part of the Sydney landscape, but most will not attack unless directly provoked. Avoid trouble by wearing covered shoes when walking in the bush, and checking areas such as rock platforms and rock crevices before making yourself comfortable. Again, seek medical advice for any bite.

Holidays

Banks, post offices, offices and most shops close on the following public holidays:

1 January	New Year's Day
26 January	Australia Day
March/April	Good Friday, Holy Saturday, Easter Monday
25 April	Anzac Day
June (2nd Mon)	Queen's Birthday
August (1st Mon)	Bank Holiday
October (1st Mon)	Labour Day
25 December	Christmas Day
26 December	Boxing Day

There are four school holidays a year: mid-December to the end of January, two weeks over Easter, two weeks in July and two

weeks at the end of September. It can be difficult to get discounted air fares and accommodation during these peak periods.

Internet Cafés

There are plenty of these useful establishments all around the city. Here are a few:
digi.kaf, 174 St Johns Road, Glebe
Fountain Café, 20 Darlinghurst Road, Kings Cross
Global Gossip, 14 Wentworth Avenue; 111 Darlinghurst Road, Kings Cross
Internet Centre on Oxford, 6 Oxford Street, Darlinghurst
Neat Internet Cafe, 730 and 750 George Street
Phone Net Cafe, 73–75 Hall Street, Bondi
Surfnet Café, 5A Market Lane, Manly
Well-Connected Internet Cafe, 35 Glebe Point Road, Glebe

If you just want to surf the internet, try a local library, where often you can get access for free. This includes the State Library of NSW on Macquarie Street.

Left Luggage

There are lockers for luggage at Central Station, near platforms 3 and 4, and also at the Coach Terminal, Eddy Avenue level. At the airport, Tempo Services (tel: 9667 0926) offers a left luggage service on arrivals level 1 of T1 International Terminal.

Lost Property

You should report loss or theft of valuables to the police immediately, as most insurance policies insist on a police report. The Police Assistance Line is manned 24 hours a day for the reporting of non-urgent crime and incidents; tel: 13 14 44.

Property left on Sydney Buses is kept at the depot from which the bus operates. Property left on harbour ferries is kept at Sydney Ferries offices at Wharf 3,

Circular Quay, tel: 9207 3101. For items lost at the airport, call Sydney Airports Lost Property on 9667 9583 or go to level 3 of T1 International Terminal.

Maps

State and local tourist offices *(see page 237)* give away useful maps of their areas, and there are free specialised maps, of Darling Harbour, for instance, or the Sydney ferry network. Look out for the *Sydney Fleximap* published by Insight or, for a more detailed street atlas, pick up *Gregory's Street Directory* at a newsstand or bookshop.

Media

Publications

Sydney has two daily newspapers, the *Sydney Morning Herald* and the *Daily Telegraph*. The first is a well-respected broadsheet with good national and international coverage and the second is an energetic tabloid, with plenty of local news and gossip, always good for entertainment value.

Australia has two national papers, the *Australian* and the *Financial Review*, both excellent publications at the serious end of the scale. The weekly *Bulletin* is a long-running magazine with good news analysis and there is also a weekly Australian edition of *Time* magazine.

Foreign newspapers and magazines are available at news agencies in the city, the airport and other major tourist districts, usually within a couple of days of publication.

Radio and Television

The Australian Broadcasting Commission (ABC) runs a national television channel as well as an extensive network of radio stations. ABC Television is broadcast on Channel 2 and offers excellent news and current affairs, as well as local and imported drama, comedy, sports and cultural programmes. The commercial TV stations, Channels 7, 9 and 10, offer news, drama, soaps, infotainment, travel shows and, between them, coverage of all the major international sporting events. Many hotels provide access to a large number of cable television stations.

The radio stations include Triple J-FM (105.7), rock and comment for the twenty-somethings; Classic FM (92.9), continuous classical music; and Radio National AM (576), excellent national news and events coverage. Commercial radio stations include 2UE AM (954), for continuous talkback and unadulterated opinion; and Triple M FM (104.9), for popular local and international rock.

Of particular interest to overseas travellers is Australia's ethnic/multicultural broadcaster, SBS. The organisation's television channel offers many foreign-language films and documentaries, and Australia's best coverage of world news. SBS Radio 2 FM (97.7) and SBS Radio 1 AM (1107), offer programmes in a large variety of languages.

Money

Currency

The local currency is the Australian dollar (abbreviated as A\$ or simply \$), made up of 100 cents. Coins come in 5, 10, 20, and 50 cent units and 1 and 2 dollar units. Notes come in 5, 10, 20, 50 and 100 dollar units. Single cents still apply to many prices, and in these cases the amount will be rounded down or up to the nearest 5c amount. Carry smaller notes for tipping, taxis and payment in small shops and cafés.

There is no limit to the amount of foreign or Australian currency that you can bring into or out of the country, but cash amounts of more than A\$10,000 (or its equivalent) must be declared to customs on arrival and departure.

Banks

The four big banks in Australia are the National, the Commonwealth, Westpac and ANZ. Trading hours are generally 9.30am–4pm Monday to Thursday and 9am– 5pm on Friday. A few of the smaller banks and credit unions open on Saturday mornings. Most banks will have an internal board or a window display advertising exchange rates; if not, ask a teller.

Credit Cards and ATMs

Carrying a recognised credit or debit card such as Visa, MasterCard, American Express or Diners Club, is always a good idea when travelling. A credit card should provide access to EFTPOS (electronic funds transfer at point of sale), which is the easiest and often the cheapest way to exchange money – amounts are automatically debited from the selected account. Many Australian businesses are connected to EFTPOS.

There are literally hundreds of Automatic Teller Machines (ATMs) around the city allowing for easy withdrawal of cash, and again a linked credit card will provide access to both credit and other bank accounts.

Many small businesses are still cash only.

LOST CHEQUES AND CARDS

If you lose your travellers' cheques or want replacement cheques, contact the following:
American Express, tel: 1 800 688 022
Thomas Cook and MasterCard Travellers' Cheques, tel: 1 800 127 495

If you lose your credit card, call:
American Express, tel: 1 300 366 105
Diners Club, tel: 1 300 360 060
MasterCard, tel: 1 800 12 0113 (world service puts you in contact with local authority)
Visa, tel: 1 800 621 199

TRANSPORT

ACCOMMODATION

ACTIVITIES

A–Z

Exchange

Most foreign currencies can be cashed at the airport, with major exchange outlets operating to fit in with flight arrival times. Sydney has many bureaux de change, which generally open 9.30am–5pm, but you'll usually get a better rate at one of the big banks.

Travellers' cheques

All well-known travellers' cheques can be cashed at airports, banks, hotels and similar establishments, and are as good as cash with many of the larger retail outlets and the shops in major tourist areas. Smaller restaurants and shops may be reluctant to cash cheques, so you should also carry cards or cash.

Banks offer the best exchange rates on cheques in foreign currencies; most banks charge a fee for cashing cheques. Travellers' cheques can also be purchased in Sydney at one of the large banks.

P ostal Services

Post offices are open 9am–5pm Mon–Fri, with some branches opening Sat morning. The General Post Office (GPO) is located in Martin Place in the City and opens 8.15am–5.30pm weekdays and 8.30am–noon, Sat.

Domestic Post

Posting a standard letter to anywhere in Australia costs 50 cents. The letter will reach a same-city destination overnight, but may take up to a week if it is being sent to a remote part of the country.

Yellow Express Post bags can be used to send parcels and letters overnight to other Australian capital cities. The cost ranges from $3.90 to $9.30 and represents very good value for money when compared to courier costs.
Postal enquiries and information: tel: 13 13 17

Overseas Post

The cost of overseas mail depends on the weight and size of the item. Postcards cost $1 by airmail to the UK and the US. Standard overseas mail takes about a week to most destinations.

There are two types of express international mail. Express Mailing Service (EMS) will reach the UK in three or four days. The minimum cost for a package is $35. Express Post International (EPI) will arrive in the UK within four to five working days and is priced according to weight and size.
EMS and EPI, tel: 13 13 18

Faxes

There are many places from which you can fax documents, including hotels, video stores, newsagents, a variety of small businesses, and also post offices, where the rates are very reasonable.

T elephones

Local calls in Australia are untimed, and cost 25c from private phones and 40c from public phones. Instead of making calls from hotel rooms, which can be double or triple the price, you should aim to use public phones. Having a phonecard will make this much easier. These are widely available from newsagents and other outlets displaying the Telstra logo. There are four cards ranging in price from $5 to $50.

Most interstate (STD) and international (ISD) calls can be made using phonecards. These calls are timed, and can be expensive, but cheaper rates are available after 6pm and on weekends. Most overseas numbers can be dialled direct without the need for operator assistance.

Sydney's main telephone directory is called the *White Pages* and comes in two volumes. At the start of volume A–K is a complete guide to essential services in the city, including lists of useful numbers. The *Yellow Pages*, also in two volumes, list commercial operations under subject headings.

Calls made from Sydney to other parts of NSW are charged at STD rates, although it is no longer necessary to dial an area code first. However, you do have to dial an area code to call interstate in Australia. All regular numbers in Australia (other than toll-free or special numbers) are eight digits long. Sydney numbers have 9 as the first digit. The NSW area code is 02. If you are calling from overseas, drop the 0.

Numbers beginning with 1 800 are toll-free. Numbers beginning with 13 are charged at a local rate, even if the call is made STD. Numbers beginning with 018, 041, 015, 019 are mobile phone numbers.
Directory enquiries: 1223
Overseas assistance: 1225
Information on costs: 12552
International calls: 0011, followed by the national code of the country you are calling.

Mobile Phones

Most of the large urban areas and major rural centres are covered by a telecoms "net". Smaller towns and remote regions are not covered, which means that mobiles have virtually no use as a safety communications device when travelling in the Outback.

Many visitors will find that they can bring their own phones with them and use them without too much trouble. Contact your provider before leaving home to find out what is involved. To hire a phone during your stay, look under "Mobile Telephones" in the *Yellow Pages*, and shop around for the best deal – this is a very competitive market.

Time Zone

Sydney is on Eastern Australian Standard Time (EST), which is 10 hours ahead of Greenwich Mean Time, 15 hours ahead of New York and 18 hours ahead of California. Daylight saving (one hour forward) operates from the last weekend in October to the last weekend in March.

TRANSPORT

Tipping

Tipping is not obligatory but a small gratuity for good service is appreciated. It is not customary to tip taxi drivers, hairdressers or porters at airports. Porters have set charges at railway terminals, but not at hotels. Restaurants do not automatically include service charges, but it is customary to tip waiters up to 10 percent of the bill for good service.

Toilets

Australians manage without euphemisms for "toilet". "Dunny" or "Thunder Box" is the Outback slang, but "washroom", "restroom", "Ladies" and "Gents" are all understood. In Sydney, public toilets are often locked after certain hours, but you can generally use the facilities in any pub or cinema without making a purchase. Toilets are generally clean, even in the Outback. Sydney's most ornate toilets are located on the ground floor of the State Theatre on Market Street.

Tourist Information

The head office of the Australian Tourist Commission (open 9am–5.30pm) is at Level 4, 80 William Street, East Sydney; tel: 9360 1111; www.australia.com. There are also ATC offices in Britain and the US:

United Kingdom: Gemini House, 10–18 Putney Hill, London SW15 6AA; tel: 020 8780 2229
USA: 2049 Century Park East, Suite 1920, Los Angeles CA 90067; tel: (310) 229 4870

In the excellent tourist centres/kiosks dotted around the city (see below), you will find maps, accommodation guides, brochures and well-informed staff to help with all your traveller's queries, including information about composite tickets to many of the attractions.

Each of the major regions has its own tourist information centre, and these are always a good first stop when travelling out of town. Most tourist centres open seven days a week. **Tourism New South Wales** (tel: 13 20 77) can put you in touch with relevant tourist authorities in Sydney and around the state.

Websites

Enter "sydney tourism" into any search engine, and you will be presented with a vast number of sites – some much more up-to-date and useful than others. Here is a selection of the more comprehensive and reliable:
www.atn.com.au
www.australia.com
www.discoveraustralia.com.au
www.oztravel.com.au
www.sydneyaustralia.com
www.sydneycity.net
www.sydney.com.au
www.visitnsw.com.au

Weights and Measures

Australia uses the metric system of weights, measures and temperatures.
1 metre = approx 39 ins
1 kilometre (km) = 1,093 yards or approx 0.6 mile
16 km = approx 10 miles
1 kilogram (kg) = approx 2.2 lb
1 litre = 1.75 pints
40 litres = approx 9 imperial gallons or 10 US gallons
20°C = 68°F
30°C = 86°F

What to Wear

Whatever the season, forget an overcoat. A sweater may come in handy, even in summer, when, after a hot day in the sun, the evening breeze off the harbour may feel chilly. A light raincoat will serve in any season. Anywhere you go, you'll need comfortable walking shoes.

Sydneysiders dress casually when not at work – shorts, a short-sleeved shirt or T-shirt and trainers or sandals are fine. Most restaurants have dropped the requirement for men to wear jacket and tie, but some establishments may refuse customers wearing T-shirts, tank tops or ripped jeans.

ACCOMMODATION

ACTIVITIES

A—Z

TOURIST CENTRES IN AND AROUND SYDNEY

Sydney Visitors' Centre
106 George Street, The Rocks
Tel: 9255 1788
Blue Mountains Tourism Authority
Echo Point, Katoomba and Great Western Highway, Glenbrook
Tel: 1 800 641 227 (toll-free) or 4739 6266
Bondi Visitors' Information Centre
Bondi Beachside Inn, cnr Campbell Pde and Roscoe St, Bondi Beach.
Closed Sat–Sun
Tel: 9130 5311
Darling Harbour Visitors Centre
Palm Grove, between Cockle Bay and Tumbalong Park, Darling Harbour
Tel: 9240 8788
Gosford Visitor Centre
200 Mann Street, Gosford
Tel: 1 800 151 699 (toll-free) or 4385 4430

Hawkesbury River Tourist Information Centre
5 Bridge Street, Brooklyn
Tel: 9985 7064.
Hawkesbury Visitors' Centre
Bicentenary Park, Richmond Road, Clarendon
Tel: 4588 5895
Manly Visitors Centre
Manly Wharf, Manly
Tel: 8966 8111
Parramatta Visitors Centre
Cnr Church and Market Streets, Parramatta
Tel: 8839 3311
Southern Highlands Visitors' Information Centre
Hume Highway, Mittagong
Tel: 4871 2888
Wollongong Tourist Information Centre
93 Crown Street, Wollongong
Tel: 4227 5545 or (toll-free) 1 800 240 737

FURTHER READING

Of the making of books about Australia, there is no end. Those mentioned below are mostly of general interest. The majority are still in print, and the rest are likely to be found in Sydney's many secondhand bookshops and markets

Aboriginal Australia

Archaeology of the Dreaming, by Josephine Flood
Dreamings: The Art of Aboriginal Australia, edited by Peter Sutton
The Whispering in Our Hearts, by Henry Reynolds

Art & Architecture

The Art of Australia, by Robert Hughes
Art in Australia: From Colonialization to Postmodernism, by Christopher Allen
Opera House Act One, by David Messent
Sydney Architecture, by Graham Jahn
Sydney: A guide to recent architecture, by Francesca Morrison

Biography

A Fence Around the Cuckoo, by Ruth Park
Fishing the Styx, by Ruth Park
Greer: Untamed Shrew, by Christine Wallace
Patrick White: A Life, by David Marr
Unreliable Memoirs, by Clive James

Fiction

The Bodysurfers, by Robert Drewe
Cliff Hardy series (various titles), by Peter Corris
For Love Alone, by Christina Stead
Foveaux, by Kylie Tennant
A Harp in the South, by Ruth Park
Illywhacker, by Peter Carey
Jonah, by Louis Stone
Oscar and Lucinda, by Peter Carey
Poor Man's Orange, by Ruth Park
The Service of the Clouds, Delia Falconer
Seven Poor Men of Sydney, by Christina Stead
The Vivisector, by Patrick White

Food & Wine

Cheap Eats (Universal Magazines)
The Penguin Good Australian Wine Guide, by Mark Shield & Huon Hooke
The SBS Eating Guide, by Maeve O'Mara & Joanna Savill
The Sydney Morning Herald Good Food Guide, edited by Terry Durack and Jill Dupleix
The Wines of Australia, by Oliver Mayo

History

The Fatal Shore, by Robert Hughes
The Future Eaters, by Tim Flannery
The Great Shame, by Thomas Keneally
Manning Clark's History of Australia, by Manning Clark
1788, by Watkin Tench, edited and introduced by Tim Flannery

Language

The Lingo: Listening to Australian English, by Graham Seal (University of New South Wales)
The Macquarie Dictionary (Macquarie Library)

Travel Companions

Best Sydney Bushwalks, by Neil Paton
A Companion Guide to Sydney, by Ruth Park
Cosmopolitan Sydney: Explore the World in One City, by Jock Collins and Antonio Castillo
Sydney, by Jan Morris
The Sydney Morning Herald Best of Sydney, edited by Ross Muller
The 100 Things Everyone Needs to Know About Sydney, by David Dale
Walking Sydney, by Lisa Clifford and Mandy Webb

Other Insight Guides

Three types of Insight Guide are designed to meet the needs of every traveller.

Insight Guides

The acclaimed 190-title classic series covers every continent. Other titles on Australia and its regions include: *Australia* and *Melbourne*.

Pocket Guides

There are also over 100 Pocket Guides, designed to assist the traveller with a limited amount of time to spend in a destination. Carefully planned one-day itineraries written by a local resident make a location easily accessible, and each book contains an easy-to-use full-size pull-out map. There are Pocket Guides to *Sydney*, *Melbourne*, *Perth*, *Brisbane*, and *Cairns and the Great Barrier Reef*.

Compact Guides

In addition, more than 130 Compact Guides offer the traveller a highly portable encyclopaedic travel guide packed with carefully cross-referenced text, photographs and maps. There is a *Compact Guide to Sydney*.

Insight Maps

Insight's best-selling laminated Fleximaps combine detailed cartography and informative text with ease of use and durability. There are Fleximaps for Sydney and Melbourne.

SYDNEY STREET ATLAS

The key map shows the area of Sydney covered by the atlas
section. An index of street names and places of interest
shown on the maps can be found on the following pages.
For each entry there is a page number and grid reference.

Map Legend

▤	Motorway with Junction	⊖	Border Crossing		Motorway	•—•—•	Monorail
▭	Motorway (under construction)	✈	Airport		Dual Carriageway	⛐	Bus Station
▭	Dual Carriageway	†	Church (ruins)		Main Roads	❶	Tourist Information
	Main Road	†	Monastery			✉	Post Office
	Secondary Road	🏰	Castle (ruins)		Minor Roads	✝	Cathedral/Church
	Minor road	∴	Archaeological Site		Footpath	☾	Mosque
	Track	∩	Cave		Railway	✡	Synagogue
–·–·–	International Boundary	★	Place of Interest		Pedestrian Area	🗡	Statue/Monument
– – –	Province/State Boundary	🏛	Mansion/Stately Home		Important Building	▯	Tower
––•––	National Park/Reserve	※	Viewpoint		Park	🗼	Lighthouse
– – –	Ferry Route	⚓	Beach				

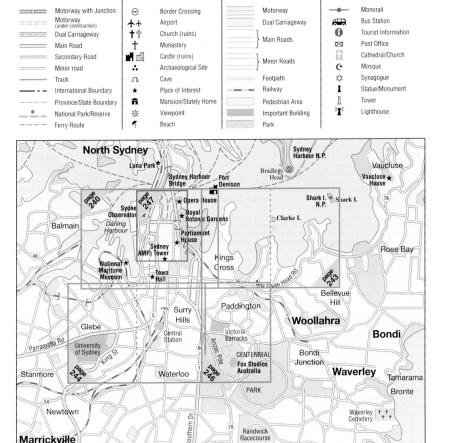

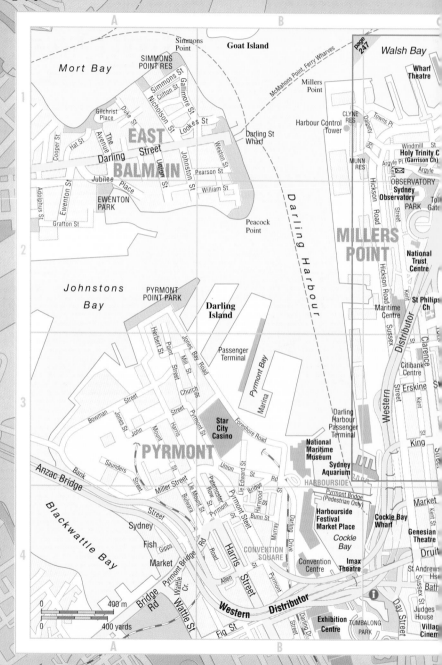

page 247

Mort Bay

SIMMONS POINT RES

Simmons Point

Goat Island

Walsh Bay

Wharf Theatre

McMahons Point Ferry Wharves

Millers Point

Gilchrist Place

SIMMONS Simmons St

Gallimore St

Clifton St

Nicholson St

Lookes St

Harbour Control Tower

CLYNE RES

Dalgety

Towns Pl

Windmill St

Holy Trinity C (Garrison Ch)

EAST BALMAIN

Duke St

The Avenue

Darling Street

Union St

Johnston St

Weston St

Pearson St

William St

Darling St Wharf

MUNN RES

Argyle Pl

Argyle

OBSERVATORY

Sydney Observatory

PARK

Toll Gate

Hat St

Cooper St

Jubilee Place

EWENTON PARK

Ewenton St

Adolphus St

Grafton St

Peacock Point

Darling Harbour

Hickson Road

MILLERS POINT

National Trust Centre

Kent St

St Philips Ch

Maritime Centre

Sussex

Distributor

Johnstons Bay

PYRMONT POINT PARK

Darling Island

Clarence St

Herbert St

Point Street

Mill Street

Jones Bay Road

Passenger Terminal

Pyrmont Bay

Marina

Darling Harbour Passenger Terminal

Western

Kent

St

Erskine St

Citibank Centre

King St

PYRMONT

Bowman

Jones St

John

Church Street

Street

Mount

Harris

Pyrmont Street

Foreshore Road

Star City Casino

National Maritime Museum

Sydney Aquarium

HARBOURSIDE

Market

Anzac Bridge

Bank

Saunders

Miller Street

Buhara

Le Mount St

Union St

Paternoster Row St

Pyrmont St

Harwood

Bunn St

St

Darling Drive

Murray

Pyrmont Bridge (Pedestrian Only)

Harbourside Festival Market Place

Cockle Bay

Cockle Bay Wharf

Genesian Theatre

Blackwattle Bay

Sydney

Fish

Market

Gipps

Pyrmont Bridge Rd

Wattle Cr.

Allen

Harris Street

Pyrmont

CONVENTION SQUARE

Convention Centre

Imax Theatre

Druit

St Andrews Hs

Sussex St

Bath

Bridge Rd

Wattle St

Western Distributor

Fig St

Darling Dr

Exhibition Centre

TUMBALONG PARK

Day Street

Judges House

Villag Cinem

0   400 m

0   400 yards

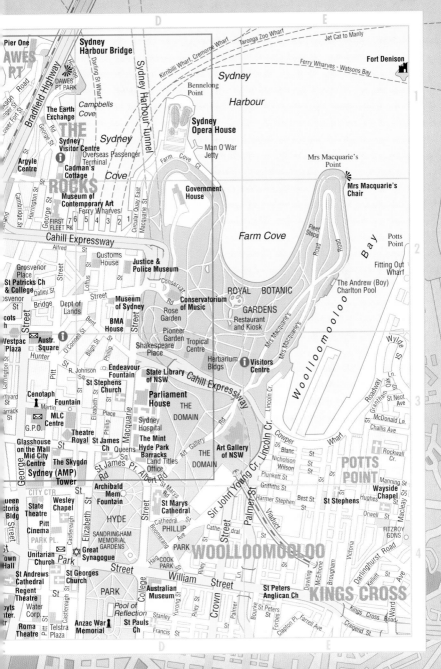

Pier One

AWES PT

HAWES PT PARK

Bradfield Highway

Sydney Harbour Bridge

Darling St Wharf

Sydney Harbour Tunnel

Kirribilli Wharf · Cremorne Wharf

Taronga Zoo Wharf

Jet Cat to Manly

Fort Denison

Ferry Wharves · Watsons Bay

Sydney

Harbour

Bennelong Point

Campbells Cove

The Earth Exchange

Sydney Visitor Centre

Sydney

THE ROCKS

Argyle Centre

Cadman's Cottage

Overseas Passenger Terminal

Sydney Opera House

Man O'War Jetty

Mrs Macquarie's Point

Mrs Macquarie's Chair

Farm Cove Ct

Museum of Contemporary Art

Ferry Wharves

FIRST FLEET PK 7 6 5 4 3 2 1

Circular Quay East

Macquarie St

Government House

Farm Cove

Fleet Steps

Potts Point

Cahill Expressway

Alfred St

Customs House

Justice & Police Museum

Fitting Out Wharf

Bay

Woolloomooloo

Grosvenor Place

St Patricks Ch & College

Grosvenor St

Bridge St

Dept of Lands

Museum of Sydney

Conservatorium of Music

ROYAL BOTANIC

The Andrew (Boy) Charlton Pool

scots h

Westpac Plaza

Austr. Square

Hunter

BMA House

O'Connell St

Bligh St

Phillip St

Rose Garden

Pioneer Garden

Shakespeare Place

GARDENS

Restaurant and Kiosk

Mrs Macquaries Road

Mrs Macquaries Road

Wylde St

Carrington St

Pitt St

R. Johnson Sq.

Endeavour Fountain

St Stephens Church

Tropical Centre

Herbarium Bldgs

Visitors Centre

Granfham St

Roadway

St Neot Ave

Oak

vnyard St

arrack St

Cenotaph

Martin

MLC Centre

Elizabeth St

Phillip St

Macquarie St

State Library of NSW

Cahill Expressway

Lincoln Cr.

McDonald Ln.

Challis Ave

Fountain

G.P.O.

Place

Parliament House

THE DOMAIN

Cowper St

Rockwall Cr.

Glasshouse on the Mall Mid City Centre

Theatre Royal

St James Ch

Sydney Hospital

Blanc

Nicholson

POTTS POINT

George St

The Skygdn

Sydney (AMP) Tower

St James Rd

Queens Sq.

The Mint

Hyde Park Barracks

Land Titles Office

Pr. Albert Rd

Art Gallery Rd

Wilson

Plunkett St

Wayside Chapel

Manning St

Hughes St

CITY CTR

Archibald Mem. Fountain

St Marys Rd

Art Gallery of NSW

THE DOMAIN

Sir John Young Cr.

Lincoln Cr.

Griffiths St

Harmer Stephen

Best St

St Stephens

Orwell St

Maclay St

ueen ctoria Bldg

State Theatre

Wesley Chapel

HYDE

SANDRINGHAM MEMORIAL GARDENS

St Marys Cathedral

PHILLIP

Palmer St

Victoria St

FITZROY GDNS

own Hall

Pitt Cinema

PARK PL.

Great Synagogue

Elizabeth St

Cathedral St

Boomerang St

Cathe- dral St

Viaduct

Darlinghurst Road

St Andrews Cathedral

Unitarian Church

Park

St Georges Church

PARK

College St

WOOLLOOMOOLOO

William Street

Dowling

McElhone

Brougham

Kellet St

Ward Ave

Regent Theatre

Water Corp.

Australian Museum

COOK PARK

Hary

PARK

Crown St

Yurong

Riley St

Palmer St

Bourke St

St Peters Anglican Ch

St Peters

Forbes St

KINGS CROSS

Kings Cross Road

oyts nter.

Roma Theatre

Pitt St

Telstra Plaza

Anzac War Memorial

Pool of Reflection

Stanley

St Pauls Ch

Francis St

Clapton Pl.

Farrell Ave

Craigend St

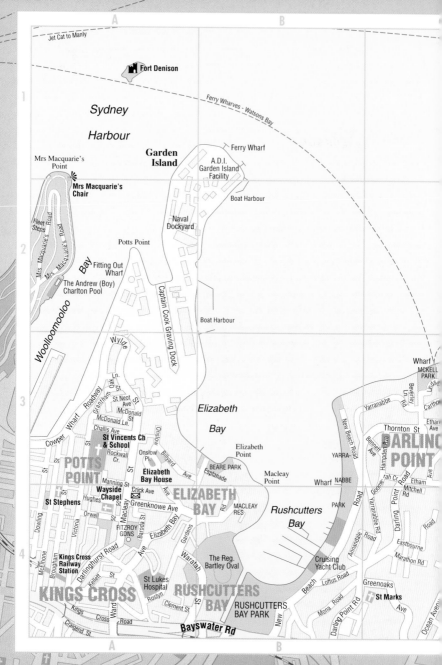

Jet Cat to Manly

Fort Denison

Sydney

Harbour

Ferry Wharves - Watsons Bay

Garden
Island

Ferry Wharf

A.D.I.
Garden Island
Facility

Mrs Macquarie's
Point

Mrs Macquarie's
Chair

Boat Harbour

Fleet
Steps

Naval
Dockyard

Mrs Macquarie's Road

Mrs Macquarie's Road

Bay

Potts Point

Fitting Out
Wharf

The Andrew (Boy)
Charlton Pool

Boat Harbour

Woolloomooloo

Captain Cook Graving Dock

Wylde

Ln.

Roadway

Grantham

Oak

St Neot
Ave

McDonald
St

McDonald Ln.

Elizabeth

Bay

Challis Ave

Cowper Wharf

St Vincents Ch
& School

Rockwall
Cr.

Onslow
Pl.

Billyard

Onslow

Ave

Elizabeth
Point

Wharf

MCKELL
PARK

Beverley

Ln

Rd

Yarranabbe

Carmon

Ethan
Ave

Thornton St

DARLING
POINT

Yarranabbe Rd

New Beach Road

Bennett
Ave

Hampden

Ave

YARRA-

rah Cr

Road

Darling

Point

Road

Etham
Ave

Mitchell
Rd

Road

POTTS
POINT

Elizabeth
Bay House

BEARE PARK
Esplanade

Macleay
Point

Manning St

Wayside
Chapel

St Stephens

St

St

Baroda

St

Crick Ave

Hughes

Maclay

St

Greenknowe Ave

Orwell

St

Victoria

FITZROY
GDNS

Elizabeth Bay

ELIZABETH
BAY

Ave

Rd

MACLEAY
RES

NABBE

PARK

Wharf

Rushcutters

Bay

Dowling

McElhone

Brougham

St

Kings Cross
Railway
Station

Darlinghurst Road

Nellett

St

Ward

Roslyn

St Lukes
Hospital

Gardens

Waratah

The Reg.
Bartley Oval

Cruising
Yacht Club

Gowrie

Yarranabbe Rd

Road

Almaindale

Road

Eastbourne

Marathon Rd

Beach

Loftus Road

Mona

Road

Greenoaks

Ave

St Marks

Road

Ocean Avenue

KINGS CROSS

Kings

Cross

Road

Craigend St

Clement St

RUSHCUTTERS
BAY

RUSHCUTTERS
BAY PARK

New

Bayswater Rd

Darling Point Rd

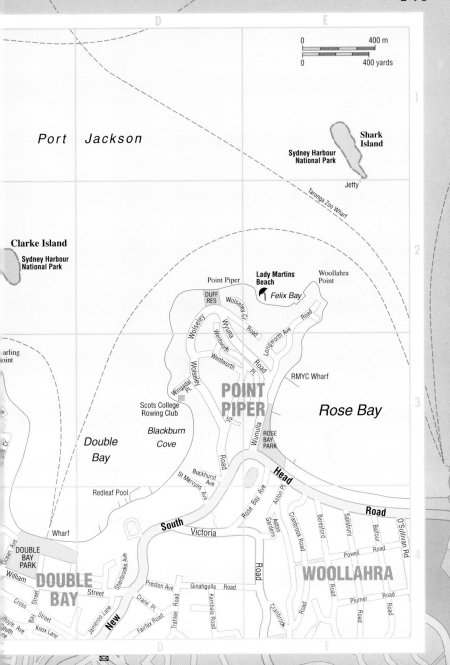

D   E

0   400 m
0   400 yards

1

Port   Jackson

Shark Island

Sydney Harbour National Park

Jetty

Taronga Zoo Wharf

Clarke Island

Sydney Harbour National Park

2

arling oint

Point Piper

Lady Martins Beach

Woollahra Point

DUFF RES

Wolseley Cr.

Felix Bay

Wolseley

Wyuna

Road

Longworth Ave

Road

Wentworth

Wentworth Pl.

Road

RMYC Wharf

Wolseley Pl.

Wingadal Pl.

POINT PIPER

Rose Bay

3

Scots College Rowing Club

Double Bay

Blackburn Cove

Wunulla

ROSE BAY PARK

s

Road

Head

Buckhurst Ave

St Mervyns Ave

Redleaf Pool

Rose Bay Ave

Aston Pl

Road

O'Sullivan Rd

Wharf

South

Victoria

Aston Gardens

Cranbrook Road

Beresford

Salisbury

Balfour

DOUBLE BAY PARK

Ocean Ave

William

DOUBLE BAY

Sherbrooke Ave

Powell

Road

4

Preston Ave

Ginahgulla   Road

Road

WOOLLAHRA

Plumer   Road

Cross

Street

Bay

Street

New

Jameroo Lane

Crane Pl.

Trahlee Road

Kambala Road

Cranbrook

Road

Road

Road

lfoyle Ave outh ne

Knox Lane

Fairfax Road

D   E

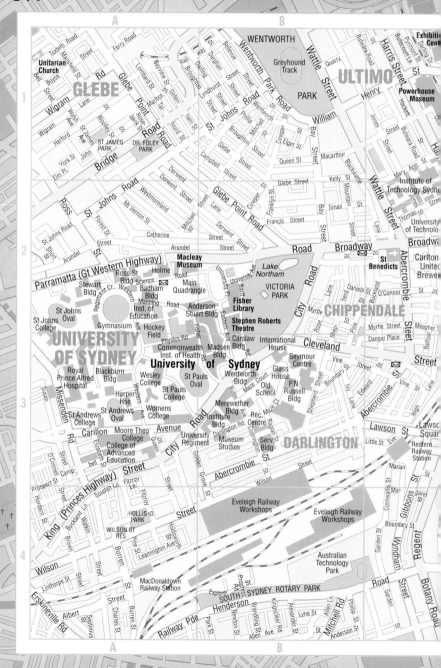

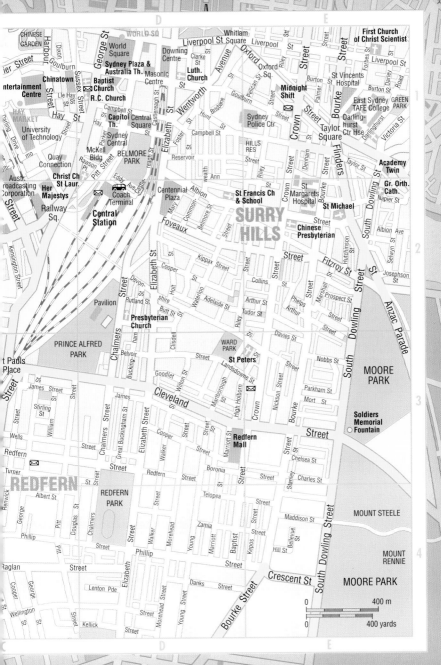

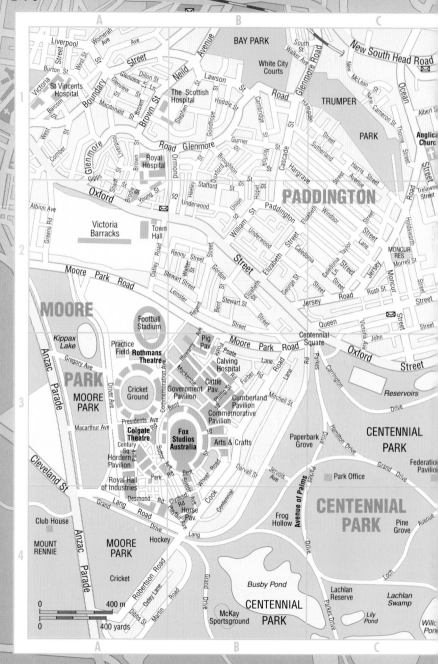

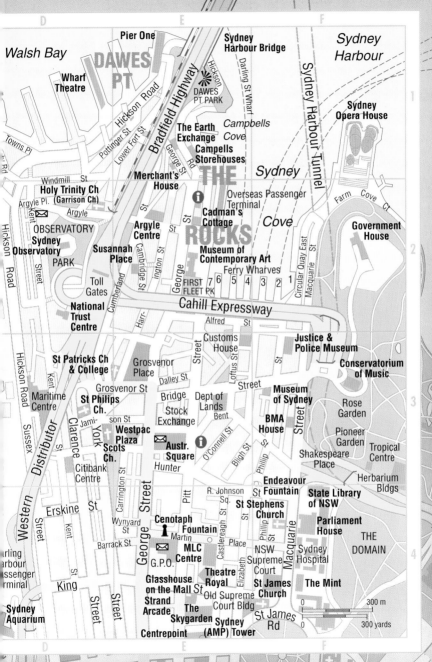

Walsh Bay

DAWES PT

Pier One

Wharf Theatre

Sydney Harbour Bridge

Sydney Harbour

Bradfield Highway

Hickson Road

DAWES PT PARK

Towns Pl

Pottinger St

Lower Fort St

Hickson Road

Darling St Wharf

Sydney Harbour Tunnel

Sydney Opera House

The Earth Exchange

Campbells Cove

Campells Storehouses

George St

Sydney

Merchant's House

Holy Trinity Ch (Garrison Ch)

Argyle Pl.

OBSERVATORY

Sydney Observatory

PARK

Windmill St

Argyle

Cove

Overseas Passenger Terminal

Cadman's Cottage

THE ROCKS

Government House

Farm Cove Ct

Hickson Road

Argyle Centre

Cambridge St

Princes St

Susannah Place

Museum of Contemporary Art

Toll Gates

Cumberland

National Trust Centre

Harr-

FIRST FLEET PK

George St

Ferry Wharves

7 6 5 4 3 2 1

Circular Quay East

Macquarie St

Cahill Expressway

Alfred St

Customs House

Justice & Police Museum

Conservatorium of Music

St Patricks Ch & College

Grosvenor Place

Dalley St

Lofts St

Street

Kent St

Maritime Centre

Hickson Road

Grosvenor St

St Philips Ch.

Jami-son St

Clarence St

York St

Bridge St

Street

Dept of Lands

Bent

Museum of Sydney

BMA House

Rose Garden

Pioneer Garden

Tropical Centre

Sussex

Distributor

Stock Exchange

Westpac Plaza

Scots Ch.

Austr. Square

O'Connell St

Bligh St

Phillip St

Shakespeare Place

Herbarium Bldgs

Citibank Centre

Hunter

Carrington St

Street

St

Western

Erskine St

Kent St

Wynyard St

Barrack St

Pitt St

George Street

R. Johnson Sq.

Endeavour St Fountain

St Stephens Church

State Library of NSW

Parliament House

THE DOMAIN

Cenotaph Fountain

Martin

Castlereagh St

Place

Phillip St

Elizabeth

Macquarie Street

arling harbour assenger erminal

G.P.O.

MLC Centre

King

Theatre Royal

NSW Supreme Court

Sydney Hospital

Sydney Aquarium

Glasshouse on the Mall St

Strand Arcade

The Skygarden

Centrepoint

St James Church

Old Supreme Court Bldg

Sydney (AMP) Tower

St James Rd

The Mint

0   300 m

0   300 yards

STREET INDEX

ART & PHOTO CREDITS

All photography for this edition is by **Glyn Genin** except on the pages detailed below:

Art Archive 41
Marc Asnin/Corbis Saba 39
Bill Bachman 148
David Bowden 150, 162
Bridgeman/National Library of Australia 21
Bridgeman/State Library of NSW 16
Darling Harbour Authority 22
Courtesy Ken Done 42L/R
Jeffery C Drewitz/The Photo Library 180
Mary Evans Picture Library 18, 20
Jean-Paul Ferrero/Auscape 124, 156
Getty Images 44, 45, 46, 48, 50, 51
Bret Gregory/Auscape 158, 192
Terry Harris 80, 96, 112, 200
John Van Hasselt/Corbis Sygma 38, 43
Geoff Higgins/The Photo Library 182
D & J Heaton 159
Britta Jaschinski 238
D Lundt/Corbis Sygma 26
Catherine Karnow 6R, 33, 34, 35, 53, 55, 57, 58-59, 62, 69, 75, 81, 88, 118–119, 137, 147, 153

Landsdowne Archive 19
David McGonigal 211
David Messent/The Photo Library 176, 178
Mitchell Library/Auscape 28
National Library of Australia 25
Reuters/Corbis 27, 37, 40
Robbi Newman 17, 32, 144, 148, 218
Tony Perrottet 7T, 8T, 10–11, 12–13, 36, 56, 136, 152, 155B
Peter J Robinson/The Photo Library 204
State Library of NSW 23, 24
Superstock/Powerstock 29
Eric Smith/Trip 117, 140
Robin Smith/The Photo Library 205
David Stahl 223
Tourism New South Wales 2–3, 7TL, 9T, 14, 54, 114, 128, 157, 164, 170–1, 172–3, 174, 177, 179, 181, 184, 190, 191, 194, 195, 197L, 197R, 198, 199, 201T, 206, 207, 208, 209
Trip/Australian Photo Library 154

PHOTO FEATURES

Pages 76/7: all Tourism New South Wales except Robert Harding World Imagery/Alamy (verandah); Coo-ee Historical Picture Library (Greenway); Glyn Genin (Hyde Park Barracks).

Pages 78/9: Robert Wallace/ Stock Photos (Maritime Museum); Tourism New South Wales (Metro); Andrew Stephenson/Wildlight (1950s house); Glyn Genin (Sydney Tower); S. T. Yiap/Alamy (Exhibition Centre).

Pages 108/9: Jerry Dennis (Nelson and Crooners); National Maritime Museum (yacht); Tourism New South Wales (Powerhouse); Tony Perrottet (Edge of the Trees); Australian Museum (dinosaur).

Pages 138/9: all Tourism New South Wales except Paul Gunning/Alamy (fireworks); Buzz Pictures/Alamy (gay parade); Jean-Paul Ferrero/Auscape (fun run).

Pages 202/3: ANT Photo Library/ NHPA (kangaroos); Gerard Lacz/ NHPA (koalas); Ken Griffiths/NHPA (spider); Dave Watts/NHPA (kookaburra); Patrick Fagot/NHPA (lorikeets); Reg Morrison/Auscape (waratah); Robbi Newman (wattle); Bill Bachman (possum).

Map Production: Dave Priestley and Stephen Ramsay

© 2005 Apa Publications GmbH & Co Verlag KG, Singapore branch

GENERAL INDEX